The American Record Label Book

The American Record Label Book

Brian Rust

ARLINGTON HOUSE·PUBLISHERS
NEW ROCHELLE, NEW YORK

THE AMERICAN RECORD LABEL BOOK

Brian Rust

Copyright © 1978 by Brian Rust

All rights reserved. No portion of this book may be reproduced without written permission from the publisher except by a reviewer who may quote brief passages in connection with a review.

Book design by Marge Terracciano

P 10 9 8 7 6 5 4 3 2 1

Manufactured in the United States of America

Library of Congress Cataloging in Publication Data

Rust, Brian A L 1922-
  The American record label book.

  1. Phonorecords—Labeling—United States. I. Title.
ML156.2.R83   621.398'32   78-16583
ISBN 0-87000-414-X

Publisher's Note

A numerical listing of nine of the most prominent prewar American record labels profiled in these pages is included in Volume IV of *The Complete Encyclopedia of Popular Music and Jazz 1900-1975* by Roger D. Kinkle (Arlington House, 1974). The nine labels listed consecutively in this work by catalog number include Victor, Bluebird, OKeh, Columbia, Brunswick, Decca, Melotone, Perfect and Vocalion. This is the only numerical listing of these labels in book form, and provides a unique reference source for researchers and collectors.

Introduction

The ability to record, preserve and at any time reproduce at will the sound of a voice or musical instrument, or indeed any sound at all, was just another age-old dream that became a reality towards the end of the nineteenth century, a few decades after man was able to preserve the sight of someone or something by means of the camera and a little ahead of his ability to transmit sound through the atmosphere by means of radio. When Thomas Alva Edison and his phonograph that used wax cylinders, and Emile Berliner and his gramophone that employed flat discs, began their recording programmes in the 1890s, they could hardly have foreseen that within the lifetime of many who were then young children, their products would be regarded as *objets d'art* regardless of the music or other performance on them, or who the performers might be, objects collected avidly and treasured. Edison saw his invention as an aid to commerce. It could be used for dictating correspondence, he thought. Berliner—with either greater foresight or greater faith in his product—saw it primarily as a home entertainer.

As recording techniques improved and legal battles over patents were resolved, the fame of the talking machine or phonograph spread throughout the United States and Europe, and eventually encompassed the civilized world. The great established artists came to abandon their scepticism towards the new invention, which for years some of them regarded as no more than a noisy, objectionable toy. Listening to some of the earliest recordings of the 1890s, one can sympathize with this view. When even the best machine made the average record sound like a parrot with laryngitis, one can understand that a Jean de Reszke or a Nellie Melba would not be eager to hand down to posterity a travesty or at best a caricature of their superb voices.

But by the middle of the first decade of the new century, there was hardly an artist of stature anywhere in the world who had not submitted to the somewhat uncomfortable procedure of making a record, perhaps singing or playing one title several times in succession in an effort to secure a satisfactory master. Some, like Adelina Patti and the Norwegian composer Edvard Grieg, even came out of retirement briefly to commit their art to the abiding care of science, for the entertainment and enlightenment of unborn generations. It would probably have surprised them beyond belief—Grieg particularly—if they could have known that sixty or seventy years later, a single copy of any of these records would be valued at a hundred times what it cost to buy it in a record store soon after its release. It was in April 1905—the same month Jean de Reszke is alleged to have overcome his distrust of the machine and recorded two arias in Paris for Fonotipia—that a British trade magazine commented: "The record collector, that is in the discriminating sense, does not yet appear to have arrived."

Indeed, this strange individual, as many regarded him and some still do, was not to arrive until the late 1920s. When he did, he was mostly concerned with collecting (with great discrimination, be it said) only records of singing, perhaps with a few outstanding instrumentalists included as examples of brilliant violin or piano technique. Then only twenty or thirty years had elapsed from the time these records were made, so they could still be found in second-hand stores, street markets, and auction rooms, and purchased there for very small change. For who wanted those old-fashioned things now that electric recording was a fact; now that harsh, noisy surfaces had given place to velvety-smooth reproduction unmarred by any physical defects or shortcomings? The answer, of course, was—the record collector.

Yes, the record collector, with his knowledge of exactly what he wanted (if only he could find it), his enthusiasm for the chase, and the apparently built-in scratch-filters in his ears that enabled him to tolerate, even enjoy the voices of singers long dead, even if to the ordinary listener it seemed that they were singing in a thunderstorm or frying bacon by the side of Niagara.

Soon after the operatic and vocal collector arrived, his younger brother, the jazz collector, made his debut. He was able to buy the records of his choice new and factory-fresh, for 75 cents or less, over the counters of record stores during the Jazz Age itself. Younger members of the jazz fraternity who came on the scene when it was far too late to do this—since "ephemeral" jazz items rarely lasted longer than a few months or a year in the catalogs, some of them never reaching the distinction of a catalog entry at all—could often catch up on the issues of a decade or so earlier by the same diligent haunting of the same types of establishment as had provided their operatic brethren with the objects of their fancy; and for less money, since the ignorant owners of these shops might charge a dollar for a Caruso or a Melba (names they knew, and associated with culture and age—and hence with rarity and value). But an out-of-date jazz record might be tossed scornfully at the would-be purchaser for a penny or two.

The Second World War brought a shortage of shellac and the need to recycle existing shellac discs to produce new records. This meant that millions of discs all over the world were fed into the melting pot. War is a great leveller. Whether the record was a ploughed-up, played-out, worthless item by an unimportant artist performing a trivial piece, or a beautifully preserved, seldom seen example of an unusual performance by a little-recorded musician, once it had been accepted for salvage, there was no appeal against the death sentence thus pronounced.

Three or four years after hostilities had ceased in 1945 came a revolution of revolutions. For half a century, the speed at which records were usually played was 78 revolutions per minute, more or less. The material they were made of was, as we noted above, a compound in which shellac was a major ingredient. Now came the long-playing record, with its grooves many sizes smaller than anything on the existing discs, pressed in virtually unbreakable vinylite plastic and playing at either 45 rpm or 33⅓ rpm. Another decade, and the old 78 rpm disc had become as much of a museum piece as Edison's wax cylinders of the 1890s. But human nature being what it is, another decade later, in the threatening atmosphere of world politics and the Age of Violence, the Permissive Society and the Great God Television, there came a boom in things nostalgic. It created a market for the objects of an era not so long ago, when if things were not perfect, they were generally better than they are now; "cheap" music being the potent thing it is (as Sir Noël Coward makes leading man Elyot Chase observe in *Private Lives*), there has sprung up an enthusiastic new market for old 78 rpm records of dance music, film songs, the popular singers and players of the years before Hiroshima, and the casts of Broadway and London musicals.

For some considerable time, I have been accorded the honour of being asked by many correspondents for a book about the makes of records that were on sale at one time or another during the first half-century or so of the talking-machine. The discriminating record collector of all kinds of music has indeed arrived, and is eager to learn exactly when his records were made, what firm produced them, what else can be found on this or that label, what these labels look like, and how common—or rare—are the items produced by this or that company.

As an inveterate and unrepentant nostalgiac myself, I have pleasure in offering just such a book. In it, arranged alphabetically by label, I have given as much as I know concerning each one. I have ended the survey at 1942, when the American Federation of Musicians forbade its members to record for commercial companies unless the latter paid a royalty to the Federation on each record sold, for the financial assistance of unemployed musicians. (The implication was that the very act of making records that would be used on radio programmes instead of live musicians was directly resonsible for the plight of the unemployed.) This seems a sensible point at which to draw the line. Records made after the ban was lifted in 1943 and 1944 are, in the main, of little value or interest to collectors. (Exceptions seem to be early examples of Elvis Presley and other practitioners of the cult of "rock 'n' roll." Having nothing but an absolute horror of this in all its forms, I feel quite unqualified to deal with it or any of its ramifications.)

The non-collecting public today seems divided into two groups. There are those who consider a 78 rpm specialist to be some kind of eccentric, especially when he patiently explains that to put his prizes on tape, sell the originals and save space, would be to lose something both tangible and intangible, perhaps inexplicable, in the music, and the pleasure it gives. There are also those who have heard that old records are valuable for no other reason than that they are old. If they have any stored in the cellar, they are convinced that they have a fortune in shellac, to be converted into currency at the expense of the collector (who is not expected by these people to be discriminating, but to be ready to pay high prices for anything and everything so long as it reproduces sound at 78 rpm).

This book, then, aims to help my fellow eccentrics, if that is what we are. I have included American labels only, with notes on their British counterparts; and I have tried to answer the questions most commonly asked about the major labels, at least, and to provide useful information on all of them. Discographers have been derided as "musical bookkeepers," and label enthusiasts as "philatelists more interested in the label on a record than in the music in the grooves," regardless of the fact that true philatelists collect objects of little or no artistic merit that nevertheless can command values many times greater than the rarest and most desirable record ever pressed. To these harmless eccentrics, musical bookkeepers and offbeat philatelists I dedicate this book. Rejoice! The discriminating collector has arrived at last.

Brian Rust

Hatch End
Middlesex
England

ACO

This was the cheaper label produced by the Aeolian Company, Ltd., of Aeolian Hall, Bond Street, London, W.1, between November 1922 and August 1927. The ten-inch G series and the twelve-inch F had identical labels, an attractive rich red with gold lettering and design that varied little over the fifty-eight months of the label's existence.

The catalog covered the usual middle range of music: light popular classics of the kind readily accommodated in three minutes of playing time, comedy songs, popular vocals both ancient and modern, and of course dance records. These were invariably issued under pseudonyms, each of which could apply to several entirely different bands. At first, American Vocalion and Gennett supplied the American masters. For the last eighteen months of its life, Aco drew only on Gennett for its American repertoire. But most of its transatlantic issues were from Vocalion, and used the original matrix numbers. Those from Gennett early on had a bogus number indented over the spot on the run-off where the Gennett matrix number had been. London recordings were in a C-5000 series that reached over C-8000 before the summer of 1926, when electric recording was introduced and the matrices were numbered C-1-E and up.

The G series began at 15000 and seems to have finished at 16230, the last one referred to in *The Gramophone* for August 1927, after which no further references in advertisements or reviews could be found. In spite of a repertoire aimed at the middle of the road, Aco is not a common label. Its appeal to jazz collectors lies mostly in its sporadic issue of odd sides by the Original Memphis Five, the Mound City Blue Blowers, Fletcher Henderson and his Orchestra, and the Hottentots, while the occasional side by Jeffries and his Rialto Orchestra offers interesting hot dance music of quite advanced quality. Sides by Irving Kaufman appeared frequently on Aco, usually under the pseudonym "Harry Topping."

The following chart shows the approximate first matrix number recorded in each year:

1922	C-5000	1926	C-7500
1923	C-5400	1926 (July)	C-1-E
1924	C-6140	1927	C-150-E
1925	C-6800		

AEOLIAN VOCALION

See Vocalion.

AJAX

Ajax was a short-lived label specializing in urban blues, jazz and country music. Its name was registered as a trademark by H. S. Berliner, son of Emile, of 131-141 18th Avenue, Lachine, Quebec, Canada, trading as the Compo Company. Although the date of this was November 2, 1921, no Ajax records seem to have been made before the summer of 1923. The earliest have matrix numbers in a block covering 31000 (or 31001) to about 31030. It is not known where these were recorded, except that it was in New York City. The next series runs from 31502 to 31848, as far as is known, and these were made in the Compo studio at 240 West 55th Street, New York City. There were a few issues from the Montreal studios at 117 Metcalf Street. A different matrix number was used for each take, so there are no take numbers or letters.

As might be expected from a product of the House of Berliner, the quality of Ajax records is high. Most of them are acoustic recordings, but in perfect condition the reproduction is excellent. The last few masters appear to have been made electrically in the spring of 1925, probably slightly after the first electric recordings by Victor and Columbia. After July 1925, no further Ajax records are known to have been issued. (The late Walter C. Allen reported that in *The Chicago Defender* of July 25 and August 1, 1925, Rudolph's Music Store there advertised that Ajax records were being given away free with each purchase of other records.) Although most of them are pressed from original masters, a handful were evidently leased from the Plaza Music Company (they appear on that firm's Banner and associated labels) or from Pathe. These bear the original matrix numbers. Certain early Ajax issues show none at all, but the majority give the Ajax series of numbers etched very finely in the smooth area surrounding the label. All Ajax records bear the catalog number in the 17000 block. A very few show that the date of recording and probably other information was scratched on the original wax at the time of the session, as part of this strays beyond the edge of the area covered by the label.

Although the Compo Company had its headquarters in Canada and recorded mainly in New York, the head office of the Ajax Record Company was at 108 West Lake Street, Chicago, Ill. It was advertised as "The Quality Race Record," but despite the presence of some important names on its artist roster (Mamie Smith, Rosa Henderson, Helen Gross and Fletcher Henderson among them), neither these nor the quality of the record itself gave much competition to the major labels. By January 1926, its masters were beginning to appear with Pathe Actuelle and Perfect labels. The Ajax label itself is plain, starkly utilitarian. There are slight variants in the wording relating to place of manufacture, but the basic design is a navy blue label with the word AJAX in gold across the top of the upper part. The titles and other relevant information (including the publishers of the music) were on the lower part, without any decoration of even the simplest kind.

AMCO

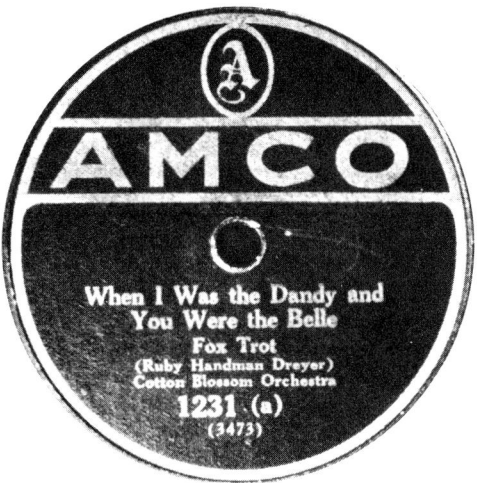

Believed to have been a store label, Amco derived its meagre catalog from Grey Gull. Such examples as we have seen follow the Grey Gull numbering and the Grey Gull system of cloaking the artists in anonymity. Yet the original masters are not Grey Gull at all but Emerson, from 1924 or thereabouts, along with a few others. Some copies exist with the Amco label pasted over a Grey Gull label, or a label from one of the Grey Gull subsidiaries. Three categories are known: a 1000 dance series, a 2000 vocal series, and a 4000 standard series. Nothing of any great importance has yet been discovered on Amco, although the label itself is a rarity. It is black with gold lettering, and the design resembles the Radiex label of the same era.

ANGELOPHONE

A very obscure seven-inch vertical-cut (Edison type) disc, manufactured by a firm named Angelico, with business addresses in New York and London, probably about 1919. As far as is known, no specimens have been found in England. *Record Research* contributor Ray Wile reported on this label in the eighth issue (May-June, 1956), reporting three varieties. The earliest had the name etched in around the upper circle of the central area, as were title, artist and other details. The second was a paper-label type, light blue or yellow with lettering in purple or black. The third, a similar design in dark blue, had the words "Angelophone Record" in white, with all other printing in gold. This type backed a specimen with the etched format label.

Nothing is known about the extent of the catalog, or whether any important records appeared on this label.

ANSONIA

A very rare label apparently deriving some of its material from Arto, with some independently recorded. Ansonia seems to have flourished—if that is the word for so rare a make—during the latter part of 1920 into the first few months of 1921. According to one specimen, the parent firm was the Ansonia Phonograph and Record Company, Inc., New York. The price is given as $1.00 when even Victor and Columbia were charging only 75 cents for quality products by quality artists, so the reason for Ansonia's rarity becomes clear. One series is numbered in step with Arto subsidiaries, but with the prefix H-. The other is numbered in a 1000 series, and the label is red and gold where the "Arto"-type label is mauve and gold.

The design of the later (independent) issue includes a watch face and the legend "Watch for our hits." But evidently the public, even those prepared to pay a quarter more than the major firms were charging, did not have to keep a long vigil.

APOLLO

There were two Apollo Records in the United States, long before the one that appeared in 1944 and flourished briefly after World War II. The earlier was a 5000 series in step with one of the several Rialto labels (in this case, the 1921 version). And in 1928, perhaps slightly earlier and/or later also, there was another that bore a cameo design with the Greek god's features enclosed in an oval surmounting the brand name in capitals stretching across the upper half, the catalog number corresponding exactly with that of Pathe's issues of the same material, and even using the same printing block as Pathe. No indication of ownership, trading outlet or other details is given.

ARETINO

The Aretino Company of Chicago can lay fair claim to having produced the 78 rpm record with the largest spindle hole, measuring three inches across! The records themselves are pressed from Columbia masters of the first decade of the century. The labels were little more than a pinkish-red border a fraction over an inch wide, surrounding the incredible orifice in the centre. Printing is entirely in gold, the brand name "Aretino Record" covering an arc round the upper rim, the manufacturer's name around the lower, and the legend "Clear—Sweet" to the left and right of the spindle aperture.

The catalog series is a three-figure one prefixed D-, and is known to include rare items by Bert Williams and Vess L. Ossman. Doubtless other interesting contributions from the Columbia repertoire of the time also appeared on Aretino, but the known examples are all anonymous. Identification can be made by playing them against the Columbia records of the same title and matrix number—which number also appears on the Aretino label.

ARIEL

The Ariel record is unusual in that it was the product of a British firm not normally associated with records, Messrs. J. G. Graves of Sheffield, who between 1910 and 1938 drew on the catalogs of Jumbo, Favorite, Beka, Imperial, Zonophone and finally Parlophone for the Ariel repertoire. (The rather rare ten-inch Ariels were known as Ariel Grand Records, selling pre-1914 at the considerable sum of 3s. 6d., or not far short of $1.00 at that time; the almost unheard-of twelve-inchers were termed Ariel Concert Records, and these were 6s. 6d. each. Certainly these prices are not exorbitant for such names as Zélie de Lussan, John McCormack, Frieda Hempel and Emmy Destinn; but the same prices were charged for the Ariel Full Military Band playing selections from *Carmen* (and *Buzz Buzz Jazz One-Step*, whatever that was), for third-rate comics, for anonymous violin-cello-harp trios, and for coy drawing-room ballads that other labels were offering at two-thirds of the price.

The use of Parlophone's catalog meant that OKeh masters appeared on Ariel. Some of these, admittedly of no artistic consequence, bypassed the Parlophone label, as far as I can discover. But Ariel remains a happy hunting ground for jazz and dance band collectors. Here, under the absolutely invariable pseudonym of the Ariel Dance Orchestra, can be found such varied fare as Frank Trumbauer's *Turn On the Heat* and *Sunny Side Up*, back to back as on OKeh and Parlophone; and Sam Lanin's *Susianna* (backed by Fred Hall's Sugar Babies' *I Faw Down an' Go 'Boom!'*), the Lanin having a vocal refrain by Bing Crosby. As Norman (or sometimes Normand) Thorne, Seger Ellis sang love songs to the accompaniment of Eddie Lang and the Dorsey Brothers; and on *To Be in Love* and *S'posin'*, they are joined by Louis Armstrong. Annette Hanshaw is renamed Leila Sandford, and Red McKenzie and the Mariners described simply as "Vocal Trio." English bands as widely different as Arthur Rosebery's, Nat Gonella's Georgians and Victor Silvester's Ballroom Orchestra were also called the Ariel Dance Orchestra, while the Dorsey Brothers' Concert Orchestra, under the direction of Dr. Eugene Ormandy, no less, became the Ariel Symphony Orchestra.

The earlier Ariel records were numbered in blocks beginning 2000, 3500 and 4000. The numbering apparently depended on whether the masters came from Jumbo, Favorite or some other source. The Parlophone-OKeh were also numbered 4000 up, reaching nearly 5000 before the label disappeared. The anonymous (sometimes pseudonymous) Zonophone titles began around 100 and reached four figures before being abandoned. For a time Ariel was drawing on both Parlophone and Zonophone simultaneously. The quality of Ariel recordings was generally high, as might be expected, since they came from the same presses as Zonophone and Parlophone records. The earlier issues from Jumbo and the rest were inclined to be rougher. The label is always dark brown with ornate gold printing, and the design barely changed in all the years it was in use. The records could be bought by mail order, and if you chose twenty at a time, you could save 10s.—about $2.50 at that time—paying 6s. with the order and 6s. monthly.

ARTHUR FIELDS MELODY RECORD

Arthur Fields was a prolific recording artist on every label: solo under his own name, and with many dance bands, sometimes anonymously. His association with the record business was not confined to singing, however. During the spring of 1923, records with black and gold labels embodying a profile of Arthur Fields and produced by the Arthur Fields Record Company of New York were issued on a limited scale. The only one known is numbered 1516, and reference to labels in the Olympic group shows the same titles with the same number on those labels: *Crying for You* and *Wanita (Wanna Eat? Wanna Eat?)* sung, not surprisingly, by Arthur Fields. Whether other Olympic masters were used for pressing more Arthur Fields Medody Records is not known.

ARTO

Arto records were the product of the Standard Music Roll Company of Orange, N.J., with offices (and probably studios) at 1604 Broadway, New York City. They first appeared in the late summer of 1920, and had vanished by the late autumn of 1922.

Most of the issues are in a 9000 series with black and gold labels, covering the kind of music most likely to appeal to the average listener, with emphasis on dance music and popular vocalists, including the pioneer blues artist Lucille Hegamin. She was recording blues for Arto several months before any other company had begun to follow OKeh's lead in this field, and copies of these early blues records can still be found relatively easily today.

The matrix series changed its format rapidly. There are numbers to be found in 17000, 18000, 20000, 23000, 25000 and 26000 blocks in the two years of Arto's life, usually visible in very faint handwriting, mirrored, *underneath* the heavily-indented catalog number in the smooth ungrooved area round the label. Why each block was abandoned after what must have been only a few months' use is not known. Although the Arto label was discontinued after only little more than two years, the Globe and especially the Bell labels were maintained somewhat longer, Bell (q.v.) surviving until 1928. Other Arto derivatives include Cleartone, Hy-Tone, and Ansonia, whose catalog series were derived by lopping the first digit from Arto's and substituting a code letter. Paramount and its affiliates also used Arto masters.

From the quality point of view, Arto records are remarkably good. The catalog never produced anything unusual from an artistic viewpoint, but bands of the calibre of the Original Memphis Five, the California Ramblers and Ben Selvin and his Orchestra made many sides for this label, a good number of them interesting because the selections were not repeated by these bands on other labels.

AUTOGRAPH

To Autograph records can go the credit for being first on the market with electric recording. From the autumn of 1924 until they vanished from the scene sometime in 1926, the blue and gold labels proclaimed the product "Electrically Recorded." While the results are crude indeed, there is no denying that they have a brighter top response and a tone range that reaches further into the bass than almost anything else offered to the public up to that date.

The president of Marsh Laboratories, Inc., where they were made, was Orlando R. Marsh, the sales manager John Hawkins. *The Talking Machine Journal* of October 1924 reported that the firm had just moved to the seventh floor of 78 East Jackson Boulevard, Chicago, and that it had been supplying Autograph records for six months, at $1.50 each. Since the major labels were charging exactly half that sum for their popular issues, and in view of the limited appeal of most Autograph issues, such a price seems absurdly large. It could account for the extreme rarity of the records themselves.

As far as can be gathered, there was no actual catalog as such, and in the case of many specimens that have come to light, no catalog number either. Since it is known that various private firms such as the Rialto Music Shop used Marsh's studios for recording their Rialto and other records, and that sessions issued by Paramount and Pathe took place in those very studios, it may well be that the primary *raison d'être* of Marsh's enterprise was to record for other companies whose own studios were too far from Chicago to warrant sending recording gear there but who had such men as Jelly Roll Morton, the famed jazz pianist from New Orleans, or Boyd Senter, "The Jazzologist Supreme," contracted to them, and who at the time of the required sessions were actually appearing in Chicago. There certainly seem to have been Autograph records issued as such before April 1924. Specimens with red and gold or maroon and gold labels with the same checker-board design have been found, obviously made and almost certainly sold sometime in 1923.

The announcement referred to above also says that the label specialized in organ records by Jesse Crawford. It lists ten sides, with catalog numbers, by this artist, some months before the first (acoustic) sides he made for Victor, and probably the first ever made of a Wurlitzer organ. When Jesse Crawford signed with Victor, he was replaced by Milton Charles, and records of this artist's work on Autograph masters even crossed the Atlantic and were issued in England on Edison Bell Winner. They are electric recordings of quite good quality, recorded in the Tivoli Theatre, Chicago.

One of the most outstanding of all Autograph records is by Joe "King" Oliver, one of the greatest of New Orleans jazz cornet players. He plays *Tom Cat* and *King Porter Stomp*, accompanied only by Jelly Roll Morton at the piano. Cornet and piano duets seldom have much sales appeal, even at modest prices. At the deluxe level there could have been little or no demand, and the original issue is quintessentially rare. The electric recording system could barely cope with the majestic power of Oliver's cornet. Nevertheless, a clean original, or a careful transfer from one, can give us a tantalizing glimpse of two masters of their art at work, unhindered by commercial considerations or an indifferent supporting band (as was Morton's fate on another Autograph session in his own name with his Kings of Jazz).

There seems to have been little straight dance or popular music on the Autograph label. Besides being one of the richest seams for basic jazz, there were recordings of pioneer local radio talent, Swedish choral conventions, and sacred works. In my own collection I have an Autograph test that defies identification. Pressed on smooth shellac that would not disgrace the best quality Victor products, it has *Muscle Shoals Blues* on one side, played by a band including cornet, trombone, clarinet, alto saxophone, violin, piano and brass bass, numbered 30. On the other side, the same band accompanies a girl vocalist singing *Oh Baby Dear*, numbered 35. The realism of this recording, which must go back to 1921 or 1922, is uncanny. The band is probably coloured.

The highest Marsh matrix number so far traced is 1061. There were two catalog series, in three figures between 400 and 700, and a 4000 block. Since the entire repertoire was recorded in Chicago at a time when the greatest jazz talent was playing there, it is interesting to speculate on what else may have been recorded by Orlando R. Marsh. Important other sessions from that golden age may well have been held on the seventh floor of 78 East Jackson Boulevard.

BALDWIN

A very rare and obscure label apparently pressed by the Bridgeport Die and Machine Company (of Bridgeport, Conn.) from Paramount masters about 1922, and probably sold in chain-stores or possibly through mail-order firms.

BANNER

It could be said that Banner was the flagship label of the Plaza Music Company of New York. It was launched in January 1922, the popular series being numbered 1000 upwards, and what might be termed the standard series starting at 2000. For the first year, Banner records were mostly reissues of material recorded by Paramount and Emerson, Paramount having matrices numbered from about 700 to about 1300, and Emerson in the 42000 block.

At the end of 1922, Plaza apparently opened its own recording studio and began recording masters numbered 5000 upwards. This series remained in use until the coming of CBS as a corporation producing records, and remained in use on its Columbia and OKeh records until the end of 78s, and was then carried on into the LP/EP era!

When the catalog numbers of Banner records reached 1999 in the summer of 1927, they then jumped to 6000, but after only 150 issues in this block, the numbering jumped again to 7000 in the spring of 1928. By the end of that year, the numbers had reached about 7250, and then quite inexplicably reverted to

6201. There followed slightly over 350 issues in this series, and the numbers were altered again—to 0500 upwards. Halfway through the 0800s, at the end of 1930, there was one more change, to 32000, and this reached into the 33000s before the label was abandoned in the autumn of 1935.

At the end of 1928 came the merger with Pathe and Cameo records. The advent of the Banner 0500 series in January 1930 almost coincided with the disappearance of the Pathe label altogether. (See also Cameo and Pathe.) The name of the firm holding rights to Plaza, Cameo and Pathe material was the American Record Corporation, and it was this that formed the basis of the reactivated Columbia label in 1939 under the CBS aegis.

Through the years of its existence, Banner proved one of the most popular labels on the market. The reproduction quality of the earlier independent issues was generally good, if somewhat nasal. Copies that have been little used or carefully treated give quite reasonable results; but being a cheap make, they wear very easily. In the autumn of 1925, electric recordings began to make their appearance on Banner, but these tend to be shrill and rather constricted. By the time the merger took place, the quality had improved. At their best they were quite mellow, but often Banner records of the late 1920s had a thick sound with a rather muddy bass. This was eventually corrected, but sides made during the last five years of Banner's existence err quite often in the other direction and tend to revert to a thin top sound with low bass response.

The magazine *Record Research* since July 1961 has been listing all known Banner matrix numbers, and a glance at these painstakingly reconstructed "recording ledgers" show that here again was a label entirely concerned with appealing to the general public, with copious monthly issues of dance records and popular vocals, many under pseudonyms, and often leased from what were then rival firms such as Pathe. From the mid-twenties until 1931, Adrian Schubert was the musical director, and he produced dance records by the hundred. Ben Selvin, Sam Lanin, Joseph Samuels, the Original Memphis Five and Fletcher Henderson all contributed dozens of sides to the Banner label, along with popular vocalists like Irving Kaufman, Billy Jones, Ernest Hare and Vernon Dalhart. After the formation of the American Record Corporation, bands of the fame of Vincent Lopez, Duke Ellington and Fred Rich were signed to make Banner Records. In the 1930s, artists from Brunswick reappeared on Banner, among them Bing Crosby, the Mills Brothers, Guy Lombardo and the Boswell Sisters.

Banner issued a number of light classical records, and some Irish and other folk dance music. Comparatively little attempt was made to capture the Negro market. Occasional records of fairly well known female blues singers graced the monthly lists, offering jazz-orientated vaudeville-style blues, a very few conventional sermons, and nothing more.

The British outlet for Banner masters was principally the Imperial label, (q.v.).

The following chart shows the first matrix number recorded in each year in the original Plaza series; those prior to 1925 are estimated, since no documentary evidence exists as far as can be traced:

Year	Matrix	Year	Matrix
1922 (Nov.)	5000	1933	12818
1923	5040	1934	14505
1924	5380	1935	16545
1925	5790	1936	18475

1926	6370		1937	20476	
1927	7030	Plaza	1938	22243	ARC-Brunswick
1928	7705		1939	23899	
1929	8430		1940	25625	
1930	9252		1941	29381	
1931	10347		1942	32108	CBS
1932	11084	ARC			

BELL

At the outset, Bell records were a product of the Standard Music Roll Company of Orange, N.J. They were numbered, as were that company's Arto label, with the first digit removed and the letter P- substituted. The first labels were black and gold, like Arto, with a bell trademark that had been claimed for use since November 23, 1920. Strangely, this device disappeared soon afterwards, leaving a curiously empty-looking label that remained in use until the autumn of 1923, when a much smarter design, including a satyr playing pan-pipes in white on a black ground with gold lettering and neat, tasteful decoration, replaced it until the label was discontinued in July 1928. (Some of the later labels were royal blue, and a four-figure series just before the end was red, with the same design but devoted to spirituals, vocal blues, and what is now called country-and-western music.)

Bell P-313 is believed to be the last issue with the P- prefix. After this, the label continued under the aegis of the Bell Record Corporation of 38 Clinton Street, Newark, N. J., drawing for its material on Emerson records. (Bell 324 is a strange advertising record claiming that for the previous ten years, the make had been produced for and sold by the W. T. Grant Company of Lynn, Mass. But there were at that time no Bell records more than three years old!

From 1923 until the end of 1927, Bell continued to be associated with Emerson. But for the last few months of Bell's existence, Gennett supplied the masters. During the Arto era, and for a little way into the Emerson period, Plaza masters (Banner, etc.) were also used. Most Bell records suppress the original matrix number, using their own catalog number suffixed -A or -B to denote the side.

Bell records are not hard to find, and contain items of moderate interest to jazz collectors, urban blues enthusiasts and those who enjoy occasional hot solos amid commercial dance band arrangements. The pressing quality is usually good, and of course the recording characteristics have the same faults and virtues as Arto, Banner, Emerson and Gennett of the period. The usual retail price seems to have been 50 cents.

BELTONA

The music house of the Murdoch Trading Company of 59-61 Clerkenwell Road, London, E. C. 1 originally produced the Beltona label in 1922. American recordings came from Vocalion or sometimes from Gennett, British masters principally from Aco, q.v. The pressings were made by the Vocalion Gramophone Company of Hayes, Middlesex.

The only one of the considerable number of different labels from this factory to survive into LP times, Beltona had a distinctive pale fawn label for its first hundred issues or so, with printing in red and black and the trademark in a circle surrounded by twining plants, some in flower, of a species unknown to any botanist. The trademark itself is the face of a girl with a great deal of hair and the word "Beltona" on her hairband, gazing vacantly at the beholder. (On publicity material she was described as "Curiously Euphonic," as were the Petmecky steel needles with which Murdoch's urged its patrons to play Beltona records. British advertising certainly adopted some strange slogans half a century ago.)

The damsel with the hair and the unsmiling stare remained on all Beltona records to the end. From the autumn of 1927, Edison Bell took over production, and titles from the American Plaza Music Company's Banner catalog began to appear on Beltona. Until this point, the design had remained unchanged, although the fawn, red and black had given place to two shades of pale blue-green and black. Now it was a larger label, white below, black and gold above, sober but distinctive. The catalog numbers, which had started at 100, had by this time reached nearly 1300, and for nearly seven hundred more issues relied on Edison Bell. That label itself became the property of the Decca Record Company in January 1933, and it was Decca that maintained Beltona for the next three decades or more.

All the dance records were issued under pseudonyms, and so were most of the vocal items. From the beginning, there had always been a preponderance of Scottish material in the Beltona catalog, and soon after Edison Bell assumed responsibility for the label, it became a kind of Scottish "race" series, issuing all kinds of Scottish artists from solo bagpipers to comedians hoping to tread in Sir Harry Lauder's footsteps, with a goodly assortment of reels, strathspeys and other genuine Scottish dances faithfully recorded on accordions, melodeons, violins and pianos, jointly and severally. The sober brown, white and black design soon disappeared and was replaced by an almost garish combination of vermillion and gold on white, with title and artist credit in black. Eventually the red was changed to royal blue and a thistle was added to the design.

The jazz collector can find choice Fletcher Henderson titles on Beltona, and one by the Mound City Blue Blowers, one by the California Ramblers, and a reasonable assortment of dance music of the period, some of it featuring good solo work. Most of the bands were described indiscriminately as "American Dance Orchestra," "Avenue Dance Orchestra" (these were mostly British), "The Sunny South Dance Orchestra," "The Southern States Dance Band" or "The Virginia Dance Orchestra." It is not a common label, probably because at 2s. 6d. each—about 60 to 65 cents—it was competing with a much superior product in Regal or Zonophone at exactly the same price.

BERLINER

Arguments continue as to who was the true founding father of recorded sound. The names of Leon Scott, Charles Cros, and Thomas Alva Edison are the most obvious candidates for the honour, but nothing can alter the fact that a young German immigrant, Emile Berliner, was the first to envisage a disc as a means of storing and reproducing sound engraved with lateral vibrations (as distinct from a vertical-cut cylinder on which sound waves were first indented) and to prove it a commercial proposition.

This is not the place to discuss in detail the scientific and economic background of the disc record industry. Roland Gelatt has already covered this in his fascinating book *The Fabulous Phonograph*, originally published in 1956. A resumé of the physical appearance of the varying kinds of Berliner record, and the sort of performances it provides, will be of interest, however, to those who can use their ears and dispense with possible prejudices when listening to these relics of three-quarters of a century and more ago.

It is known that early in 1888 Emile Berliner finally developed his lateral-cut disc. It recorded by having a stylus trace the sound wave in a film of fatty substance on a zinc base, then fixing the pattern by immersion in acid. This "master" could then be used to produce duplicates. Berliner is known to have left Washington, where he had his laboratory, in 1889 to return to Germany to demonstrate his brainchild. There he licenced a toy-making firm in Waltershausen named Kämmerer and Reinhardt to produce toy hand-driven machines of no great physical stamina. Berliner supplied five-inch discs for these that must have been recorded in Germany. Some of them are monologues in English or German, and are almost certainly delivered by Berliner himself. None of these records gives any artist credits. Like all Berliners, they have title and copyright details etched or embossed on the central area, sometimes by machine but more often by hand, sometimes in two different handwritings. They do carry numbers, however, and a sticker on the back (which is smooth and ungrooved) gives the words of the recitation or song. (All the vocal and instrumental solos on specimens I have inspected were unaccompanied.) One in particular is unusual, among a batch of a dozen or so that I examined recently, in that it seems to have been pressed in a kind of plastic much superior from the rest, almost as smooth as modern vinylite. In addition it bore what could be a date: 14-8-90. It also has the catalog number 102 and the usual copyright number, so it is difficult to guess what this means if it is not a date. It fits with what is known of the very earliest commercial recordings, so it would seem that on August 14, 1890, four trumpet players stood in a room somewhere in Germany—Hanover?—and played what the sticker describes simply as *Marsch No. 1* (without any composer credit) into a long metal funnel.

Messrs. Kämmerer and Reinhardt marketed the newfangled toy for three or four years, exporting machines and records all over Europe, including England, where the principal London supply centre was Parkins & Gotto, 60 Oxford Street. The cost of a disc was one shilling, and a single sheet of paper, measuring eight inches long and five wide, served as a catalog for these first disc records. There are eighteen recitations, one of them being *My Name Is the "Gramophone"*; nine songs in English, two in French and six in German; twelve records of brass instruments (six quintets, one trombone solo, two cornet solos, a set of bugle calls, something described simply as *Concert Piece* and something else called *Mikado*); two piano solos; and five "assorted plates": farmyard imitations (these I have heard, and they are incredibly poor), a banjo duet, an unidentified "clarionette solo with variations," an old-fashioned street organ (*sic*), and "Roll of Drums." This flimsy little list is undated, but the presence among the English songs of *Ta-Ra-Ra-Boom-De-Ay* seems to suggest that it was published in 1892 or 1893, when that wonderful piece of nonsense was first popular.

By this time, Emile Berliner was back in Washington and had launched a modest enterprise named the United States Gramophone Company, with its main office at 1410 Pennsylvania Avenue N.W., Washington, D.C. At the end of 1894, this company issued the first commercial records that were not marketed as toys. A year later he awakened the interest of a young mechanic named Eldridge R. Johnson of Camden, New Jersey, who designed and built the first spring-driven machine for playing Berliner's records. By now the records had grown to seven inches in diameter. Titles, artists and sometimes other scraps of information were still written by hand in the middle of the record, as were the location and usually the date of recording. In 1897, these details were beginning to appear etched in an ornate typeface that was considerably easier to read than the handwriting of secretaries, engineers or whoever else happened to inscribe the records. (Often the details were written in by a young man who was talent scout, accompanist—the soloists and choruses had a piano accompaniment by now—and general factotum for "E. Berliner's Gramophone": Fred W. Gaisberg. He it was who brought the machine and the records to England and to Europe, and eventually to Asia and the Far East, and of whom it has been said, "His middle initials should really be H.M.V.")

The numbering system of the first Berliner records was complex indeed. Blocks of numbers were allocated not to a studio or location generally (they were being recorded in New York and Philadelphia as well as Washington), but to a number of musical or vocal categories:

1-149	Bands
150-199	Popular songs
200-374	Instrumental solos, duets, etc.
375-449	Traditional and comedy songs; whistling solos

450-499	Banjo records
500-699	Popular songs
700-709	Fife, drum and bugle corps records
710-749	Popular songs
750-819	Probably unallocated
820-849	Brass quartets
850-899	Vocal quartets
900-999	Various vocal items, including operatic excerpts as well as popular songs

From this point, the numbering begins to leave gaps:

1103-1104	Italian songs by Ferruccio Giannini
1107-1112	Italian songs by Antonio del Campo
1200-1203	Spanish songs by Ferruccio Giannini
1450-1499	Records by the Metropolitan Orchestra
1551-1571	German songs
1600-1788	Popular songs
3001-3004	Tyrolean songs
3179-3181	Musical comedy choruses
3194-3199	Tyrolean songs
3251-3261	Xylophone solos by Charles P. Lowe
3300-3314	Trombone solos by Arthur Pryor
3401-3421	Cornet solos
3653-3656	Ballads by Mabel Cassedy
3900-3904	Saxophone solos by Jean Moeremans
4150-4153	Euphonium solos by Simone Mantia
8000-8014	Sousa's Band (recorded April 1899)

With the exception of the last block, none of these is dated later than 1898. In February 1899 a new system of numbering was adopted, starting at 01 and continuing in fairly strict chronological sequence until something over 01304 about May 1900. Eldridge Johnson, finding himself in the midst of a legal battle between his associate, Emile Berliner, and the company's erstwhile agent, Frank Seaman, for the rights to Berliner's invention, set out with his own wax recordings, known as Improved Gram-O-Phone Records. They sported neat paper labels printed in gold and black, through which can still be seen the title, artist and recording date, still printed in the Berliner fashion. Having won their case after some eight months, Berliner and Johnson pooled their scientific and engineering genius and set up the Victor Talking Machine Company, which apart from its absorption in 1903 of Seaman's renegade Zonophone record, is the only major label in the history of the industry that never took over or was taken over by another record company. (See also Improved Gram-O-Phone; Victor; Zonophone.)

When Fred Gaisberg arrived in London in July 1898 to set up Berliner's European branch, he too continued the block system of numbering the products. It was more methodical than the system in use in America, however. Each type of performance had its rigid confines of a thousand or ten thousand numbers. Thus, a male soloist in English was issued in a 2000-2999 block, a female from 3000 to 3999, two or more voices of either or both sexes, 4000-4999, and so on through the range of instrumental solos and groups. Three figures were reserved for bands and such orchestras as could make successful records. (Strings were much harder to record accurately than brass or woodwind.) As the thousand-blocks were used up, they were used again with a 2- before the original number. If the soloist or group were other than English, their four-figure number was prefixed with a fifth digit, so that records of European or Asian origin, or performed in such language, were numbered in blocks as follows:

10000	Hebrew	60000	Spanish
20000	Russian	70000	Hungarian, Czech, etc.
30000	French	80000	All Scandinavian languages, and Finnish
40000	German	90000	Dutch
50000	Italian		

Thus, a Berliner numbered 22451 would be a male singer in Russian; 33261 a French woman; 44209 a chorus or a duet in German; and so on. For the first three months of recording in London, the catalog number was the matrix number. From November 1, 1898, a separate matrix series was introduced. When Johnson's wax recording method was adopted in May 1900, a new J- series was introduced. Gradually the old series was phased out and the J prefix dropped, but the numbering system was maintained. It was the practice in both America and Europe during the Berliner era to indicate remakes by a lettering code after the catalog-cum-matrix number. They apparently worked backwards from the end of the alphabet as far as V. If further remakes were needed, they were designated ZZ, YY, XX, etc., although the system was also used to denote parts of a work that could not be forced into the two minutes of playing time for a seven-inch record revolving at (more or less) 78 rpm. Thus we find that the suffix *x* applies to the first verse of a song and suffix *y* to the second.

What of the repertoire of Berliner records? As collectors' items, because they are the original disc records, all Berliners come into the category of interesting, even if all they offer are thin, emasculated, frequently distorted versions of well worn light classics and popular concert items, vocal or instrumental: the kind of thing that raises no flicker of interest among collectors when it occurs on a major label a quarter of a century later. The popular songs of the day, however, rendered by artists specially chosen for the carrying power of their voices and their ability to enunciate clearly, provide primary evidence of exactly how these scraps of nostalgia were sung at the time. In addition, there are on Berliner some valuable examples of ragtime, recorded by top-flight artists such as the Banjo King (so named) and Vess L. Ossman and even Sousa's Band (or as many of its members as were considered necessary and could be accommodated with reasonable ease in the recording room, as the studio was known in those days). There are also other artists working in the ragtime idiom on Berliner. Banjoist Richard L. Weaver, and even the United States Marine Band, recorded excellent examples of what ragtime music sounded like at the outset of its twenty years of popularity as a new musical language, in 1899. The same year, in London, American banjoists Clark and Rays included ragtime in their recorded program, and a music-hall act known as the Musical Avolos, who played all sorts of instruments, recorded just six days earlier a number called *March from Rice's Ragtime Opera* as a guitar and mandolin duet.

In the theatrical world, various actors and actresses on both sides of the Atlantic recorded speeches and/or songs from their shows. There were some very interesting speeches on topics of the day recorded by such luminaries as Robert Ingersoll, the agnostic philosopher and orator whose record, *Hope*, remains today the oldest original master preserved in the RCA Victor vaults, and is remarkable for its clarity. There were other interesting records by Chauncey Depew, a prominent businessman and after-dinner speaker; singing actresses Ada Rehan, Alice Neilson and Jessie Bartlett-Davis; actors Maurice Farkoa and Joseph Jefferson; and Negro folk songs by George W. Johnson, who whistled and guffawed his way through each number with incredible *joie de vivre*.

The most valuable of all Berliner records, however, are those made in Europe by prominent opera singers. In London, Fred Gaisberg captured Ellen Beach Yaw and Marie Tempest, the latter still in musical comedies such as *The Geisha* then. In Russia, records were made by Leonid Sobinoff, Joachim Tartakoff and the Figners, Nikolai and Medea Mei, among others—records which now command hundreds of dollars when a copy turns up once in a very rare while.

As rare pieces of shellac, few records can match the short-lived ten-inch Berliner that was introduced in England in the summer of 1901. It rapidly became the Gramophone Concert Record, with a black and gold paper label (q.v. under Gramophone and Typewriter), but it was, while it lasted, a product superior to its smaller cousin.

BINGOLA

A very rare member of the Grey Gull group of labels, Bingola produced a mere handful of records about 1929 or 1930 in a series numbered 1000 or 1001 to 1008, perhaps a few more. (Carl Kendziora reported in *Record Research* that 1008 was the highest he had seen.)

BLACK PATTI

Black Patti was a Negress who during the latter part of the nineteenth century had a singing technique that legend credits as comparable to that of Adelina Patti. The records that bear her sobriquet offer fine jazz, blues, some sacred records (sermons, spirituals), a few examples of Negro humor, and even a few Wurlitzer organ solos played by Ralph Waldo Emerson. All these were recorded by Gennett (Starr Piano Company), mostly in Chicago, many of them expressly for the Black Patti label. They were produced by the Chicago Record Company, one of whose controlling influences was impresario Mayo Williams.

From the Gennett recording ledgers, we find that the company paid Starr $30 for each side recorded. Sales figures are not available, but the extreme rarity of the records suggests that these must have been very small, especially since the year of their issue, 1927, was a boom year in American records of most other makes. The fact that the length of time between the first issue (8001) and the last (8054) was only some six months, and the absence of any star names in the catalog combine to suggest that Mayo Williams soon became disenchanted with the Chicago Record Company.

Yet there was one truly outstanding issue on Black Patti, the rare but famous coupling by the legendary cornetist Willie Hightower under the name of Hightower's Night Hawks (*Boar Hog Blues* and *Squeeze Me,* 8045). As a recording, it is substandard because wholly underrecorded. But what can be heard of the performance is superb.

The Black Patti label is purple, framed and printed in gold and embodying on the entire top half a peacock with tail feathers fully extended.

BLACK SWAN

The first record label to be owned by Negroes and to cater, ostensibly at least, to the Negro "race" market debuted in May 1921. That such a market existed had been amply demonstrated by OKeh Records the previous autumn (see OKeh), but this venture was different in that its president, Harry Pace, and his erstwhile partner, William C. Handy, were Negroes. Handy was of course the celebrated composer, publisher and bandleader who had already recorded with his band on Columbia and other labels.

I say "ostensibly" because, although the records pressed on the Black Swan label from original masters were undoubtedly by genuine Negro artists—not all of them jazz bands or blues singers by any means—there were also issues derived from Paramount and Olympic masters by bands led by such white musicians as Irving Weiss and Sam Lanin, masked by some pseudonym which was also used for Negro talent. (Fletcher Henderson, the great pianist and arranger, was resident accompanist and leader of various groups that accompanied singers and made dance records for Black Swan, but not everything credited to "Henderson's Novelty Orchestra" or "Henderson's Dance Orchestra" is by a *Fletcher* Henderson band.)

The brand name was derived from the remarkable Negress, Elizabeth Tay-

35

lor Greenfield. Born in Natchez, Miss., in 1809, her voice ranged from baritone to high soprano, a compass of 27 notes. She was equally as well known in London as in New York, giving many concerts in both cities and all over the world. She died in 1876.

The original office of the Pace Phonograph Corporation was at 257 West 138th Street, New York City. By the end of 1921 the then thriving business had moved a few blocks to 2289 Seventh Avenue, also in Harlem. The name was changed in March 1923 to Black Swan Phonograph Company, of the same address. But within about a year, business had apparently fallen off to such an extent that no records were announced to the trade after July 1923, and in April 1924 the Black Swan catalog was merged with Paramount. A block of numbers in the Paramount Race series (from 12100 to 12189) was allocated to such Black Swan issues as were still currently available, and the design of the Paramount label was adapted to include a special reference to Black Swan, even including its trademark and the original catalog number, as well as its new Paramount number.

The recording studio and pressing plant of Pace-Black Swan was in Long Island City, N.Y. The records were issued in a variety of labels in the two years of independence. To begin with, they had an undeniably cheap appearance, black printing on a yellowish-fawn or pale orange background. This was changed to a much more attractive deep orange label, with black surmounting and the name BLACK SWAN in white, with title, artist credit and the usual details in black; but on some copies the white part becomes orange. Next came a much less interesting black label with all trademark, artwork and details in gold, and finally the same design but on a red background. The first catalog series covering popular issues covered numbers 2001 to at least 2125. There was a similar 10000 series that seems to have begun at 10065 and ended at 10083, rather inexplicably, and afterwards another series that probably began at 14101 and continued to 14150. There were also series beginning at 7101, 16001, 18001, 25001, 40001 and 60001, which covered opera of a kind, light classics, drawing-room ballads and other obviously white-oriented material.

The biggest success Black Swan ever had in its short life was probably one of Ethel Waters' first records, *Oh Daddy* and *Down Home Blues*. A close second would be Trixie Smith's *Trixie's Blues* and *Desperate Blues*. To this day, both turn up in fair numbers, but usually in a condition suggesting that their former owners loved them too well but unwisely, without regard to the need for changing steel needles often; for the surfaces of most Black Swan records are inclined to be gritty.

BLU-DISC

One of the very rarest and shortest-lived of all American record labels, Blu-Disc seems to have had one monthly release, December 1924. The discs themselves were indeed dark blue, appearing black unless examined in a strong light. The labels were dark red with black lettering, without decoration of any kind, nor any suggestion as to where the manufacturers (given as "The Blu-Disc Record Co., New York") operated in that city.

The presence on that solitary list of LeRoy Smith and his Dance Orchestra, the Washingtonians, the D'C'ns, Duke Ellington's Orchestra, and singers Alberta Prime and Sonny Greer, suggests that this is another all-Negro all-jazz-and-blues label. But although the Duke is the accompanist on the D'C'ns and the Alberta Prime, and his is the Washingtonians band (playing *Rainy Nights* and *Choo Choo*—the latter an Ellington number), the two sides credited to Duke Ellington's Orchestra (*Nashville Nightingale* and *Rose Marie*) are not by him, but by a commercial white band of no jazz interest whatever. The last two discs on the list are vocals by Irving Post (who may be Irving Kaufman) and Arthur Hall, another prolific recording artist, both of them white and neither having any connection with jazz. The December 1924 leaflet refers to "selections by Paul Robeson, star of 'All Gods Chillen Got Wings' " (sic), but to the best of my knowledge, copies of this record have yet to be found. A postcard-sized publicity handout refers to the records of LeRoy Smith's Dance Orchestra being obtainable at the cigar counter, presumably of the theatre where the Smith band was appearing. If sales depended on the patronage of the theatregoers, it is not surprising that the records are so rare. They are numbered 1001 through 1009 on the list, without any numbers being given for the Robeson item or to one by Fred Weaver, also vaguely referred to; but the labels of the discs themselves show the numbers preceded by the letter T-.

BLUEBIRD

Two makes of 78 rpm record were marketed under this name in the United States. The earlier of these was apparently a Paramount derivative, of exceptional rarity and about which I admit I know nothing more than that it had a short life in 1921–1922. It was produced by the Blue Bird Talking Machine Company of 5607 Santa Fe Avenue, Los Angeles, Cal. The other is the widely known and popular Victor subsidiary, which made its first appearance in the summer of 1932, on sale in Woolworth's yet manufactured from first-class material and featuring excellent dance bands and popular singers. These were eight-inch records. They soon disappeared from the market, such as it was, and the following March, a full-sized ten-inch Bluebird record, with a striking creamy-yellow label printed in blue, made its bow at 35 cents. In the autumn of 1937, the design was changed to a rich dark blue with gold lettering. The flying bluebird with a strangely woebegone expression was now reduced in size, and was shown against a stave. A little over a year later, the symbol of good luck was reduced still further and partly overprinted with the name of the make—and surmounted by the familiar dog-and-gramophone trademark. This design remained until the end of the era covered by this book. (Mexican issues of the earlier years had green instead of blue printing on yellow.)

Bluebird as eight-inch records were numbered 1800 upwards. The regular successors began their numbering at B-5000 and continued to B-11594 until November 1942, except that from B-7893 to B-9042 were allocated to "race" (later renamed "rhythm and blues") records and country-and-western items. B-9043 to B-9999 were never used. (Records in these categories issued prior to B-7893 in October 1938 were intermingled with regular popular dance and vocal items.) There were other series of Bluebird records not regularly stocked by stores but available on order from Camden, N.J. B-1000 and under were children's records issued between May 1936 and April 1946; B-2002 to B-2199 were exclusively Cajun artists' records, issued between June 1935 and September 1936 but running backwards (!); and B-2200 to B-4999 was what was called an International series that was current from April 1934 to March 1942. In November 1942 both Victor (q.v.) and Bluebird altered their entire numerical systems to four-figure serials prefixed by two-figure category codes instead of the more customary letters. The Bluebird label was discontinued in March 1950 but in 1976 it was reactivated as an LP featuring popular and jazz collectors' items.

The matrix number series dovetails at all times with Victor's, but at no time is the matrix number shown on either the label or the wax. It was apparently customary to suppress even the take digit on Bluebird (though not on Victor), so that with the exception of the very last issues it is impossible to determine visually which take was used.

To introduce a new make of record, almost as a competitor to the principal product, at a time when public interest in records was at its lowest ebb in the history of sound recording, seems ill-advised. But the marketing strategy was anything but feckless. During the Depression a large share of what remained of the record market was going for cutrate dime-store labels like Oriole (q.v.). Victor, indisputably the leading label in prestige, watched as sales went to cheap labels it could not compete with at 75 cents. Hence the decision to launch a 35-cent label.

Although the very earliest Bluebirds are not commonly met with, they proved sufficiently successful to persuade the Victor executives that they could survive. Not only did they look good and sound good technically; they featured front-rank artists, especially from 1938 through 1942. Other cheap labels in the booming 1920s had flooded the market with records made for the most part by a small number of almost entirely male vocalists and outlandishly named studio dance bands. Bluebird, in the 1930s and early 1940s, offered names to attract the public: George Hall, Dolly Dawn and her Dawn Patrol, Shep Fields and his Rippling Rhythm, Alvino Rey, Teddy Powell, Dick Todd, Ozzie Nelson, Vincent Lopez, Freddy Martin, Earl Hines, Fats Waller, and most important of all, Artie Shaw and Glenn Miller.

The records Glenn Miller made for Bluebird between the autumn of 1938 and the spring of 1942, when he was elevated to the Victor label, are among the most famous popular records of all time, and certainly the most reissued, all over the world, in both 78 and microgroove form. Outstanding among them are his signature tune, *Moonlight Serenade*, originally announced in June 1939; *Chattanooga Choo Choo*, in September 1941; and *In the Mood*, issued in November 1939.

The "race" and "country" records did not sell in comparable numbers, as of course they were aimed at sections of the public rather than the public as a whole. They rarely appeared in overseas catalogs (although a surprisingly large number of "country" items were issued in England on the Regal Zonophone label; but sales were negligible, and the records are extremely rare collectors' pieces today as a result). The blues issues by Lonnie Johnson, Washboard Sam, Jazz Gillum, Tommy McClennon, Tampa Red and many others are more easily found. The most coveted of Bluebird records may be the reissues from original Victor masters of titles made by legendary jazz musicians five, ten or more years earlier.

Bluebird was a spearhead in the mid-thirties thrust to revive the record market. Where it succeeded, others followed, technically and materially less attractively in many ways. For though inexpensive, Bluebird records looked and sounded like records from a more expensive label.

BLUE NOTE

One of the first specialist labels catering to the jazz connoisseur, Blue Note was launched in 1939 by Alfred Lion and Frank Wolfe. Over the next decade it produced some remarkable original recordings of jazz music played without commercial considerations by piano soloists of the boogie-woogie school (Albert Ammons, Meade "Lux" Lewis and Pete Johnson), guitarist Teddy Bunn, and pickup groups that featured Sidney Bechet, Art Hodes, George Wettling, Frank Newton, J. C. Higginbotham, and many others who did not often record for the major companies. When bop came into fashion towards the end of World War II, Blue Note saw to it that ample specimens were available to its customers. Since then it has remained a major label for modern jazz.

Although the quality of the music produced on Blue Note during the years between 1939 and 1942 was high, the pressing material was frequently substandard. Wartime and post-war products are usually gritty and not longwearing. Ten- and twelve-inch records were issued at irregular intervals. They carried a distinctive modern design on the label, with the words "Blue Note" at right angles to each other in white on a blue ground. The rest of the label in the angle was a pale yellow or white, with the details, including full personnel of any bands used, in blue or black.

After the war, the firm of Vogue in France obtained the rights to issue Blue Note records. Through this arrangement, the British branch was able to release a few also; but most, if not all, were dubbed from original pressings, not pressed from masters.

The Blue Note offices were at 767 Lexington Avenue in New York City. The venture seems to have used several private studios for recording, and a bewildering array of unorthodox matrix series appears on the records.

BROADCAST

Originally Broadcast was an eight-inch British record, proudly described on the label as "the long playing record," though in fact it was of scarcely greater duration than a normal ten-inch. The grooving was finer and the label smaller, so that slightly longer playing time could be accommodated on one side than would otherwise be the case. Broadcast existed from July 1927 to July 1933 and used no American masters. But its label mates, the Broadcast Super Twelve, which was introduced in March 1931 and remained on the market until March 1934, and the shorter-lived Broadcast International, extant from January 1933 until April that year, both drew on the American Perfect catalog and others from Europe, and introduced to British audiences the voice of Charlie Palloy, hailed as a serious rival to Bing Crosby, and the more impressive names of Morton Downey (already known in England for his personal appearances there in 1928 and 1930) and Dick Powell, singing four numbers from his film, *Gold Diggers of 1933*. The Morton Downey records, augmented by further titles made for Broadcast while he was in London again in 1933, are quite easy to find; the Dick Powells are considerably rarer.

There were also Broadcast Twelve records, devoted mainly to popular concert classics and drawing-room ballads; Broadcast Super Dance records, none of them American and few of them by anything but the regular studio band under a variety of imaginative names; Broadcast Four-Tune records, mostly dance tunes crammed tightly in pairs on each side, and again all British; and briefly, in 1934–1935, Broadcast Imperial, including records by American artists Sophie Tucker and Eddie Cantor, the former recorded in London and originally on Broadcast Twelve, the latter on Perfect and associated labels. The rest of the issues on this make are mostly British or German in origin.

Broadcast Super Twelve records are numbered 3001 to 3374. When of American origin, they display the matrix numbers in the smooth area round the label, usually in well spaced, clear type. One exception known to exist is the so-named High Steppers' record of *Lawd, You Made the Night Too Long*, which is dubbed from an American Crown pressing. Its matrix number is visible indented under and showing through the bright scarlet and gold Broadcast Super Twelve label. British recordings issued on this label have matrix numbers in a series starting apparently at L-0500 and also to be seen through the label, sometimes in type, sometimes faintly handwritten.

At the outset, Broadcast records were produced by the Vocalion Gramophone Company Ltd. of Hayes, Middlesex. Then, early in 1932, the Crystalate Gramophone Record Company took over Vocalion and all its labels, gradually phasing them out along with its own Imperial in favour of Rex (both q.v.). As a Vocalion product, all the various forms of Broadcast were good sellers, the eight-inch variety particularly so. But when these were increased in size to nine inches, and soon afterwards Crystalate assumed control, sales must have slumped, for the latter-day Broadcasts are not as a rule as readily obtainable as their forerunners. In quality they were all excellent, pressed on good, durable material and selling at 1s. 6d. (then about 35 cents) each.

BROADWAY

    This is one of the lower-priced labels of the 1920s that originally relied on Paramount for its material. Then, from 1924 until its disappearance in 1931, it drew on other sources such as Emerson, Crown and Banner.

    Until the bankruptcy of the Bridgeport Die and Machine Company of 170 Elm Street, Bridgeport, Conn., in the early summer of 1925, this company pressed Broadway records. After that, apparently Paramount (the New York Recording Laboratories) produced it from its own and Plaza Music Company masters. The Crown masters were used sparingly for a time in 1931, just before the end of Broadway as a label.

    The earliest design was an intricate and detailed drawing in gold of part of the Manhattan skyline on a black background, with Broadway in gold capitals on a white bar. Later the white disappeared and the label was bright blue with gold, until it returned to black and gold for the rest of its life. The earlier Bridgeport issues were numbered 11000 upwards, until in 1926 a new series was in-

troduced, starting at 1000. There was also a short-lived 8000 series that seems to have been devoted to country-and-western music, and another beginning at 5000 but offering only a handful of "race" items—fine blues and hot bands from Paramount and associated sources.

The 1000 series included superb records by Lovie Austin's Blues Serenaders, Fletcher Henderson and his Orchestra (as "Earl Randolph's Orchestra"; on the 5000 series he was renamed "Steve Carr's Rhythm Aces"), Junie Cobb (as "Lee's Black Diamonds"), and some interesting dance records under perplexing pseudonyms, with the usual complement of popular vocal and light instrumental titles. This series is the rarer, on the whole, and is mainly electrically recorded. The earlier 11000 series is all acoustic.

BRUNSWICK

The Brunswick-Balke-Collender Company of Dubuque, Iowa was formed in 1845 as a piano manufacturer. It was not until 1916 that the first vertical-cut Brunswick records were announced. These green labels are very rare now. The subsequent lateral-cut discs that first appeared in January 1920 were a very much better commercial proposition, so that even these veterans can still be found in fair numbers.

Originally, the celebrity (5000) series had violet labels, with an eccentric white slashing effect surmounted by a small shield with the initial B, some conventional leaf decoration and the word Brunswick in copperplate script. The standard (2000) series was black, but otherwise the same. A little later came the gold Hall of Fame series numbered 10000, 15000, 30000 and 50000, the first two being ten-inch ($1 and $1.50 each) and the others twelve-inch ($1.25 and $2 each). The violet labels disappeared in 1923, after fewer than two hundred had been issued. The bestsellers among them were promptly reissued as black labels at black label prices (75 cents). There was a parallel 20000 series of twelve-inch standard issues that sold at $1.25.

47

The artists appearing on these series were stars indeed. Operatic celebrities from the Metropolitan were no longer the exclusive preserve of Victor and Columbia. On acoustic and electric Brunswicks we find Florence Easton, Mario Chamlee, Sigrid Onegin, Claire Dux, Elisabeth Rethberg, Friedrich Schorr, John Charles Thomas and Michael Bohnen. Not all of them recorded in New York; some were German Polydor artists to whose records Brunswick had access. But all were front-rank singers of international repute. On the same gold label Brunswick offered records of Wilhelm Mengelberg conducting the New York Philharmonic Orchestra. On one, no less a celebrity than Arturo Toscanini himself conducted the same orchestra in the Scherzo and Nocturne from Mendelssohn's *A Midsummer Night's Dream.* This was issued in June 1926.

The popular or "standard" series followed much the same course as similar series on the labels of Brunswick's major rivals. Outstanding among its dance bands of the 1920s was the Chicago-based organization led by composer and tenor saxophonist Isham Jones. His 1921 recording of *Wabash Blues,* with muted cornet work by Louis Panico that had the grotesque sound of a woman laughing hysterically, was a bestseller and achieved unexpected publicity when it was used on stage throughout the Broadway performance of a play about prostitution called *Rain.* Brunswick also secured the services of the Oriole Orchestra from the Edgewater Beach Hotel, Chicago. It built up a catalog of first-class dance music and hot jazz by such bands as Fletcher Henderson's, Duke Ellington's, Ray Miller's, Ben Selvin's and Gene Rodemich's. It issued excellent recordings by the Original Memphis Five, usually augmented slightly and renamed the Cotton Pickers.

The biggest seller of the acoustic Brunswicks was a bizarre recording by a trio called the Mound City Blue Blowers. Recorded in Chicago in 1924, it consisted of a comb, a kazoo and a banjo. The comb player was an ex-jockey from St. Louis named William "Red" McKenzie. Eight years later he was an attraction with Paul Whiteman's orchestra, crooning love songs in a likable style and rivalling Bing Crosby himself. But in 1924 McKenzie was a jazz musician on the most unorthodox of instruments. So great was the Blue Blowers' success that they were invited to play in the Grill Room of the Piccadilly Hotel in London's West End in April 1925. This followed the issue of their first few records, including the sensational *Arkansas Blues* and *Blue Blues*, on the British equivalent of Brunswick. This was known as Brunswick Cliftophone, the latter a gramophone marketed by the music publishers, Chappell Piano Company, Ltd. of New Bond Street, London, who were from October 1923 the "sole sales concessionaires" in Britain for Brunswick records. Not everything made in America by Brunswick was issued in the United Kingdom, but everything in the British catalog bore the same number as its American counterpart. Thus it was that many great singers and dance bands became available and well known to British record buyers, many of whom found the excellent recording quality more to their liking than the constricted sound of His Master's Voice (q.v.) and the by no means rumble free Columbia, however smooth.

One of the most unusual records of its time was issued on Brunswick in July 1925, just prior to the introduction of Brunswick's own version of electric recording. (They called it the Light-Ray process. It dispensed with a microphone, which was replaced by light rays and a photo-electric cell.) This record came from a session in Los Angeles where Abe Lyman's California Orchestra, another popular feature of the Brunswick catalog, was conducted by no less a personality than comedian Charlie Chaplin, who played violin while the Lyman band recorded two dance numbers Chaplin had written himself. (It is worth mentioning that just two years before this session, another prominent film star had ventured into the Brunswick studios, this time in New York, and recorded Amy Woodforde-Finden's *Kashmiri Song* and, in Spanish, José Padilla's *El Relicario*. He was Rudolph Valentino, recording for the only time. It was never issued at the time. Though it was scheduled as a memorial record soon after Valentino's death on August 23, 1926, the release was cancelled. Eventually, dubbings of both sides were made available in 1930 by a private concern. They hardly show the Great Lover to advantage as a vocalist.)

With the coming of electric recording, Brunswick also launched its famous machine, the Panatrope, which reproduced records electrically. Nationwide tests before audiences sceptical, enthusiastic or simply curious attempted to prove that there was no discernible difference between a live performance and a Light-Ray Brunswick record played on a Brunswick Panatrope. Edison attempted the same kind of tent-show. Both he and Brunswick apparently captured the imagination, and to some extent the pocketbooks, of some of their audiences. Listening to either product today leaves one amazed that hard-sell could produce such a brainwashing.

A few months earlier, another significant event took place. Brunswick linked arms with Vocalion (q.v.). Thereafter, the latter functioned simply as a subsidiary of Brunswick. Several of its artists were raised to the Brunswick peerage while others appeared more or less simultaneously on both labels—until the collapse of Wall Street in October 1929 brought Brunswick itself near to extinction.

Before this, however, in the spring of 1927, Chappell's in England had given up rights to issue Brunswick records. The management of Brunswick's London branch had passed to one Count Anthony de Bosdari, a wealthy businessman. He immediately set about reorganizing the British Brunswick catalog under that name. The numbers of the records imported from America no longer remained the same as in that country, and a series devoted to recordings made in London by native and visiting artists was launched, the numbers beginning at 101. By featuring the sensational young Spanish-American pianist Fred Elizalde and his music from the Savoy Hotel, and other stellar popular artists like pioneer crooner Melville Gideon, New Orleans girl singer Alice Morley, twenty-year-old revue star Jessie Matthews, and Ambrose's Mayfair Hotel Orchestra, de Bosdari hoped to make British Brunswick a power in the land.

Nor were the classics ignored. The gold label Hall of Fame series was joined by a violet labeled series drawn mostly from German and French sources and featuring pianist Walter Gieseking playing Debussy, the London Chamber Orchestra playing Bach, and the Berlin Philharmonic Orchestra playing von Suppé.

The regular Brunswick records (resplendent in black and gold with a shield design flanked by curlicues that gave the labels a strangely old-world appearance that was an exact replica of the American styling) continued to present lengthy lists every month. They were records by established favorites such as the bands of Abe Lyman, Ben Bernie (absorbed in 1925 from Vocalion), Ben Selvin, and Hal Kemp. For the jazz connoisseur, the records would soon become classics: Red Nichols and his Five Pennies (as often as not, there were eight, ten or more musicians on these), Irving Mills and his Hotsy-Totsy Gang, and the legendary King Oliver and his Dixie Syncopators. On the popular vocal side, Brunswick featured Harry Richman, Belle Baker, and the pioneer talking-picture maker, Al Jolson. It was Brunswick that recorded Jolson singing *Sonny Boy* and released it in England to coincide with the showing of the film in which it was featured. This was *The Singing Fool*, and it was said to have increased the sale of ladies' handkerchiefs nicely. The demand for the record was such that the factory worked around the clock to keep pace with orders. It is said that a crowd besieged its gates in an attempt to buy copies hot off the press, literally. The frequency with which battered specimens turn up in junkshops to this day seems to bear out these legends. Other Jolson records on Brunswick, back to 1924, had sold well, but this was fantastic.

It did not help the fortunes of Brunswick enough, however, to stave off disaster. In August 1928 a British firm known as the Duophone Syndicate had taken over the affairs of British Brunswick. But within a year, Jolson and all his tears notwithstanding, the new setup was itself in difficulties, and British Brunswick perished. In April 1930 the American branch, Brunswick-Balke-Collender, sold out to the film company, Warner Brothers. Warner did its best to maintain the Brunswick image by signing up film stars they had under contract. What followed, in addition to the dance bands already established as Brunswick artists, were a batch of unusual records by such as Gloria Swanson and Noah Beery, and still more by Harry Richman and Al Jolson. But they didn't sell. The Depression had by now bitten deep. So in December 1931 Warners sold out to the newly formed American Record Corporation, which was already producing Banner, Cameo, Oriole, Perfect and Romeo records for the chainstore counters.

Brunswick became ARC's most expensive line, maintaining its price tag at 75 cents while the other labels sold at or around 35 cents each. While Warners had Brunswick, it signed up two acts that caught the ears of such record buyers as could still afford luxuries: the Mills Brothers, that incredible Negro quartet from Ohio that sounded like a small jazz band without using any orthodox instruments other than one guitar, and Bing Crosby. No sooner had ARC assumed control than Guy Lombardo and his Royal Canadians, now a new favorite among dancers, was lured to Brunswick from Columbia. Duke Ellington and his Orchestra came over from Victor. With the Mills Brothers, Bing Crosby, and a remarkable young trio of girl singers from New Orleans, the Boswell Sisters (also inherited from the Warner days), the Brunswick popular roster looked unbeatable. In England, Decca assumed responsibility for issuing Brunswicks and retained the franchise for two and a half years, until American Decca came into being (q.v.). In the United States, a new cheap line had been introduced during the Warner Brothers period, Melotone (q.v.). Its British opposite number, Panachord, was duly admitted into the Decca enclave along with Brunswick.

In September 1939, with the resurrection of Columbia under the CBS banner, Brunswick was gradually phased out. The last of the line was 8517, issued in April 1940. But there had been only light classics and popular concert pieces issued on Brunswick for the last eight months of its life. All the popular bands and singers had changed the black and silver Brunswick label for the plain red and gold of the new Columbia in September 1939. In the summer of 1944 and for a year or two thereafter, Decca issued a black and gold Brunswick series numbered 80000 upwards, mainly reissues of jazz collectors' items from the original Brunswick and Vocalion catalogs. But this label, apart from the familiar Brunswick name in flowing script, bore no likeness to the originals.

The numbering of Brunswick records reached 4999 in unbroken continuity from the first 2000 in January 1920. It took until February 1931 to do it, whereupon the system leapt over the 5000 block (partially allocated eleven years before) and resumed at 6000. A 7000 series of "race" records (mostly vocal blues and bearing a striking label where lightning flashes replaced the curlicues growing up the sides of the shield) began on March 18, 1927, reaching 7233 and a collection of calypso records before being discontinued in July 1932. This part of the series was resumed in January 1935 at 7301 immediately following 6999, and continued until the end in 1940. The last of the popular twelve-inch 20000 series was 20141. Most of its short life was taken up with conventional potpourris, selections and "vocal gems" from operas, operettas, musical comedies and films. One outstanding collectors' item was the selection of numbers from *Face the Music,* issued on 20106 in April 1932. It was quickly withdrawn, and since it featured Bing Crosby, it has become one of the most sought-after of all his records by those who specialize in them.

The Brunswick catalog under ARC direction included some fine examples of all kinds of popular music, with a goodly proportion of film songs recorded by the original stars themselves. Fred Astaire, Virginia Bruce, Mary Martin, Tony Martin, Dorothy Lamour, Phil Regan and Alice Faye come most readily to mind. Leon Belasco's Orchestra in 1937 introduced the Andrews Sisters to a recording studio, and few of the big names of swing were not at one time or another to be heard on Brunswick, some making their recording debuts as leaders on that label: Gene Krupa, Jack Teagarden, Artie Shaw, Harry James (with a promising young vocalist named Frank Sinatra on one of the last of all Brunswicks, *Melancholy Mood* and *From the Bottom of My Heart*) and Glenn Miller all come into this category. There was a long and impressive array of records by Mildred Bailey and her husband Red Norvo, not to mention the classic combos of Teddy Wilson (usually featuring Billie Holiday as vocalist, and with Benny Goodman sometimes present, anonymously or as "Shoeless John Jackson"). In June 1937, items from Irving Mills's Master catalog began to be reissued on Brunswick, so Duke Ellington, Raymond Scott, and the Will Hudson-Eddie DeLange band added strength to the attractive new black and silver label with the "organ pipe" design.

From the outset until March 31, 1928, Brunswick records were given a different matrix number for each take, starting at 2000. By the end of the Warner era, this series, prefixed E since the coming of electric recording, had reached 37525 before ARC replaced this with their own numbering, then just past 11000 (see Banner). This was maintained until the end of the label, and it was then continued on the new Columbias—at least at the New York studios at 1776 Broadway. Sessions taking place in other cities had their own blocks of numbers, with the appropriate initial of the location as a prefix (C - Chicago, ATL - Atlanta, NO or NOR - New Orleans, LA - Los Angeles, and so on; although acoustic recordings made outside New York sometimes were numbered by New York, or were given an A prefix for Los Angeles or a CH suffix for Chicago).

On and after April 1, 1928, all Brunswick (and Vocalion) records were given matrix numbers with letter suffixes according to takes, according to the practice of most labels. The ARC series set its Brunswick masters aside by prefixing the New York recordings with B and continuing the C, LA and other prefixes as before.

When Warners' reintroduced the Brunswick label into Britain in December 1930 after fifteen months' absence, the numbering was begun at 1000. From 1500 onwards, a zero was placed in front, evidently to distinguish the series from the French one, also started at 1000. Records that remained in the catalog from the earliest days of the Warner regime were eventually also given the same zero prefix.

As a rule, Brunswick records made after the end of 1923 do not show the matrix numbers in the wax until the beginning of the ARC era in January 1932. On some of the earlier issues in this eight-year period, the last two, sometimes three digits are visible in minuscule type in the wax close to the rim of the label. Because they do not appear on the label at any time prior to ARC, compiling a discography of any Brunswick artist between December 1923 and December 1931 is extremely difficult, the more so since the original recording ledgers, held in Universal City, California by MCA, the present owners of Decca, are by no means complete or easily accessible. Whereas titles issued in England on Brunswick Cliftophone in 1924 and up to 1927 frequently show the matrix number heavily etched into the central part below the label and visible through it; or it may be embossed on the same area in reverse. The faint handwritten date visible, also in reverse, close to the locked run-off groove on British issues is the date of processing the master used for the particular specimen and not, as has often been assumed, the date of recording.

The following chart shows the approximate first matrix number recorded in each year from 1919 to 1931, when the ARC serial replaced the Brunswick-Balke-Collender original (see Banner):

Year	Matrix	Year	Matrix
1919 (c. Sept.)	2000	1926	17320
1920	2500	1927	21100
1921	4500	1928	25820
1922	7000	1929	28920
1923	9700	1930	31750
1924	12200	1931	35889
1925	14570		

BUDDY

As far as can be ascertained, all issues on this label are from Gennett masters, dating from 1923 to 1926. The numbering of Buddy records begins at 8000 or 8001, and about eighty or so were issued, possibly a hundred.

Little is known about Buddy. The Gennett files do not refer to it as they do to other labels for which the Starr Piano Company supplied pressings. But the typeface is as for Gennett, and the dark blue label is the same tint as the standard Gennett of the period, printed in gold with the brand name in florid script across the upper half. The design is as unique as it is remarkable. The outer edge of the label is divided into six segments, each of which bears the name of a company having no obvious connection with the phonograph business, although obviously affiliated with one another: the Southern Aluminum Company, New Orleans, La. (and Chicago, Ill.); the Aluminum Specialty Company, Atlanta, Ga. (and Dallas, Tex.); and the Associated Manufacturing Company, Galveston, Tex. (and Oakland, Cal.). If these widely scattered companies in fact sold Buddy records through their commercial outlets, it is surprising that so very few show up now anywhere. Yet they are well worth finding. They include titles by Duke Ellington and his Washingtonians, the New Orleans Rhythm Kings, and Jelly-Roll Morton's Incomparables. No one seems to have a complete listing of Buddy's output. Who knows what other gems may have been issued on Buddy—perhaps exclusively?

BUSY BEE

A little known pre-World War I label, derived from Imperial and probably sold in some department or chainstore. Single-sided and extremely rare, Busy Bee does not offer any material of outstanding value, as far as is known.

CADILLAC

Another very obscure vertical-cut record of the Edison type, reported by Ray Wile in *Record Research*, May-June 1956. These were eight-inch records with black labels printed in gold, laminated and made by the Clements Manufacturing Company of Chicago. Nothing more is known about this label at present.

CAMEO

Cameo records, products of the Cameo Record Corporation of 110 West 38th Street, New York, first appeared in February 1922. For most of their life they were inexpensive merchandise aimed at the less discerning but immense market that wanted the new songs presented in a way its customers could understand, at only 50 cents each. Macy's was the principal outlet for Cameo. The president was Edward N. Burns, late of the Columbia Gramophone Company.

So Cameo records offered competition on terms competitive with the other newly launched cheap lines. As a label, Cameo offered little of what might be termed "culture," which at least in the 1920s meant classical music. Perhaps the nearest Cameo reached to this was a handful of violin solos of light pieces played by Eugene Ormandy, then a long way from becoming the world-famous conductor of the Philadelphia Symphony, amongst others. The shoestring budget on which Cameo seems to have operated during its early years would probably account for the absence of any big names in the dance band world, although Sam Lanin, the omnipresent, made Cameo records as the Broadway Broadcasters, and there were interesting hot arrangements of popular numbers by the

Varsity Eight, a slightly reduced California Ramblers group. One of the commonest Cameo records to this day is *It Ain't Gonna Rain No Mo'*, sung by Al Bernard ("The Boy from Dixie") to Frank Ferera's ukelele accompaniment. This was backed by an apparently white girl named Blanche Klaise singing a bluesy number, *Daddy, Change Your Mind*. This bogus blues record challenged the supremacy of a genuine vaudeville-blues artist who made many Cameo records, Lucille Hegamin. With her Blue Flame Syncopators (or sometimes only one piano, various accompanists being present on different sessions) Miss Hegamin made many successful records that sold to white and Negro buyers alike.

In January 1924, a 50-cent label known as Lincoln was launched by Cameo, and in July 1926 Romeo was introduced. Early in 1928, the Pathe Phonograph and Radio Corporation merged with Cameo. From that point on, it is easy to find identical performances on both labels, and sometimes on Lincoln and Romeo as well, albeit disguised by different aliases. The chill blast of the Depression brought about the formation of the American Record Corporation, and the inclusion of Brunswick, Banner and their associated labels. When some of these were weeded out in the early 1930s, Cameo was among them.

The first Cameo labels were quietly distinctive, black with gold lettering and the name Cameo in olde-Englyshe script on an heraldic shield. This did not last long. In a matter of months it had been replaced by a hideous affair involving twelve perpendicular red stripes like prison bars on a dark blue ground, with details in gold and easy reading impossible. The space above the shield is occupied by a profile in white of a girl facing left, in an ornate gold frame. Evidently this was not popular, for within a year or so it was replaced by a dull black label, lettering in gold, the shield gone, and a matronly woman in a similar frame, facing right. This survived until 1927, at the end of which year the details of the recording were printed in black on a large white shield. Thus the last Cameo label was as attractive as the first.

Cameo catalog numbers begin at 201, reaching around 1300 before changing to 8100 in February 1928. By the end of the year, at about 8400, it was decided that the numbers should be advanced to 9000; but this block only lasted the year 1929. In January 1930, with Banner's numbers starting afresh at 0500, Cameo's were kept in step, four hundred behind Banner, starting at 0100.

The matrix series began at 100 and reached nearly 4200 by the autumn of 1929. Thereafter, for what remained of Cameo's career, pressings bore only ARC serials. Some pressings of the Pathe partnership era show both Pathe and Cameo numbers. If there is a take letter after the Cameo number, the record is of Cameo origin; otherwise it is from Pathe.

The outlet in England for Cameo records was a curious-looking label known as Dominion, pressed from appallingly gritty material in a factory in Luton, Bedfordshire. Even at 1s. 3d each—say 25 cents at the exchange rate of that time—they were no bargain, and in June 1930 the company collapsed. Cameo had already disappeared from the Dominion catalog, which at the end was issuing Grey Gull material under the names of existing and respected English bandleaders. (See Dominion, Lincoln and Romeo.)

The following chart shows approximately the first recorded Cameo matrix number in each year of the label's career:

1922	100	1925	1300	1928	2785
1923	380	1926	1755	1929	3560
1924	775	1927	2885		

CAPITAL

Not to be confused with Capitol, this is one of the most enigmatic labels of all. According to Carl Kendziora in his column "Beyond the Cobwebs" (*Record Research*, November-December 1959), only one specimen with this label name is known. Perhaps there were no others. The known item is an unremarkable coupling by a large dance band called Pete Sullivan and his King Taste Pilots playing *Missouri Squabble* and *I Don't Believe You*. This is shown as made by the New York Record Company, and is numbered 752 (A and B). The label is plain red, with gold lettering and no decoration or trademark of any kind. No matrix numbers are shown on the wax, and the titles give little clue as to the date. Other companies recording *Missouri Squabble* did so in 1928, so this may date the Capital issue at least approximately. Other versions give the composer credit correctly to Holst and Kretzmer, whereas the Capital label gives it (and its coupling) to one Spier—almost certainly Larry Spier.

The same article mentions another pair of issues, but credited to the New York Phonograph Recording Company. Instead of Capital, one appears under the label of New York: two more dance tunes, this time by Ben Rader and his Missouri Athletic Association Orchestra, on catalog number 129. The other bears the number 607 and is by Vereinigte Sänger von Brooklyn, N.Y., which is the make—so it says. Physical similarities suggest that all these come from the same source, but what that source was is not known. Mr. Kendziora suggests one plausible answer, that each was privately made, probably with a limited pressing run.

CAPITOL

The youngest of the labels included in this book was launched just before the AFM recording ban of August 1, 1942. It bowed in with the blessing and material assistance of composer-vocalist Johnny Mercer. Although based in Los Angeles, Capitol recorded in New York too, after the war also recording in Kansas City, New Orleans and other central points, just as Victor, OKeh, Columbia and others did between the wars.

From the beginning, Capitol was always anchored in popular recording. Later, in the LP era, the label ventured into symphonies and chamber music via the superb Angel catalog from Europe. Its earliest catalogs, however, concentrated on popular artists of the 1940s, notably the sophisticated cabaret near-blues artist Nellie Lutcher, avant-garde bandleader Stan Kenton, and the deliberately corny pseudo-Dixieland unit directed by trombonist Pee Wee Hunt. Margaret Whiting, Jo Stafford, Johnny Mercer, Andy Russell, Kay Starr, Mel Torme, Peggy Lee, Gisele Mackenzie, Johnny Standley and Stan Freberg were all Capitol favorites. In the early 1950s, Frank Sinatra moved to Capitol from Columbia. Within the period of this book, Capitol issued the last records by Paul Whiteman, one featuring Billie Holiday as "Lady Day."

The original Capitol label was glossy black with silver lettering, showing an outline of the Capitol with the label name in heavy script below it. Numbering of the records started at 100, of the matrices at 1. There were no Capitol records issued in England until December 1948, under Decca's aegis. The firm passed to EMI Records in January 1956, and Capitol has been an important part of the EMI complex ever since.

CARDINAL

As might be expected, Cardinal records sport red labels and the appropriate bird. They are printed in gold. Although the trade announcements of their first appearance in December 1920 state that the Cardinal Phonograph Company of 106 East 19th Street, New York, had three factories (in Zanesville and Newark, Ohio, and Point Pleasant, N.J.), the studios were the Criterion at 1227 Broadway and the New York Recording Laboratories at 1140 Broadway, both in New York City. The products themselves are in no way as deluxe as their physical appearance might suggest.

Not at all common, Cardinal records were pressed on gritty shellac and offered the same sort of material as dozens of other labels of the time. The matrix series began probably at C-500 but did not reach C-1000, as far as is known. Catalog numbers started at 2000 and never got beyond 2100.

A new Cardinal label, much the same in design, made its appearance with number 500 in the late summer of 1922. This drew from Gennett, and was much better. As far as can be determined, no great jazz or popular masterpieces were issued on the new Cardinal either. But the quality of the record itself was an advance over the first group.

CARNIVAL

This was the short-lived house label for John Wanamaker's of Philadelphia and New York. It was pressed by the Bridgeport Die and Machine Company of Bridgeport, Conn., during the autumn of 1924 and possibly for the opening months of 1925. When the pressing plant went bankrupt in the summer of 1925, the life of Carnival ended too.

The catalog, such as it was, derived mostly from Paramount and Emerson. One of the most important items in it was the Jelly Roll Morton *Mr. Jelly Lord/ Steady Roll* (Carnival 11397), particularly because the take used for the first title is peculiar to this label, as far as is known. Otherwise Carnival, as rare as it is gaudy (black with rainbow-coloured designs rampaging about over the upper half), offers no more than quiet, conventional issues from Paramount, its subsidiaries or its associates.

CHALLENGE

Unsuitably named, this record first appeared towards the end of 1925, a product of the Gennett catalog that later included Banner/Plaza and Paramount material before it disappeared less than three years later.

The label is a dull, nebulous green with gold lettering. Down the left side stands a knight in armour, all set to challenge all comers. The quality of the surfaces is nowhere near as good as the parent labels usually offered. Since nothing appeared on Challenge that was not also on the source labels, as far as is known, collectors would be wiser to pursue the originals. If not endowed with velvet-face surfaces, the latter are at least somewhat less crackling.

The original Gennett masters showed no matrix numbers, so neither does Challenge. No attempt was made to mask the matrices of the other sources of supply. Artists were frequently billed under pseudonyms. The Challenge repertoire was aimed at a mail-order clientele who wanted current popular tunes, and never mind who played or sang them. The numbers are all three-figured.

CHAMPION

This is the longest-lived of all the Gennett subsidiaries, even outliving the parent. The first Champions were issued in September 1925 and the last in December 1934, four years after the final Gennett. The numbers ranged from 15001 to 16832. For about half of Champion's nine years, the labels were red with gold lettering and a tasteful design round the edge. The later issues had the same design on a black background. When Decca bought the rights to certain Gennetts and to the Champion trademark, the red label was reactivated in the summer of 1935 for about a year. Similar in design to the original, it was slightly smaller, and of course credited manufacture to Decca.

As long as Gennett existed as a label, Champion issues were all drawn from its progenitor. In many—even most—instances among the dance bands and jazz groups and blues singers, pseudonyms were used, fairly consistently. Thus, Bailey's Lucky Seven became The Seven Champions. Earlier on, a curious device was used to camouflage the Gennett origin even further. The matrix numbers, which never appeared anywhere in the wax or under the label, were given on the label in reverse. Thus, Gennett matrix number 9655 appears on Champion as 5569.

Some very fine and exceptionally rare jazz, blues and country-and-western records were issued on Champion, before and after the death of Gennett. Those released during the Depression are of course among the outstandingly rare records of any kind, in any period. It may not say much for the Starr Piano Company's business acumen that such gems continued to be recorded and issued when some of their sales were in the three figures, but collectors owe the company a debt of gratitude. Perhaps because their head office was in Richmond, Indiana, the shock waves of the Depression did not affect sales as violently as if they had been in New York. In any case, the artist fees were minimal, and most of what are now collectors' items were aimed at small sections of the public. No doubt Starr was accustomed to pressing and selling in trivial numbers.

The Decca Champions continued the good work. Some fine blues, jazz and hot dance music appeared in the new 40000 series. There were also some records by Clyde McCoy, his "wah-wah" trumpet extravagances and his orchestra. These were issued in England on Rex (q.v.), along with some vintage Gene Autry sides from the Starr era. There were several good sides by a small band led by Red Norvo, the master xylophonist, as "Len Herman and his Orchestra." Champion also issued a number of sides by British bands, notably Brian Lawrence's, which bemused some American critics so much that they wondered whether Henry Allen or some other American Negro trumpet player was present!

CHAPPELLE and STINNETTE

Thomas E. Chappelle and Juanita Stinnette were a Negro husband-and-wife singing act, very popular in the early 1920s. Very soon after the establishment of Harry Pace's all-Negro Black Swan label in the spring of 1921, they produced nine records (numbered 5001 to 5009), using their own names as a name for the label. Every one of the sides was by one or the other or the team, with the exception of *Decatur Street Blues* (5005), a Clarence Williams number sung by the composer himself and accompanied by a small band in which he apparently did not play.

How much of a boost to the team's public image was provided by these nine records is impossible to say, but the records are exceptionally rare. Since they appeared at a time when records were booming even though the economy was faltering, it can only be assumed that sales were minimal. They are of interest as much, if not more, to collectors of theatrical artists as to those specializing in blues, since much of the material is humorous, in keeping with the act as presented on the stage. It may be that the records were sold only in the theatres where Stinnette and Chappelle were appearing.

The labels are somewhat plain and undistinguished in black and gold. The surfaces and recording quality are reasonably good for the period.

CHATAUQUA

The ultimate in rarity and obscurity must be epitomized in this label, of which nothing is known—at least to me—beyond one side by the Original Memphis Five called *Deedle-Deedle-Dum*. It was recorded in New York by Paramount on or about June 10, 1922 and issued, according to Charles Delaunay in his *New Hot Discography* (Criterion Books, New York, 1948) on Chatauqua 11138.

Where this information came from, what the other side of the record is, what the label looks like, what else—if anything—was issued on it, are all questions to which three decades of research into American records generally and jazz records in particular have brought no answer.

It may be significant that Puritan 11138 offers the same performance. Whether other Puritan issues also appeared on Chatauqua under the same or an adjacent number is another question which collectors have pondered, as yet to no effect.

CITIZEN

Although the label of each Citizen record claims that it was "made throughout in England," it neglects to say by whom, and for what enterprise. Its rarity in the southern counties suggests that it must have been sold in some department store in the Midlands or the North, where most of the few known examples of the label have been found.

The catalog numbers are in a 3000 series, and the typography of at least one specimen strongly suggests it was made about 1912 by the British branch of Fonotipia that produced Jumbo. From this it would not seem to rate a place in a book devoted to American labels and their British opposite numbers. But at least one Citizen record that was pressed from Gennett masters of the early 1920s is known to exist.

It is unlikely that anything of musical consequence was issued on Citizen. All are acoustic, as far as can be determined, and contain the usual dance bands, popular vocals, and light instrumental novelties. One I have before me as I write is a pair of bell solos by "Mr. W. Whitlock," the composer of *The Hop Scotch Polka*, a denizen of the Top Twenty in 1950. Indeed, one side of my lone Citizen record is this very number, under its original title, *A Drop of Scotch*.

The label is pale cream in colour, printed in dark blue with a broad red band describing an arc across the upper rim of the label, with the words CITIZEN RECORD in dark blue olde-Englyshe script on it. Between the arms of this arc is a shield supported by two Welsh dragons (is there a clue to its origin here?) emblazoned with a red cross, with a red sword hilt in the left top quarter. This is surmounted by what is evidently intended to be a crown, but which looks more like an inverted scrubbing brush. The lower half of the label has as a backdrop on the cream ground a pattern of squares printed in pale red, alternating between dots and nine oblique strokes to a square.

CLARION

Two entirely different makes of record have appeared bearing the Clarion name. The first, in December 1920, was an affiliate or subsidiary of Cardinal (q.v.), numbered 1101 upwards. It had a dull red label with gold print and little decoration. The quality of both the recording and the surfaces was low, and nothing of great interest in any field of collecting seems to have been issued on it. It vanished after a few months.

The second Clarion was a very different matter. It represents a high-water mark in the achievements of the recording industry during the first half-century of its life. The second Clarion, in soft grass-green and gold with a tasteful design of a medieval herald facing right and sounding a fanfare on a straight trumpet, was a product of the Columbia Phonograph Company, Inc. Though a 35-cent label, it was top-quality merchandise throughout.

Admittedly, several of the earliest issues were repressings of material going back to 1906 and the early acoustic era (Christmas carols and other Yuletide "novelties," favorite hymns and military bands); and others in the first hundred or so were originally issued by Columbia or Harmony between 1919 and 1926, again acoustically recorded. But if anyone needed to hear how good an acoustic recording could be, there could be no better model than Clarion.

The majority of the 477 records issued between August 1930 and June 1932 are first-class Western Electrics by superior dance bands, along with popular singers of the eminence of Annette Hanshaw, Bing Crosby, the Boswell Sisters, Kate Smith, Carson Robison and Gene Autry. Several of these were issued on Clarion only.

The Clarion numbers begin at 5001-C. Another series of six issues from 9000-C to 9005-C was issued in August 1931, all children's records. As a label, Clarion is a rarity compared with such affiliates as Columbia, Harmony, OKeh and Velvet Tone. Few of the short-lived labels of the era offered such quality in performance, manufacture and recording technique.

CLAXTONOLA

"Golden Throated Claxtonola"—as the labels proclaim—was the product of the Brenard Manufacturing Company of Iowa City, Iowa, between 1922 and 1925. The series most frequently met with (if records as uncommon as these can be so described) is the 40000 block, which covered the popular items. There were others, including a 70000 series of German folk songs and dances. At the beginning, the label drew from Paramount, and was of the same rich blue with gold lettering and design (including a shield bearing the letters BMC). The catalog numbers were the same as Paramount but with a 4 as the first digit instead of Paramount's 2.

Somewhere in the early 40300s the source of material became Gennett. The numbers no longer related to any other series, the labels changed to the deeper blue of Gennett, and Paramount's typeface, elegant and curled, changed to the small, thick block in use by the Starr Piano Company at the time. Only the design of the label itself remained. Even the band names were altered. Where Paramount's superb records by King Oliver's Jazz Band, Wade's Moulin Rouge Orchestra and Young's Creole Jazz Band were issued on Claxtonola in their real identities, the Gennett issues of the Wolverine Orchestra became "The Jazz Harmonists" on Claxtonola, and the Vagabonds, itself a Gennett pseudonym for the California Ramblers, became "The Dixie Boys," and so on.

Unlike many short-lived and derivative labels of the 1920s, Claxtonola were a quality product. During World War II, a huge cache of them was found in a disused warehouse somewhere in Iowa, untouched since the day they left the factory. Among them were copies in duplicate, triplicate and more of the stuff of which jazz collectors' dreams are made. This undoubtedly accounts for the number of such items that have from time to time appeared on auction lists, and which now fetch more than a hundred times the 50 cents they cost back in 1924.

CLEARTONE

Most Cleartone records, priced at 85 cents, are Arto derivatives issued between 1920 and 1923. The Arto catalog number and label design were adapted to the Cleartone identity, even when the label was used as a paste-over on pressings made by Pathe! These, like their Arto brethren, have catalog numbers in a C-series, starting apparently at 1 and coincident with the Arto numbers for the same records. Thus, Cleartone C-97 is the same as Arto 9097, and Cleartone C-103 is identical to Arto 9103. It may be that Pathe sold off its surplus pressings to Cleartone for issue in this way, much as Columbia did to Standard and other phonograph manufacturers fifteen years earlier. The Pathe artist identity is masked in all known cases by a pseudonym.

CLIMAX

The earlier Climax label was apparently an offshoot of the infant Columbia, bearing a similar black label with silver printing and the words "Manufactured solely for the Columbia Phonograph Co., New York and London." Above this a circle containing the letters "G. R. Co." deepens the mystery of origin. The most surprising characteristic of a copy in my possession is the embossed circle in the wax at the edge of the label, bearing the letters "V.T.M.," which can only mean Victor Talking Machine! All the Climaxes I have inspected are identical to the performances for the same numbers on Columbia.

In 1943 another Climax label offered rather crudely made location recordings in New Orleans by George Lewis and his Band.

CLOVER

Another label from the Emerson-Consolidated group, specifically the Nutmeg Record Corporation. With matrices in the 3000s and catalog numbers in the 1000s, Clover appeared during the mid-1920s. Again, the catalog consisted mainly of dance and popular vocal items, along with an occasional light instrumental performance.

The label is dark blue with gold lettering. A red scroll, edged in gold with the name CLOVER in block white capitals, also gilt-edged, surmounts the spindle hole. The artist and title credits appear below in typography found on other labels of the group. Surfaces are inclined to be gritty and not very durable. The recording is somewhat shrill.

COLISEUM

The first Coliseum records, with dark green labels printed in gold, were issued in England in 1912 and continued with changes of design and colour until 1927. Only the postwar issues included any that were pressed from American masters.

The numbering started at 100 and reached about 2100 before the label was discontinued. The "sole manufacturers" (so described in contemporary advertisements) were Cooper Brothers Ltd. of 45 and 63 City Road and 17 Clerkenwell Road, London, E.C. 1, with branches in Manchester and Cardiff. Every trade magazine of the time ran full-page advertising for Coliseum records at 2s. 6d. each for the popular ten-inch series, 4s. each for the twelve-inch (numbered 4500 upwards) and 6s. 6d. for twelve-inch "celebrity" records (numbered 4000 upwards). $1.50 or thereabouts must have seemed a large sum to pay for nonentities playing titles such as *Caro mio ben* as a cello solo, or violin arrangements of an unidentified *Vienna Waltz Song* without composer-credit. And a dollar was probably quite enough to give in 1921 for Marek Weber's String Quartette playing Johann Strauss waltzes, or His Majesty's Scots Guards Band playing what the catalog described as *Verdi's Selections*, in two parts. Even half-a-crown—about 50 cents—in those days of business slump, for a couple of dance tunes on material not noted for its durability, was no bargain—the more so since other makes were offering name artists at only 6d. (about a dime) and on better surfaces.

As the decade proceeded, Coliseums were reduced in price to 2s., then 1s. 6d. At lower prices they sold extremely well, though they seldom featured readily identifiable artists. This hardly troubled the customers, who simply wanted an inexpensive dance record. Thus, imports from the Gennett and Vocalion repertoire appeared on Coliseum under vague pseudonyms such as the New York Casino Orchestra, the Mayfield Dance Orchestra and the Maryland Dance Orchestra. Strangely, the earlier Coliseum issues from Gennett, numbered into the 1400s, frequently gave the same artist credit as Gennett. So we find records attributed correctly to Green Brothers' Novelty Band, Bennie Krueger's Orchestra, and others. Vocalion then began supplying American masters until the numbers had reached the mid-1800s. At this point Gennett resumed, but under the same handful of pseudonyms as used on Vocalion. At no time was the original matrix number used. It was completely obliterated, though occasionally it can be made out by rubbing a soft lead pencil over a row of Xs showing through the label in sharp relief. They cover the American matrix number.

Two Coliseum labels were used during the 1920s. The first is pale blue with a surmounting of dark blue, the details being printed in black. The second, introduced at the turn of 1925-1926, is pale fawn with a surmounting of tan or chocolate brown, and printing in black as before. The last hundred or so of these are said to be electrically recorded. The quality is not particularly high.

One of the more interesting Coliseum issues is *Words*, attributed to the Maryland Dance Orchestra—actually Fletcher Henderson and his Orchestra featuring young Louis Armstrong. Another is *Horsey! Keep Your Tail Up* by the Carnival Novelty Four, apparently a London recording but sounding very much like a quartet from New Orleans. There is also a remarkably good accompaniment provided for "Tom Nevill" (actually Irving Kaufman) singing *I'll Take Her Back If She Wants to Come Back*.

COLUMBIA

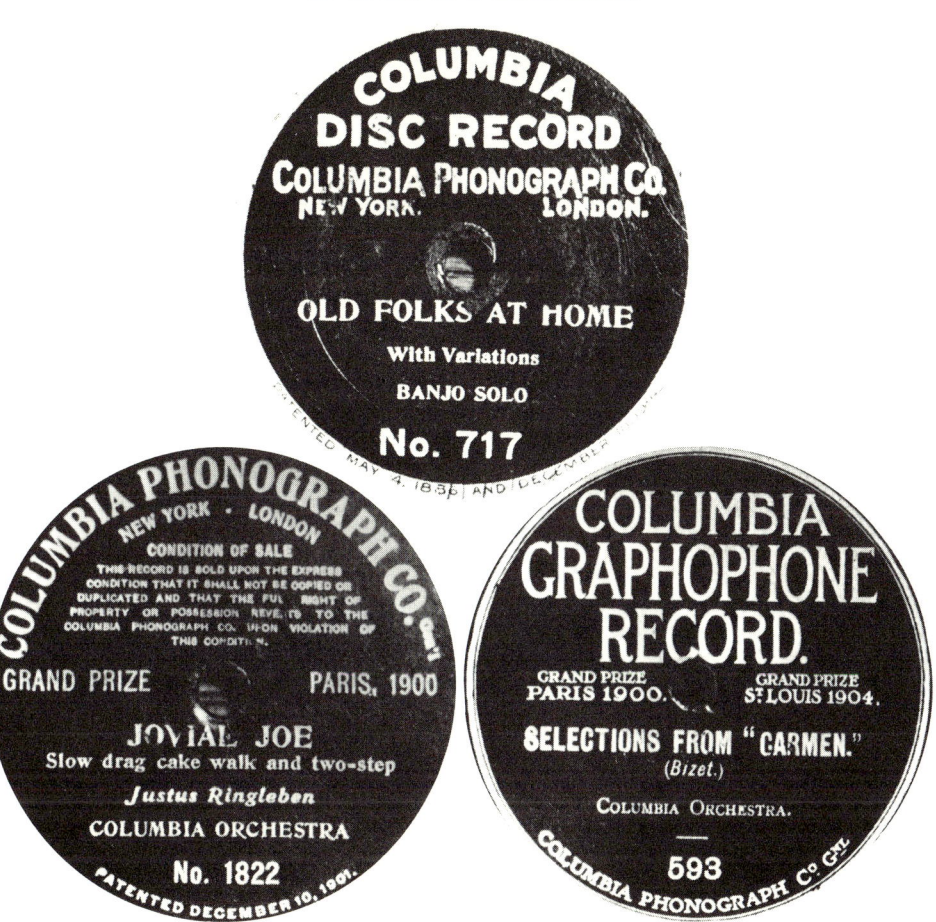

From the very beginning of the story of recorded sound, the name of Columbia has been omnipresent, a major character in the drama; for drama is what it is.

For most of the period covered by this book, records appearing with the brand name of Columbia were manufactured by the Columbia *Graphophone* Company, with headquarters in Bridgeport, Conn., where the factory remains to this day. The word "graphophone" was coined sometime in 1888 by the scientist, Charles Sumner Tainter, and his engineer colleague, Chichester A. Bell, cousin of Alexander Graham Bell, inventor of the telephone. Tainter and Bell had never lost interest or faith in Edison's crude tinfoil phonograph of the late 1870s, as the inventor himself seemed to have done. They set out to improve it, with financial assistance from Alexander Bell providing a research laboratory in Washington, D.C.

They abandoned the tinfoil principle, substituting cardboard coated with wax, in which a recording stylus could trace sound patterns according to the vibrations caused by the impulses of sound thrown upon it. The patent granted

them on May 4, 1886 actually specified a disc, but Tainter and Bell chose a cylinder. After a couple of years of further experiment, they produced the machine they called the Graphophone and exhibited it in Washington early in 1889.

Edison had already been approached by these inventors and improvers. They hoped to join forces with him and launch the machine commercially. But Edison was not interested. He saw the pair as raw newcomers trespassing on his preserve, and set out to produce a machine with his own refinements and improvements.

Litigation threatened. Were Tainter and Bell infringing on Edison's patents, or he on theirs? Tainter and Bell had in fact sold their invention to the newly formed American Graphophone Company. At this point, the intervention of big business, in the shape of Pittsburgh millionaire Jesse Lippincott, resolved the issue. He was sufficiently impressed with the potential of both inventions and their various modifications to buy a controlling interest in both and set up the North American Phonograph Company.

Lippincott saw the invention as a business aid, not as a means of entertainment and education, still less as a way of preserving historical events and voices. He zoned his new empire into areas of the United States in which subsidiary companies leased the right to use the phonograph, subject to central control from Lippincott in Washington. Only one of these companies prospered, the Columbia Phonograph Company of Maryland, Delaware and the District of Columbia.

But if the boss of the parent company was only interested in leasing machines to offices as dictaphones, his area subsidiaries found wider uses for them as entertainment media, however crude. Again Columbia led the way, recording military marches, popular songs of all kinds, whistling, banjo, cornet and other instrumental solos, and leasing them along with the machines to the proprietors of amusement arcades and storekeepers, who used them to lure potential customers. Columbia pioneered in the issuing of catalogs, the first as far back as 1891. The accompanist for several stars of this booklet was an eighteen-year-old boy named Fred Gaisberg (see Berliner; Victor).

With all but one of his subsidiaries proving unprofitable over a period of two years, Jesse Lippincott's health and financial resources cracked under the strain. In the autumn of 1890 he was stricken with paralysis. A few months later Edison, his principal creditor, took over the North American Phonograph Company. Lippincott had devised a sales organization that marked out zones of operation for each of the subsidiaries, and the Columbia Phonograph Company had proved itself the one most able to make money. While Edison held to Lippincott's belief that the invention was not so much for home entertainment as for a business adjunct, Edward D. Easton of Columbia proved him wrong. By 1894, even Edison had begun to realise this. He threw his North American Phonograph Company into bankruptcy in order to regain the right to control the enterprise himself and from his own factory, rather than be beholden to a number of mostly inactive subsidiaries. While Edison was waiting for two years for the settlement of receivership, the American Graphophone Company stepped in where its associates and Edison could not tread. For Columbia (or the American Phonograph Company) had dealt with Lippincott directly, not with North American, and was not bound by restraints that bound Edison to inactivity. The company thrust forward into the entertainment business from its headquarters in Bridgeport, Conn. There the factory manager, a Scot named Thomas Hood Macdonald, developed a reproducing machine with a clockwork motor for power.

Now there was a practical replacement for the heavy, awkward, and for the individual home user, impossibly expensive electric motor and storage batteries beloved by Edison.

Advertisements for Columbia goods began to appear in the press, mostly in the better-known magazines. Sales of machines and cylinders increased accordingly. By the end of the century, it was obvious that some means of duplicating the cylinders would have to be found that did not force the artists to perform a title dozens, even hundreds of times into the battery of horns in the studio, or to make a "master" cylinder that could reproduce copies pantographically but which was limited to a couple of dozen playings before it wore out. Eventually a method was found. Edison called it "Gold Moulded." But by now the year was 1901, and Emile Berliner's Gram-O-Phone was firmly established as the better method. Using flat discs with a lateral-cut track, it was easier to store and less vulnerable than a wax cylinder. If you dropped a Berliner, you *might* break it. If you dropped a wax cylinder, you would certainly break it.

So Columbia decided that cylinders would continue to be made to supply those who had bought any of their phonographs—from the Eagle at $10 and the Home Graphophone at $25 to the Graphophone Grand at $100 that played the new 4½-inch diameter cylinder. But it was essential that they also enter the disc record market at once. A news item dated November 6, 1901 reported that "Columbia are already making discs." So indeed they were—seven-inch ones at 50 cents, ten-inch at $1, and within two years, a fourteen-inch monster at $2. These were all single-sided, with black labels printed in silver, and announced in the same way as the cylinders: " 'The Sweetest Flower That Blows,' sung by Mr. J. W. Myers, Columbia Record." A pooling of patents with the newly formed Victor Talking Machine Company opened the way for the two companies to dominate the record market for the next fifteen years.

Columbia had begun their disc numbering at 1, very sensibly. Until the coming of double-sided records and a new series starting at A-1 in October 1908, this serial also acted as the catalog number. The records themselves were made of a durable layer of shellac composition similar to that of Berliner and Johnson's discs. They had a tough inner core of rice paper and a mica compound which, if not rendering the discs unbreakable, at least made them better able to withstand sudden glancing blows.

The earliest of all Columbia catalogs do not vary very much from those issued by Victor or Edison. When President McKinley was hit by an assassin's bullet while on a tour of the Buffalo Exposition on September 6, 1901, and died of his injuries eight days later, all three labels rushed to record part of his last public speech at the opening of the exposition. Len Spencer, a veteran recording artist even then, read the speech. Columbia issued it anonymously, as it did most of its earliest records. They had to be played in order to determine who was performing, as the announcement invariably named the artist. Spencer's record of the McKinley speech gave no suggestion as to who was speaking. Indeed, the wording of the label might almost have led prospective buyers into thinking that by some miracle of coincidence, Columbia had set up a recording machine near the President and recorded his actual voice declaring the Exposition open.

There were hundreds of discs and identical cylinders to choose from in the Columbia catalog of 1902. Vess Ossman obliged the company as he had Victor, and Berliner before that, with examples from his concert repertoire. The Columbia Orchestra or Band, usually conducted by Fred Hager, played everything from the latest musical comedy selections to orchestral settings of sacred music and

even arias from oratorios. J. W. Myers sang love ballads in his big baritone voice. George J. Gaskin ("the boy tenor" as he was billed, though he was a man in his thirties) and Harry Macdonough extended them to tenor range. There were endless comedy records by Arthur Collins and/or Byron G. Harlan singing or Cal Stewart reciting his incredible observations in the guise of a countryman known as Uncle Josh. Henry Burr (sometimes as Harry McClaskey, his real name, sometimes as Irving Gillette) provided every kind of concert song, sacred and secular alike. And of course there were plenty of cornet, trombone, clarinet, flute, piccolo and xylophone solos, even a few rather emasculated violin solos by Charles d'Almaine.

All of which was very good for sales. But with Victor having launched its Red Seal celebrity series with masters imported from Europe featuring the miraculous voice of Enrico Caruso and others, Columbia felt it should spend some of its growing resources for records made in New York by the stars of the Metropolitan Opera. So in the early spring of 1903 Columbia recorded a series of concert music and operatic arias by contralto Ernestine Schumann-Heink, sopranos Suzanne Adams and Marcella Sembrich, baritone Antonio Scotti and basso Edouard de Reszke, brother of the great tenor Jean de Reszke. These were in the ten-inch black and silver regular series, but bearing on the labels a facsimile autograph of each artist as well as a spoken introduction by the artist in some cases, and also bearing a $2 price tag.

The project cost the company dearly, and their reception by the public was lukewarm indeed. Edward Easton drew the conclusion that opera was bad business, despite the fact that Victor's Red Seals, now beginning to be recorded with lifelike clarity and accuracy, were selling as fast as the Camden factory could press them. Nevertheless, Easton allowed no further expenditure on material of this kind. As a result, the Columbia catalog for the next five or six years contained little or nothing to appeal to customers looking for something a cut above the usual military bands, banjo solos, comic songs and love or patriotic ballads. For this they turned to Victor, and Columbia lost its precious head start in the race for supremacy. Even its pioneering double-sided records of 1904 were not looked on with great favour. They simply offered a double ration of what was already plentiful on single-sided discs or cylinders.

To provide something to match the all-pervading Victor product, Columbia engaged Sig. Guglielmo Marconi to produce the indestructible Velvet Tone record. A little more than a year after signing with the inventor of the wireless telegraph, in October 1907 he brought forth the results of his labours. The discs anticipated the famous "Silent Surface" records of the 1920s by fifteen years. But the machines of the time were unable to do them justice, and they too foundered.

The next attempt by Columbia to capture some of the Victor glory took the form of an agreement with the European Societa Fonotipia di Milano and Odeon to issue their operatic records at a price that would compete with Victor's single-sided Red Seals. The European records were double-sided and could be sold at $3.50, while Red Seals by the most exalted soloists ranged from $3 to $5. Despite the fine quality of recording, the low prices and the first-class artists, however, the entente produced nothing as successful as Victor's American and sometimes European recordings by singers even better known, expensive and single-sided though these records were. Columbia began again recording its own operatic celebrity records immediately after the Fonotipia-Odeon debacle, by names like Lillian Nordica, Emmy Destinn, Mary Garden and Celestina Boninsegna. But these too failed to capture more than a fragment of the market.

In July 1912 the company ceased to manufacture cylinders and turned its whole attention to discs. If the world of opera was not for Columbia, the eminent Belgian violinist Eugen Ysaye proved in one session the following December that Columbia could make worthwhile records of first-class instrumentalists. The great pianist Xaver Scharwenka also contributed to the Columbia celebrity catalog. Soon afterwards Vladimir de Pachmann, the greatest Chopin exponent of his time, made a number of definitive recordings for Columbia. Percy Grainger, the Australian pianist and composer, joined the roster, along with Daisy Kennedy, Josef Hofmann and Leopold Godowsky. Perhaps the greatest instrumental capture of the second decade of the century for Columbia was the great cellist Pablo Casals. As with Ysaye, Casals set the ultimate seal of authority on his records by autographing the original wax of several.

There was no doubting the popularity of Columbia records of dance music and sentimental and comedy vocals. The ragtime dancing craze sparked off in 1911 by Irving Berlin's *Alexander's Ragtime Band* led to the engagement of prominent dancing teacher G. Hepburn Wilson to supervise recording sessions by Charles A. Prince's Orchestra or Band. This was a fine organization of staff musicians who could read any kind of score put in front of them, and some of the best examples of genuine ragtime music recorded at the time of its first wave of popularity are to be found on Columbia records played by Prince's Orchestra.

By now, the labels had changed from black and silver to dark blue, sometimes black, with gold lettering and white facing to the words "Columbia Record" that surrounded the newly adopted Magic Notes trademark. In England, Columbia products appeared with similar designs on the labels. In the black-and-silver days, everything was pressed in Bridgeport, even if recorded in London or on the Continent. Since the enterprising American businessman Louis Sterling had taken control of the English branch and set up a factory, Columbia-Rena records issued in England as successors to Sterling's Rena label looked very much like their American counterparts. Shortly before the outbreak of World War I the distinctive white facing was dropped, and the label became either dark blue or virtually black, or red if it was on a celebrity issue. There had been chocolate brown labels also, earlier on, handsome but short-lived. The word "Rena" was also dispensed with, and the label remained unchanged in all but minor details for the next seven years.

In 1915 Columbia in America changed the label design again. The popular series became bright blue, printed in gold with the make in bold capitals across a segment of the upper half. The celebrity label was changed from red and gold to dark blue and gold, with a red, white and blue tricolor arc sweeping across it and emblazoned with replicas of the various honours accorded to Columbia at international exhibitions in the preceding fifteen years. The English celebrity label of this time was pale blue and gold, a colour scheme that tried the eyes. Exceptions were records by members of the casts of London musical productions. These were included in the celebrity series (prefixed L-) and this label was cross-hatched in blue on white, with lettering in navy blue. A postwar series devoted to stars of the musical stage was similarly designed, but in pale green with dark green print, as attractive to the eye as the music was to the ears of devotees of the delightful trivia of artists like Alice Delysia, Edith Day, Beatrice Lillie, Leslie Henson and such.

On the pale blue L-1001 label were American masters issued in England by the great artists already mentioned. Louis Sterling also signed up maestros of the stature of Sir Thomas Beecham and Sir Henry J. Wood to conduct (admittedly edited and sometimes gruesomely mauled) versions of standard concert works and even lesser known "modern" pieces such as Debussy's *Prélude à l'après-midi d'un Faune* and Richard Strauss's *Till Eulenspiegels Lustige Streiche*. Chamber music began to be featured largely on Columbia pale blue celebrity records in England, played by the Lener or the London String Quartet.

It was Columbia that initiated in America the recording of famous symphony orchestras, notably the Chicago and the New York. This was in 1916, the year after the president, Edward D. Easton, had died. A group of financiers who knew little of music or the recording of it assumed control. But where the hardheaded Easton had little time for anything that was not an immediate moneymaker, as witness his axing of the Grand Opera series within weeks of launching it in 1903, the new A & R managers seemed ready to try anything, from Dr. Frederick Stock conducting the Chicago Symphony to a trial recording by a strange dance band newly arrived in New York from New Orleans, via Chicago. So it was that the Original Dixieland Jass Band visited the Columbia studio on January 30, 1917, and recorded several takes each of two popular numbers in their own literally inimitable style. *Darktown Strutters' Ball* and *Indiana* were the titles, but the powers of Columbia wanted none of this musical gibberish, and the tests were turned down—until they became aware that Victor had recorded the band, had rushed the results to the stores a few days later, and were doing a roaring trade. Still following where Victor led, Columbia hastily issued their pioneer jazz recordings and did very well with them. The band was not asked to return to the studio in the Woolworth Building, however. After a handful of titles for Aeolian, they signed exclusively with Victor. Columbia was left trying to match their success by recording Negro cornetist, composer and publisher W. C. Handy, "The Father of the Blues," and his purely ragtime orchestra from Memphis. Columbia also scrambled to record as many bands already in New York as were playing what was regarded as "jass" music.

One of these was Wilbur C. Sweatman's Original Jass Band. Sweatman was a Negro clarinetist-showman of no outstanding ability who led a band that played a heavy-handed approximation of the zestful, compelling rhythm and counterpointed melodies of the Dixielanders. In 1919 Columbia added various small units to its dance band roster such as the Louisiana Five, Gorman's Novelty Syncopators, and the Synco Jazz (the word by this time was spelt thus) Band. There were also a great many records by bands whose instrumentation and identities varied almost from session to session. These were made under the direction of a drummer and xylophonist named Harry A. Yerkes, who had himself recorded solos fifteen years or so prior to the outset of the Jazz Age. On January 1, 1918 he had become Columbia's "field manager," talent-spotting any musician or band operating outside New York whose work seemed to hold commercial possibilities. Four months later he was assistant to H. L. Willson, vice-president and general manager of the Columbia Graphophone Company, as it had been named since 1913. He remained at that post until he resigned in 1925, a major figure in the artistic echelons of the company. He had signed Ted Lewis' Jazz Band in the late summer of 1919, and the High-Hatted Tragedian of Jazz remained a faithful Columbia artist for fourteen years.

The postwar boom of 1919 had become a slump by the early summer of 1920. Columbia, which had confidently ordered hundreds of machine cabinets from its nationwide suppliers, now found itself with a vast stock that few felt inclined to buy. The studios and offices were moved from the Woolworth Building and 104 West 38th Street to one complex at 1819 Broadway, the entire move taking place on April 4, 1921. But economies of this sort did nothing positive. In December 1922 the American parent firm accordingly sold its British branch to Louis Sterling, who two years later bought a controlling interest in the American side of the business, with help from his banker friends, for $2,500,000. This enabled the now British-owned company to pay for the right to use the Western Electric sound system for recording.

After selling to Sterling the branch in London of which he was manager, American Columbia was put into the hands of receivers, who piloted its affairs until the sale to Sterling. The issues for December 1923 were given a new look and a new numbering system. The blue and gold, and the tricolor stripe, were replaced by a striking gold label, decorated in full color by a streamer in the colours of the national flag of Holland (why this country was favoured is uncertain) and a pale blue-green box in which the title and other details were printed in black. The numbers of the ten-inch popular series having reached A-4001, and the twelve-inch numbers starting at A-5001 having reached well into the A-7000s, were re-started at 1 for the ten-inch and 50001 for the twelve-inch, both suffixed -D. Both series continued in use until 1938. The "race" records, hitherto part of the ordinary A- block along with such regional items as were issued, were now devoted to Bessie Smith, the Empress of the Blues, and others of her race. They were given a special section of the catalog. Their series started at 13000-D, but objections were raised by the superstitious. After eight issues, in deference to these triskaidekaphobiacs—so it is said—the *thirteen*-thousands became the 14000s, and remained so until the final issue in the series, 14680-D, in April 1933 (the only one on the then new royal blue Columbia, which we shall meet again later on). Country-and-western artists were issued in a 15000-D series. Serious music appeared in 20000-D and 30000-D series, ten-inch, at $1, 65000-D were twelve-inch, at $1.50, and 68000-D were twelve-inch at $2.

These gaudy, almost garish labels were probably much more expensive to print than their blue or black predecessors. Therefore, when Louis Sterling assumed control of the company, he shook up the management in New York (hence Yerkes' resignation), scrapped obsolete equipment, and instituted a new label that approximated the British one: black with gold lettering in a simple, dignified design that would usher in the era of Western Electric recording.

One of Columbia's biggest sellers on both sides of the Atlantic was the famous recording of *John Peel* and *Adeste Fideles*. It was made in the Metropolitan Opera House in New York on the evening of March 31, 1925 by the Associated Glee Clubs of America with audience participation. The audience was estimated at 4,000 and there were 850 singers on the stage. Choral records made by the acoustic process were necessarily restricted to the number of singers it was possible to accommodate in the studio without overloading the diaphragm of the recording equipment. At best the results were dull, the lyrics difficult to understand. Now, with this new wonder, electrical recording, you-are-there realism could be captured. There had been electric recordings made during an actual performance before this—in Westminster Abbey, London, at the burial of the Unknown Warrior on November 11, 1920—but the results were so crude as to be unintelligible, barely sounding like voices singing at all. Columbia had done the pressing, and there was nothing to suggest that a revolutionary method of recording was anywhere near.

The Metropolitan recording crossed the Atlantic and repeated its success in England. Other electric recordings followed soon. But the new method was never publicized, to avoid a sales slump in existing acoustic issues and by agreement with Victor, also a party to the Western Electric contract, to preclude a demand for the new recordings that would cause chaos in the industry. Meanwhile, prosperity returned to Columbia. Encouraged, the company equipped mobile recording vans to make regular tours of the country to record hidden talent among rural artists, black and white, as well as little-known dance bands and choral groups based in such cities as Atlanta, New Orleans, Dallas and Los Angeles. It was in Los Angeles in October 1926 that Columbia made the first records of two artists of importance. One was the eccentric "hot-gospeller" Aimee Semple McPherson, the other a young man and his friend who provided an anonymous vocal refrain to a record by Don Clark's Los Angeles Biltmore Hotel Orchestra called *I've Got the Girl*. The duo were Bing Crosby and Al Rinker. Both records were issued in England, Don Clark's under the name of "The Charleston Serenaders." Neither sold many copies. Miss McPherson's message and methods were given ample press coverage in the United States without the need for a record that was never more than a curio; and in England, her name meant little and her message even less. Playing the first Bing Crosby record today gives little hint that one of the greatest entertainers of all time was present. The song itself was just another lively fox trot of the time, with a harmonized vocal chorus that was quite good but not outstanding.

A year before this, in October 1925, a new holding company known as Columbia International, Ltd. was formed in England. Its subsidiaries included the Carl Lindstrom Company in Germany, the Columbia Graphophone Company, Ltd. in England, and from November 11, 1926, the General Phonograph Company in New York, producers of OKeh records (q.v.). Buoyed by the phonograph boom brought about by the new recording process and the return of better economic conditions generally, Columbia in England and Europe embarked on vast centenary celebrations to mark the hundredth anniversaries of the deaths of Beethoven and Schubert. In 1927 and 1928 the blue L- series was dominated by complete symphonies, choral works and chamber music by both composers. Whether sales justified the enormous expense is a matter for conjecture. In any event, no similar celebrations were held in succeeding years, perhaps because of the Depression.

While things were on the upgrade, Columbia bought out the Pathe Freres Pathephone organization in December 1928. Later on, the head office in England decreed that the leaders of the three principal political parties should enshrine their platforms in Columbia wax for the guidance of the electorate in the 1929 General Election, and for the education (and, as it turned out, the cynical amusement) of future historians. Nor were these the only strange speech records produced by Columbia in that last golden year before the winter of discontent. There was a breathless reading of a short story specially written for the purpose by the author, Edgar Wallace. Dutch health expert Tromp van Diggelen chatted for a few minutes in good English. There was also a long series of twelve-inch purple-labelled records of talks on a wide range of academic subjects, even including smells, by ranking experts. These cost only about $1 each.

Columbia in America brought off a recording coup in May 1928 by signing Paul Whiteman. The King of Jazz had been the mainstay of Victor's dance band roster since 1920. Snaring him was a great achievement, and promoted accordingly. One form the hoopla took was an exclusive Paul Whiteman label, a vulgar affair in five colours featuring the famous trademarked caricature of the leader himself. Alas for the publicity and special labels, events on Wall Street meant that an expensive luxury like Paul Whiteman, the band reduced from thirty-four to twenty, had become dispensable. In the autumn of 1930, he recorded his last for Columbia. A year later and for the next six years, Paul Whiteman's name again graced the Victor label—and no fancy pictures or jazzy designs. In the years Whiteman was recording for Columbia, he produced some excellent examples of Bing Crosby singing alone and with others, some strangely non-jazz pseudo-symphonic potboilers, and George Gershwin's *Concerto in F* for piano and orchestra in six rather short twelve-inch sides, with Roy Bargy at the piano. The composer himself was in London at the time, recording piano solos from his latest musical comedy about to be staged there, *Funny Face*—and a remarkable set of three *Preludes* and the *andante* movement from *Rhapsody in Blue*, never issued in England but released in the United States in January 1929.

Paul Whiteman was not the only Columbia celebrity to be accorded his own label. The same honour was belatedly bestowed on Ted Lewis, soon after Whiteman's first Columbias were issued. It took the form of a much more tasteful design printed in black on silver, a natural pen drawing of Lewis in his characteristic pose holding top hat aloft in his right hand. It was Ted Lewis, too, with or without a special label, who could claim to have made one of the biggest successes in dance records ever released on Columbia. This was the gentle waltz ballad *Goodnight*, issued in April 1928. It was equally successful in England. Another enormously popular Columbia record, on an international scale, was the first sketch by Moran and Mack as *Two Black Crows*, issued in 1927. The subsequent additions to the series were fairly successful, and there can hardly have been a home with a phonograph in the USA or the UK that did not have at least one of these recordings, with their delightful philosophical comments from the sleepy-voiced member of the team.

Although the Depression hit the record market in Britain far less severely than in America, by the middle of 1930 it became obvious that survival there depended on the amalgamation of the major companies. After months of discussion, the Columbia Graphophone Company and the Gramophone Company ("His Master's Voice") went into partnership with Parlophone to form Electric and Musical Industries, Ltd., as from March 20, 1931. This gave Louis Sterling and RCA's David Sarnoff places on the board of directors. To avoid possible antitrust action in the United States as a result of giving RCA partial control over the affairs of its competitor Columbia, English Columbia disposed of its Columbia Phonograph Company stock in May. The trustees of that stock sold out to Grigsby-Grunow, the manufacturers of Majestic radios, refrigerators and washing machines. In November 1933 this firm went bankrupt, and Columbia in America became just another label in the ever growing collection owned by the American Record Corporation, to which the receivers for Grigsby-Grunow had sold it for just over $70,000.

The Columbia label was never worked on by its new owners. The sales gimmick of royal blue records, introduced in December 1932, was abandoned a few years later. These records were certainly attractive to behold. They were made of rich blue material, with labels a tone or two lighter: reminiscent in some ways of the design in use between 1915 and 1923. (Ted Lewis lost his silver special, but his last Columbia records bore his face, drawn in gold, above the bar bearing the word COLUMBIA.) Records of the black label era were sometimes pressed on royal blue wax with original labels, making an even more remarkable appearance by the contrast of glossy black and rich blue. The idea was fine but the timing was bad. Few customers were buying records in 1932 and 1933, and the surfaces seemed somewhat inferior to the velvety smooth black records that had preceded them for the last seven or eight years.

A small number of issues, mostly by dance bands, appeared on Columbia in its last years as a member of the ARC entourage. Brunswick was ARC's principal "quality" label, Columbia very much an afterthought. Then, in 1938, Edward Wallerstein, an RCA executive, suggested to William S. Paley, president of the Columbia Broadcasting System, that the Columbia label be reactivated, to resume its place of honour in the record market. Brunswick and the other ARC labels would be withdrawn. Paley bought ARC in December 1938. With Wallerstein as general manager, a new and vigorous Columbia record took its place in the American record market from September 1939 with Benny Goodman, Kay Kyser, Count Basie, Mildred Bailey, Kate Smith, Gene Krupa and Harry James among the popular stars and a considerable number of symphony orchestras and chamber music groups to balance the catalog. The popular numbers were started at 35201 and priced at 50 cents (25 cents less than the Brunswick label that was then phased out). There was a completely new label designed for the popular records, and dark blue and gold for the classics. This was the position at the time of the ban on recording imposed at the end of July 1942, and in fact continued beyond it.

In England, there had been other changes besides that of ownership for Columbia in the 1930s. The old popular series which had begun at 1000 in the autumn of 1908 had reached over 5700 by the beginning of 1930 in the ten-inch size. The three-figured twelve-inch had switched to 9000 in December 1924, nearly reaching 10000 by the same date. Well over one thousand records had been issued on the classical L-1000 series by that time. Even the ten-inch classics, starting curiously at 1300 back in 1915, had achieved over three hundred issues in the fifteen years since. The brown-label D series were essentially pre-1915 operatic records, with a handful of instrumental solos and vocal ballads. The entire system seemed due for an overhaul, and received it. Starting in March 1930, popular records were issued in a series starting at DB-1 for ten-inch, DX-1 for twelve-inch, LB-1 for classical ten-inch, LX-1 for twelve-inch. Dance records were given a series of their own starting at CB-1. This survived until February 1935, when a drastic price reduction brought the magenta labeled Variety series into existence at FB-1000. The CBs had scored just over 800 issues in those five years. All these series were maintained until the end of 78s in February 1960. The DBs were continued into the 45 rpm pop era, lone survivors of a different age.

The CBS label as it is known today seceded from EMI in England in 1952. For some dozen years its products were issued in that country by the English branch of Philips, the mammoth Dutch electrical firm, after which CBS established a London branch in its own right.

The following chart shows the first matrix number used in each year (approximate only prior to 1911). As production increased and field trips were frequent, and new permanent studios were opened outside New York, the system of allocating blocks of numbers to each location resulted in some loss of synchronization, some studios using blocks more rapidly than others. In the 140000 block, the first known record in terms of chronological allocation, not strictly numerical, is shown. After 1934, the ARC system is used (see Banner).

10" USA	12" USA	10" England	12" England
(c. October)			
1			
180			
950		(early) 25000	
1720		25500	
3095*		25790	
3330	30000	25900	
3590	30080	26080	6000
3800	30130	26470	
4000	30205	26560	
4275; 19100 (November)	30330	26720	
19180	30621	27400	6120
19704; 38100 (July)	30930; 36300	27750	6170
38525	36530	28350	6290
39170	36850	28740	6390
39718; 45500 (March)	37120; 48500	29200; 35600 (September)	6450
46311	48535	35950; 65150 (January)	6700 75251 (October)
47260; 77000 (April)	49052	65830	75350
77605	49295	69230	76065
78240	49567	69450	76333
78906	49730	69650	76747
79621	49920; 98000 (December)	71140	74229
80127	98006	71550	75034
80757	98052	73120; A-1 (May)	76853; AX-1
81446; 140000 (September)	98115	A-520	AX-271
140220	98163	A-1550	AX-800
141452	98201	WA-2693	WAX-1210
143241	98307	WA-4644	WAX-2325
145459	98422	WA-6740	WAX-3170
147740	98613	WA-8278	WAX-4490
149728	98677	WA-9896	WAX-5320
151183	98725	WA-11020	WAX-5930

152059	CA-12329	CAX-6285
152341	CA-13320	CAX-6650
152666	CA-14234	CAX-7035
(From here on, see the	CA-14839	CAX-7393
chapter on Banner for	CA-15515	CAX-7695
ARC-CBS matrix numbers)	CA-16135	CAX-7920
	CA-16766	CAX-8150
	CA-17257	CAX-8550
	CA-17747	CAX-8710
	CA-18273	
	CA-18850	

* The New York blocks 1261-1350 and 2000-2999 were allocated to recordings made in Shanghai and Tokyo and probably other locations outside the USA. As will be seen, the London numerical sequences are irregular. No exact dates are known prior to 1919, and the jigsaw puzzle is by no means complete even after that date, until the adoption of the A- and AX- prefixes. The 70000 and 72000 blocks were recorded in France and/or Italy.

COMMODORE

The Commodore Music Shop of 136 East 42nd Street, New York City, entered the record business in the spring of 1938 when its owner, Milt Gabler, issued the first red label items for the jazz connoisseur. The ten-inch records were numbered 500 upwards, and there was a handful of twelve-inch issues numbered 1500 upwards. The recording of the first few dozen issues was done by the American Record Corporation.

Eddie Condon, the Chicago guitarist, and his dixieland colleagues were featured on the majority of Commodore records made before 1942. One remarkable session had Fats Waller sitting in at the piano. It was Commodore's commendable custom to list the personnel and recording date on the labels. Since Waller was contracted to RCA Victor at the time, he was renamed "Maurice," after his son. But this fooled no one—nor was it meant to.

One of the most remarkable of all Commodore records was not a Condon product but one by Billie Holiday, heroine of many Brunswick and Vocalion sessions. She abandoned her customary rôle of endowing popular songs with her own sophisticated brand of jazz phrasing and recorded *Strange Fruit*, a gruesome account of a lynch mob. For several years this was the most desirable of all records among certain British enthusiasts, and copies changed hands at fantastic prices.

Among the more unusual Commodore issues was a parody of Sir Noel Coward's play *Private Lives*. Renamed *Private Jives*, it was enacted by tenor saxophonist Bud Freeman (assuming a most Coward-like delivery), pianist Joe Bushkin, and a radio actress named Minerva Pious. A pair of twelve-inch records consisting of a jam session of some fifteen minutes by leading jazz exponents on the song *A Good Man Is Hard to Find*, foreshadowed the lengthy improvisations of the LP era.

Commodore 78s, perhaps the major catalog of dixieland jazz, were reissued on the Mainstream label in the 1960s, and later on the revived Commodore label after Gabler retired from three decades as A & R man for Decca.

In 1976, items from the Commodore catalog became available in England for the first time on LPs issued by Decca, thanks to a long overdue agreement with Milt Gabler.

CONCERT

This, one of the rarest and most obscure of all American labels, was apparently issued in two releases. Both were given in full in a double-page spread in *The Talking Machine World* of September 15, 1920. Regardless of the type of music offered, there was one numerical series, from 1001 to 1069 (with nine unaccounted for): 1001 to 1055 under the heading "First Catalog," and 1056 to 1069 as "Advance List of October Concert Records." Whether there were any further issues is not known. None has been found on a higher number than 1069, and no other catalogs or supplements have come to light. Everything was priced at $1, at a time when Victor and Columbia were offering a superior product by identical artists at 85 cents each—for the Concert releases advertised in this costly announcement consisted mostly of conventional records by Billy Murray, Charles Hart, Ernest Hare, Henry Burr, the Sterling Trio, the Peerless Quartet, Rudy Wiedoeft's Palace Trio, the All Star Trio and George Green's Novelty Orchestra.

The producers were the Concert Record Manufacturing Company of 145 West 45th Street, New York. Specimens that have been found show that they were drawn from the Lyric repertoire (q.v.). Examples of these have been found with other labels pasted over the Lyric label, with the Concert catalog number stamped in the wax as well as the Lyric one.

The higher price and obviously inferior quality of recording and pressing could alone account for the rarity of Concert records. But in addition, a comparison of Concert's output with major company issues shows that Concert was issuing in October 1920 the sort of titles that had appeared on Victor, Columbia and others two to four months earlier.

There was another Concert record, this one derived from Imperial (q.v.) during the years 1906 and 1911.

CONNORIZED

Between October 1921 and July 1922, possibly a little later, brown and gold labelled Connorized records were issued from Gennett masters by the Connorized Music Roll Company. Usually crediting the artists with their correct identities but not always retaining the same couplings as the parent label, Connorized records are rarely met with, even in the New York area. The series started at 3001, and as far as is known only about a hundred records were ever issued under this name, mostly popular dance and vocal items.

CONQUEROR

This was originally one of the Plaza group labels, deriving its material from Banner and sometimes using pseudonyms. The first issues appeared early in 1926, with large red labels bearing ornate gold decoration that varied little during the sixteen years of the label's existence. In the 1930s it was reduced in size to conform to the standard of those times, and the colour was changed to chocolate brown.

Numbering started at 7000 and reached nearly 10000 before the label was discontinued in the spring of 1942. It became one of the ARC group labels when Banner and its affiliates became part of that empire, and alone among them, Conqueror stayed the course to the end of ARC and beyond, finishing as a subsidiary of CBS along with the newly revived OKeh label. Where other ARC labels during the years 1932 to 1938 issued nearly everything in the same coupling format as one another, Conqueror was sold through the Sears Roebuck catalog and therefore adopted a more independent line, missing many of its affiliates' issues altogether and cross-coupling others.

CRENSHAW

The only known example of a Crenshaw record was described and illustrated by Carl Kendziora in his "Behind the Cobwebs" column in *Record Research* for January 1962. It appears to be a single issue designed to promote the songs written by B. A. and T. C. Crenshaw. The latter sang both his own *I'm Happy 'Cause My Lovin' Mama's Comin' Home* and *Lindy*. Although the label does not credit him, *Lindy* was a song by his brother celebrating Col. Charles A. Lindbergh's epoch-making flight on May 20-22, 1927—which thereby dates the recording. Accompaniment is by Alonzo Paytes and his Hot Five, which was hardly that. The typeface and recording characteristics indicate a Marsh recording, electric, as are a number of Paramount records of the same era. The label is maroon with gold printing. There is, of course, no catalog number.

CRESCENT

The Crescent Talking Machine Company of 109 Reade Street, New York, makers of "talking machines" that played normal lateral-cut records, launched its Crescent record in November 1917. *Record Research* for November 1969 and July 1970 carried two definitive and very interesting accounts by George A. Blacker on the subject of these exceptionally rare records. As the publicity material claimed in the issue of *The Phonograph* for November 21, 1917, these records were designed to be played with a steel needle, in the manner of the contemporary Aeolian Vocalions, not with a ball-shaped sapphire as were the Pathe records from which most if not all of their catalog derived.

Mr. Blacker suggests that Crescent's sales manager and spokesman, Dr. Rowland G. Faldl, asked Pathe to make sixty couplings for Crescent, needle-cut. This was probably interpreted as an Aeolian-type cut by the vertical-cut-trained Pathe engineers. When it was found that the resulting Crescents could only be played on Aeolian machines—not even on their own Crescent Talking Machines—sales were so disastrously small as to make that first list of 120 titles the last. Hence the great rarity of Crescent records. Not that anything is lost musically, as practically all of them can be traced to Pathe and played on their machines, which were not hard to find. Besides, the material itself is confined to the usual round of Henry Burr, studio dance and military bands, and Collins and Harlan, with a few other nonentities filling out the list. The numbers span 10001 through 10060, and the price of each record was 75 cents.

In 1944 the Jazz Man Record Shop, 1221 Vine Street, Hollywood, Cal., issued the first of about a dozen green and silver labelled Crescent records devoted to the music of Kid Ory's Creole Jazz Band, the whole set appearing at irregular intervals over the next two years.

CRITONA

A very rare label marketed by Criterion Records, Inc., of 1227 Broadway, New York, between September 1920 and September or October 1921. One George Beadle was the President and A. H. Cushman the Secretary of the company. The records themselves, with dark red labels printed in gold with a central design of a huntsman in full cry complete with horn, appeared in three series. These seem to have begun at 700, 1000 (these were single-sided operatic items) and 8000 (light concert music). All were priced at 50 cents. Apparently there were about a hundred issues in all. The few that have been found give no clue as to source. They bear no matrix numbers, only the Critona catalog number suffixed -A or -B in the wax round the label.

CROWN

At least three labels issued in the USA and the UK have borne the name Crown. The earliest, as far as is known, was an Arto subsidiary numbered as was its parent, but with the prefix K- replacing the first two digits of the Arto number. Thus, Arto 9014 becomes Crown K-14, as in *Record Research*'s illustration in the April 1963 issue. In this connection, Carl Kendziora reported that the trademark was registered by Arto and had been continuously in use since January 1, 1921, a matter of four months or so after Arto made its own debut. The label is black with gold lettering in the usual Arto typeface. The royal-looking venture seems not to have lasted very far into 1921, as the last known issue is K-39.

The second Crown label was a very much more attractive design in orange, black, white and gold. Numbers started at 3000 in the autumn of 1930. It seems that while Crowns were recorded in an independent studio, the pressings were done by RCA Victor, no less. The latter's card-index files contain a complete account of everything issued on this label before it disappeared in the autumn of 1933, after having released just over five hundred records. Some of these appeared also on Broadway (q.v.). In England a considerable number were issued on Imperial (q.v.). The matrix numbers begin at 1000 or 1001, and reach just over 2200. The most interesting collectors' items on Crown are the sides attributed to Gil Rodin and his Orchestra, actually the Ben Pollack Orchestra, and to Joel Shaw and his Orchestra, Gene Kardos' orchestra under the nominal leadership of his pianist. Crown issues were largely dance music, with a few popular vocals and a substantial number of country-and-western items by Carson Robison, Frank Luther, Frank and Johnny Marvin, Frank and James McCravy, and Clayton McMichen's Georgia Wildcats.

British branches of F. W. Woolworth & Co. sold the third Crown record, a nine-inch disc, at 6d (then about a dime) between September 1935 and March 1937. This, a product of excellent quality in every way, was manufactured by the Crystalate Gramophone Record Manufacturing Company, Ltd., of Tunbridge Wells, Kent. It featured many front-rank British dance bands and popular artists of all kinds—several of the dance records under pseudonyms. "Buddy Barnett and his Music" was often a British group directed by staff director Jay Wilbur. But on Crown 235 it was a dubbing from American Vocalion of Dick McDonough and his Orchestra (*The Scene Changes*), and on Crown 266 it covered the identity of Jack Shilkret and his Orchestra (*Did I Remember?*), from the same American label.

CURRY'S

These British records were originally sold between 1922 and 1929 by a firm of bicycle manufacturers (now makers of television and radio parts and other electrical goods, with branches all over the country). There are two distinct kinds. The first had yellow labels, very crudely printed in black with elaborate designs. They were pressed by the Crystalate Gramophone Record Manufacturing Company, Ltd., of Tunbridge Wells, Kent, using its own Imperial masters and such American matrices as they could obtain from Plaza Music, Emerson and probably Paramount. The lifespan of this Curry's series was no more than five years. Generally the quality of the material, both physical and musical, was appalling. It included the most obvious dance successes and vocal pops of the day, pressed on substandard shellac.

The second wave of Curry's records was a very different affair. Numbered 100 upwards, as seemingly was the first series, they consisted of selected issues from Piccadilly records with a tasteful white label printed in blue and gold. As a rule the label was merely stuck on existing Piccadilly pressings, which had a reputation for good recording and excellent surfaces. The repertoire was geared to the same market as it had been, but the quality improved considerably. Such American recordings as appeared on the later Curry's label came from the Grey Gull catalog.

Neither label is commonly met with. It is likely that both were sold at about 1s. to 1s. 6d.—then about 25 cents.

D & R

Evidently a mail-order label of a very early kind, as the only copy I have seen or heard of bearing the name on the label (blue, with gold decoration and lettering) is numbered 3667, gives no ownership or origin, but is in fact pressed from Columbia masters of early 1910. One side is the incredible performance by Irving Berlin himself of his own number, *Oh! How That German Could Love*, issued on Columbia A-804 in April 1910 with the same backing (Billy Murray singing *My Little Dutch Colleen*).

DANDY

Despite intensive research, I have not been able to find out how Dandy records were marketed or by whom. They drew from the Emerson-Consolidated repertoire of 1924–1926, and as a result have matrix numbers in a 3000 series. The only catalog number range I know of is the 5000 block. They were obviously aimed at the popular market. A considerable proportion are dance music, with occasional hot jazz items such as those by the Original Indiana Five. The design is matt black with a white panel arc above the spindle hole bearing the word DANDY in black, with white decoration and gold title and artist credits.

DAVEGA

A rare label produced by Pathe, using mostly its own masters. But occasionally Davega records were pressed from Paramount and/or Banner, and these odd ones bear Paramount or Banner matrix numbers in the 1000s or 5000s respectively, and sometimes the Banner catalog number in the wax. The customer was the S. B. Davega Company of New York, whose name appears on the labels of all known issues. They were apparently issued between the early summer of 1922 and approximately March 1923. More latterly the store, specializing in sporting goods and later television, became known as Davega Stores.

Davega records, which have attractive dark green labels printed in gold with a tasteful and clear-cut design, were issued in two series: the popular dance and vocal items (numbered 5001 upwards and reaching at least to 5078), and an operatic series starting at 8001 and reaching at least to 8010. Both were apparently sold at 50 cents, and offer little to excite a collector other than a few sides by the Original Memphis Five and other bands.

DAVIS & SCHWEGLER

A Hollywood music-store label that existed briefly in 1939. It is noted mainly for the first and rarest records by Nat "King" Cole and his Trio.

DECCA

The Decca Record Company, Ltd., of the United Kingdom, was formed in 1929 by a stockbroker, Edward Lewis (now Sir Edward Lewis). For five years, during the worst of the great trade slump of the early 1930s, this company went from strength to strength, acquiring the rights to various American labels, notably Brunswick, Melotone, and the entire American Record Corporation range as then constituted. ARC material was thus continually issued on Decca and its subsidiary labels, Brunswick and Panachord. In January 1933, English Decca bought Edison Bell, within a year of acquiring English Vocalion. When Edward Lewis launched Decca in the United States in the summer of 1934 with assistance from Jack Kapp, late of Brunswick, records produced by the new American branch of course became the property of the London-based parent company.

In March 1937, Decca in London bought the Crystalate Gramophone Record Manufacturing Company, Ltd., and so added Rex and Vocalion to their labels. As a result, suitable American Decca products began to appear on these labels as well as on Decca itself, Brunswick and Panachord. In the summer of 1938, the rights to the ARC catalog passed to EMI Records, Ltd., so all the titles on Brunswick and other Decca labels made between the end of 1931 and the summer of 1934 had to be deleted from those catalogs. The relationship between the two Decca companies continued through to 1974, when the powerful Music Corporation of America took over the company's affairs in the USA, and EMI secured British rights.

American Decca began to issue their familiar ten-inch popular record at 35 cents. The first blue and gold "sunburst" label, with the make printed in a striking "perspective" design, disappeared in 1937 in favour of more conventional block lettering. This in turn was abandoned during the war for a script style of lettering for the word DECCA, except on the Personality series where it appeared in shaded block letters with serifs. The catalog numbers started at 100 and continued until the 4400s. A country-and-western series starting at 5000 and another from 46000, and a race series beginning at 7000, ran beside the popular series, but neither covered a thousand issues before being discontinued. There was a Sepia series of Negro records numbered 8500 upwards for a short time, from 1940 to 1942, and a similar one beginning at 48000 after the war. The twelve-inch popular series began at 15000, but this was changed to 29000 before a hundred records had been issued in it. The Personality series, beginning at 18000 in 1939, eventually supplanted the four-figure popular series. On reaching 18999, the Personality series continued in the 23000s, reaching 24999 and proceeding to 28000, as 25000 upwards was yet another Personality series! There was a DU-40000 series during the postwar years, pressed on an unbreakable plastic called Deccalite and offering album sets by every sort of artist from Fred Waring's Pennsylvanians to Andres Segovia playing concert music on guitar. Originally, the Personality series starting at 18000 and 23000 had deep crimson labels with gold lettering, befitting a product whose music was intended to be looked on by the public as deluxe. Once it became the popular series, black and gold was the order of the day, and the old blue Decca never returned. In conservative Britain, the popular F- series, starting at F-1501 in July 1929, was always true-blue, come the more expensive ten-inch M- series in magenta (1929–1930) or vermillion and white (1932 onwards) or the twelve-inch K-500 series (black from 1930 to 1932, blue from then until 1941, then vermillion and white to the end). British Decca ("The Supreme Record") bore as its trademark a bust of Beethoven, glowering above the middle C of the brand name, regardless of the music on the record. His services were not dispensed with until 1954.

Jack Kapp, head of American Decca, had experience in the record business since the mid-1920s and the old Brunswick-Vocalion era. His interests in music matched his shrewd business brain. He liked commercial music and had little or no time for the classics, or serious music of any kind. The earliest Decca catalogs reflected his tastes. Although in 1939 there were some impeccably played guitar solos by the great Vincente Gomez, these were as near to classics as Decca was ever to reach in Kapp's lifetime. He was only forty-seven when he died in 1949, just as the LP was beginning to take root. From this point onwards, first-class records on microgroove of standard and even more esoteric works began gradually to appear on Decca.

Kapp was a friend of Bing Crosby and many other Brunswick stars in the Warner and ARC eras of that label's fortunes. When American Decca was launched, Kapp filled its first monthly supplements with Bing's latest songs, and fine records by top artists of the calibre of the Mills Brothers, Guy Lombardo and his Royal Canadians, the Ted Lewis band, Bob Crosby and his Orchestra, the Dorsey Brothers' Orchestra, the Casa Loma Orchestra, and the orchestras of Jimmie Lunceford and Chick Webb. Film stars followed, among them Judy Garland, Deanna Durbin, Frances Langford, Ginger Rogers, Mae Questal ("The Betty Boop Girl"), Phil Regan, Dick Powell, Gene Kelly, and Bob Hope.

It was Bing Crosby who established a record among records just before the ban of 1942, when he recorded in Decca's Los Angeles studios a song his friend Irving Berlin had written for Bing's latest film, *Holiday Inn*. It was *White Christmas*. In the three and a half decades since it was made, sales of over ten million copies throughout the world, in 78, 45 and LP form, have made it the undoubted biggest seller of all time. Crosby remained an exclusive Decca artist until 1955. He had countless other successes over those twenty-one years, solo and with other artists ranging from the great concert violinist Jascha Heifetz to his sparring partner, Bob Hope; from Connee Boswell, the Andrews Sisters and Jane Wyman to Louis Armstrong, Joe Venuti, Jimmy Dorsey, and Al Jolson.

The Andrews Sisters were direct descendants of the Boswell Sisters, who broke up as a team around late 1935. The former were even more sensationally successful—and always on Decca—than their predecessors had been on Brunswick. At the beginning, they had a 1937 smash hit in Sammy Cahn's Yiddish-based *Bei Mir Bist du Schoen*. They followed in 1938-1941 with *Hold Tight, The Beer Barrel Polka, Boogie Woogie Bugle Boy* and *Apple Blossom Time*. In the later war years they reached their peak of popularity with *Rum and Coca Cola* and *Don't Fence Me In*, and had another hit after the war with *Can't I?* The three sisters were one of Decca's hottest properties in the 1940s.

Though Decca made its mark from the start (despite the inferior quality of its pressings), it came into its own in the early 1940s when Jimmy Dorsey's records began outselling even Glenn Miller's Bluebirds. Though Decca was generally less successful than Victor/Bluebird and Columbia/Vocalion/OKeh in picking the most successful big bands, it did launch Count Basie and Woody Herman, and recorded Louis Armstrong from the mid-thirties through the forties.

Decca's matrix numbers generally fall into three blocks. They seem to have resumed almost where Warner-Brunswick left off nearly three years earlier. Decca's first New York session took place in August 1934 at matrix 38352. On reaching 39999 a little over a year later, the series changed to 60000, which continued into the microgroove era and six digits. Chicago recordings continue from the old Brunswick C- block, jumping from C-9999 to C-90000 in the spring of 1935; and on reaching C-91999 exactly five years from that date, changed again to C-93000. The other regular recording location, Los Angeles, had a series all to itself. It started at DLA-1 in August 1934 and reached just over 3000 (with the prefix changed to simply L- in June 1942) before the ban. Other recordings made in California were included in this series. A handful made in New Orleans in March 1936 were included in the New York block.

The following chart shows the first matrix number used in New York, Chicago and Los Angeles for the years 1934 to 1942:

	New York	Chicago	Los Angeles
1934 (August)	38290	C-9300	DLA-1
1935	39220; 60000 (September)	C-9640; C-90000 (May)	DLA-90
1936	60300	C-90550	DLA-291
1937	61503	C-91050	DLA-650
1938	63122	C-91380	DLA-1120
1939	64845	C-91620	DLA-1700
1940	67010	C-91900; 93000 (May)	DLA-1915
1941	68528	93500	DLA-2320
1942	70120	93900	DLA-2825

DIAMOND

The Diamond label in England was a subsidiary of Pathe, using Pathe masters issued between February 1915 and at least May 1918. As far as is known, nothing American appeared in its catalog of something under four hundred issues (starting at 01).

The American Diamond label was derived from Columbia about a decade earlier. It was used by the Diamond Record Company of Chicago, which issued these single-sided pressings from contemporary Columbias under the famous patent date of November 25, 1902. No other patent date is known to appear on them, but Columbia records known to have been made in 1906 were issued as Diamond.

The design of the label is striking. It consists of a white diamond lying across the half-inch wide spindle hole, surmounted by the words in white block letters DIAMOND RECORD (round the rim of the label) and DIAMOND RECORD COMPANY (following the contours of the diamond). Below the diamond is a white panel, shaped rather like a piano roll seen at eye level, on which the title, description (artists were anonymous) and number (Columbia matrix number) were typed in reddish-brown, or latterly in dark green. The background of the label is itself dark green.

As Columbia featured some interesting ragtime music and songs, and even recordings by the great Negro comedian Bert Williams, any of them could have appeared on Diamond. Some by Ragtime Bob Roberts, often with very fine rag piano accompaniments, have already been found. The quality of the recording and pressing is as good as that of Columbia, of course.

DIVA

"Made to Rival the Best," Diva was a Columbia subsidiary produced for the W. T. Grant chainstores during the years 1925 to 1932. Its catalog ran parallel with that of Harmony, even to the numbering of the records. Where Harmony would number a record, say, 353-H, Diva would issue exactly the same coupling as 2353-G: 2,000 numbers on, one letter of the alphabet back. This continued until the slump in the record industry generally and Columbia's fortunes in particular forced the discontinuation of Diva, along with Harmony, Clarion and Velvet Tone, its 50-cent partners. (Later the price became 35 cents.)

Though the designs on the labels of these cut-price Columbia products were usually all but non-existent, the Diva label, if not attractive to the eye in the way the Vocalion label was, is remarkable. Glossy black with all printing in gold, it included (apart from the above slogan, the usual patent dates, and the details of the performance) a panel bearing the word DIVA apparently across the bell of a trumpet or some similar horn, behind which a crosseyed creature with distended cheeks is to be seen, presumably blowing the instrument.

There was another series towards the end of Diva's career that did not rely on Harmony for its material. This was the 6000-G series that is notable for the interesting urban blues it featured: music not found on Harmony or Clarion, only on Diva and Velvet Tone. Why these should have been favoured is not known, but a good guess might be that the Grant stores numbered many Negroes among their clientele. They evidently arrived rather late in the day, for 1930 was not a good year for basic blues issues, however superb the quality of the performance and the physical material of the record. There is no denying either of these characteristics in the case of Diva; although, like Harmony, the first nine hundred to a thousand issues were made by a horribly boxy acoustic process, four years after it had been abandoned by the parent Columbia. The remaining four or five hundred releases, however, were electric, and pressed on velvety surfaces as fine as anything on Columbia and OKeh, the two principal labels from Bridgeport, Conn.

DOMESTIC

This was a short-lived label that made its appearance in November 1917. A listing of its first (and only?) issue in *The Talking Machine World*, contained the usual collection of popular songs and dances of the time, sung or played by names that occurred many times on every label or nowhere else at all. This list also featured standard light classics. Beyond that, nothing is known about this label.

DOMINION

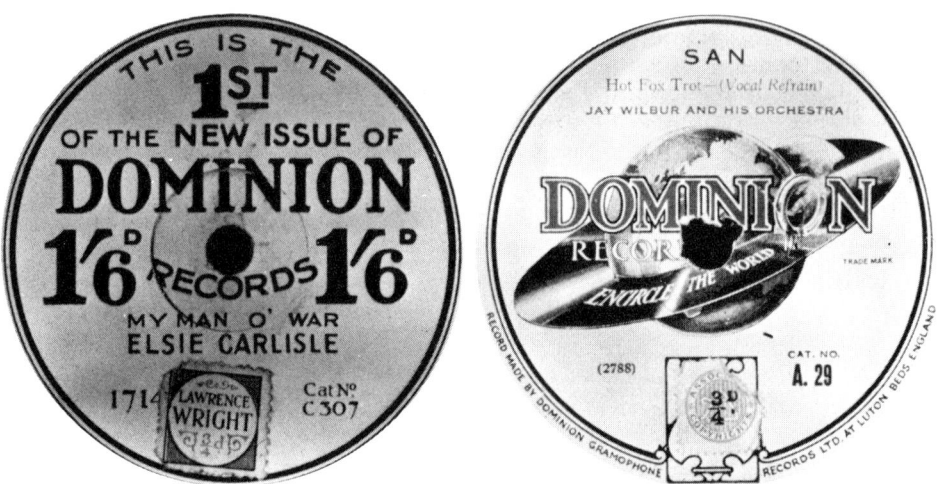

This was a British label announced with panache in October 1928 from the head office of Dominion Gramophone Records Ltd., 55–57 Great Marlborough Street, London, W.1. Priced at 1s. 3d. (then about 25 cents), the most impressive feature about Dominion records was the clear cream label printed first in gold but for most of its life in dark blue, with a record encircling the globe and the second O of DOMINION taking the form of a soundbox resting on the track, with the slogan "Encircle the World." The quality of the surfaces was commensurate with the low price, and the recording was no better.

Numbering began at A-1 and continued to at least A-267 (April 1930). There were two other series: a blue labelled "Classic" series (so-called) at 1s. 9d. (say 30 cents) starting at B-1 in September 1929, and a red, costing the same, starting at C-301 in April 1930. There were American issues from Cameo throughout most of the A- series, these showing the original matrix numbers in the wax, sometimes through the label, and also on the label itself, in the 2000–3000 block. Those also appearing on Perfect in America sometimes have the Perfect six-figure matrix number showing through the Dominion label.

Dominion's own recordings began at 1001 in August 1928, and the last traceable number in the series is 1726. For the last few issues, Dominion ceased to rely on Cameo-Perfect for its American masters, and records from the Grey Gull catalog can be found in the later A and some of the C series, some of the dance titles even being ascribed to the Savoy Orpheans or Jay Wilbur and his Band. Wilbur was the company's musical director until the spring of 1930. In June he took a similar position with Crystalate, after Dominion had ceased trading. Besides appearing under his own name, Wilbur was also the power behind the Deauville Dance Orchestra, the Brooklyn Broadcasters, and the Moonlight (sometimes Midnight) Serenaders; and on A-29, *San* from Cameo by the Alabama Red Peppers was ascribed to Jay Wilbur.

Although virtually nothing of outstanding interest appeared on the cream A series, the blue B began with an album of readings by authors of extracts from their novels, and continued with records by lesser lights of Italian opera by Tom Burke, a British tenor well known throughout Europe and the USA. The C series, lasting for less than a hundred issues, produced some rare Al Bowlly records anonymously, and on C-307 an obvious piece of recorded pornography, *My Man o' War*, sung by Elsie Carlisle, a popular revue and cabaret star whose usual *métier* was romantic light-comedy numbers put over rather in the style of Annette Hanshaw. It is said that the censors, who were very active in the Lord Chamberlain's office in those days, vetoed the issue of further copies when the dreadful deed was discovered. The subsequent fine reportedly put Dominion out of business. But in fact, their financial position was such that not even a best-seller could have saved them. When their affairs were finally wound up in 1934, four years after the collapse, it was found their assets were nil. Shareholders received nothing whatever for their investments of six years before.

DOMINO

The first Domino records issued in the United States were seven-inch vertical-cut, having light blue labels with dark blue lettering. They came and went about 1917. The much better known Domino was a ten-inch subsidiary of Plaza Music, and from 1924 to 1933 contributed the same type of material to popular entertainment as Banner, Regal and the others of the complex. That is to say, most of the issues on Domino were exactly what was issued simultaneously with the other labels. But some of the earliest Dominoes were of performances never issued on any other make at the time. To the jazz collector, they are of considerable interest. Several are by the New Orleans Jazz Band. They bear a matrix serial unlike any other, in the 10000s. Within a few months there was an 11000 and a little later a 12000 series.

Artists from Banner sometimes appeared on Domino under pseudonyms early in the label's career. Most of the catalog consisted of dance music, popular songs and the occasional light classic. Numbering began at 300, but it advanced to 3432 instead of 432 in February 1925, and continued in this series until about 4500 early in 1930. The label was reactivated briefly in 1932 (numbered 100 upwards) but disappeared again some time in 1933.

These later arrivals have handsome gold labels with black print, and contain selected items from the ARC output of the time, including some jazz titles by Chicago musicians and others under the nominal direction of Billy Banks. The first Domino issues are no less attractive. They feature dark olive-brown labels with a broad floral band design and title details in gold. The name DOMINO runs in heavy block letters in gold on six individual white panels surmounted by a masked girl with a ruffle in gold and the words "Domino Record Co. New York" in white at the foot of the label. To give the records an even more unusual look, they were usually pressed on brown wax. Later labels dispensed with the white part of the design, and have dark red or violet labels entirely printed in gold. The recording quality is as good as Banner, of course, and the surfaces reasonably smooth, if not notably durable.

DUOPHONE

For some time prior to the summer of 1925, a British firm known as the Duophone Syndicate Ltd. of 63 Queen Victoria Street, London, E. C. 4 had been manufacturing and selling a machine for playing records. It involved a double soundbox, so the volume of reproduction was of course increased. In August that year, the Syndicate announced that it was about to enter the record business, and ran a contest to get suggestions for suitable music with which to launch its catalog. The winner would receive for his prize the most expensive Duophone on the market, all suggestions to be received by September 1. On October 1, the first list was published. It consisted of some twelve-inch records at 4s. (about 80 cents) and a great many more ten-inch at 2s. 6d. (about 50 cents). The larger records were mostly by Lt. Col. J. McKenzie-Rogan, late of H. M. Coldstream Guards, and his Symphony Orchestra or Military Band. The smaller were mainly dance music and popular songs, many of them derived from the American Vocalion and Gennett catalogs. The twelve-inchers were numbered A-1000 upwards, the ten-inchers B-5000 upwards. They had truly extraordinary labels printed in black and gold on a livid violet background, and depict the Duophone tone arm amid much decoration. A small oblong panel gave succinct details of the performance on the record. They were evidently manufactured by the Aeolian Company Ltd. in their Hayes, Middlesex, factory, and are of reasonable quality.

In November 1926, by which time the Syndicate had moved its headquarters to 18 Savile Row, London W.1, a new Duophone record was announced. This was to be the revolution of the decade. (The Aeolian Company had just embarked on its Marconi Process of electric recording, but as yet there were no electrically recorded Duophones.) The new records were unbreakable, though they looked just like normal records, being black and glossy, with a label similar to their predecessors (which were then withdrawn). The new series began its numbers at UB-2001.

Within a year, things had changed again. There was another series of Duophone Unbreakable Records, numbered M-100 or M-101 upwards and carrying a bright red label with black lettering and some gold decoration. In place of the tone arm, there appeared a picture of a lion grasping a record—obviously a Duophone—between its forepaws. The lion was in the act of chewing the record—without damaging it. The price asked for these stoic discs was 1s. 6d. (about 30 cents). But while it is true that dropping them would not break or even crack them, playing them with any but the lightest soundbox and probably fibre needles would strip the grooves off in a spiral, revealing the core of fibrous substance on which was mounted the coarse-grained plastic in which the soundtrack was pressed. It was also true that if, as often happened, a Duophone Unbreakable Record was put to the test and it was dropped on its rim enough times on or about the same spot, it would split laterally. Then, with no difficulty, the two sides could be separated, so that it became possible to play one side of the record while holding the other. The texture of the core was soft and absorbent. It made the finest blotting paper I have ever come across. But at 15 cents a circular sheet, ten inches in diameter, it was somewhat expensive, even if, for a time at least, the reverse side could be coaxed into playing a very rough approximation of what had been recorded in the Emerson studios in New York (for by now Emerson was supplying the American element in the Duophone catalog) or by the Syndicate itself in London. The usual name given to the Emerson bands was the Claremont Dance Band, or sometimes the U.B. Syncopators.

In August 1928, the Duophone and Unbreakable Record Co. Ltd., as the Syndicate was now known, gained control of British Brunswick and changed its address again, this time to 15–19 Cavendish Place, London W.1. The old garish label and its predatory lion were abandoned. A new design, completely different and in excellent taste, was adopted for yet another new series of records. These appeared in two forms. Those with a black label were as unbreakable (but just as destructible) as their antecedents. But those with violet labels denoted a superior product pressed on good quality shellac in a factory in Feltham, Middlesex. The numbers began at D-4001, and about fifty were issued before the end of 1929, nearly all of them by American dance bands under contract to Brunswick-Balke-Collender, such as Vincent Lopez, Ben Bernie, Red Nichols, Meyer Davis and Harry Reser's Six Jumping Jacks. There were also some British recordings by Bert Firman (late of Zonophone), and right at the end, by the Savoy Plaza Band, recorded by the newly launched Worldecho Records (q.v.). It is possible to read the correct identity of these artists through the labels, as the Brunswick engineers kindly included them along with the title, matrix number and take, and the Duophone processing engineer did not spoil their efforts by erasing them.

This proved helpful to researchers, because all of these fine bands were under contract elsewhere, and hence were obliged to record pseudonymously for Duophone. Their records were geared to the British market. Very few ever appeared in the United States.

Late in the autumn of 1929, the affairs of Duophone were in a bad way. They gamely launched a final series, F-2001 upwards. It still bore the discreet black and gold design of the D series, and had a family resemblance to Brunswick's shield; but only the unbreakable kind of disc was issued. The new series had no American issues, as far as can be traced, but is remarkable for four sides by Lewis Stone and his Orchestra that launched the long and distinguished recording career of one of Britain's finest arrangers and bandleaders, known throughout the 1930s and 1940s as Lew Stone. There were also some serious piano recordings, a few drawing-room ballads, and military band music. Similar music had been on the earlier D series. Those with a three-figure catalog number were devoted to such works, but few were ever issued. Perhaps the most interesting are some breezy ballads sung by the much-loved comedian, Stanley Holloway, casting aside his clown's mask and singing with warmth and charm. There are also some popular songs of the time sung by Melville Gideon.

Neither these nor the latest F series could extricate Duophone. In the spring of 1930, the chairman pleaded with the shareholders to increase their investments to cover the cost of wonderful new expansion plans, but to no avail. By the end of the year, the Duophone Unbreakable Record, the Duophone Syndicate, and the claims and promises of the past five years were no more than a vague memory among most record buyers.

DURIUM

This was Britain's answer to America's Hit of the Week (q.v.), a record sold at about 20 cents on newsstands, with one new issue weekly. Like Hit of the Week, Durium records were made of thin pliable celluloid, pinkish-brown in colour, with a coating on one side only of cellulose acetate which carried the grooves. These were compressed so as to accommodate two full-length performances on one side.

Although it is impossible to *break* a Durium record, it is simplicity itself to destroy it—by playing it with too heavy a soundbox or too large a needle, or simply by tearing it as easily as a piece of cardboard. The recording quality is excellent, and if sufficient care is taken when playing, the surfaces are smooth, even today. The music found on Durium is almost all dance music played by a studio band directed by Lew Stone, frequently featuring Al Bowlly as vocalist, sometimes teamed with Stone. There are tracks by Carson Robison and his Pioneers, and EN-7 is a direct pressing from a Hit of the Week master. It features vocalist Paul Small, but like most of the other band titles, is credited to the Durium Dance Band. Manny Klein is featured on trumpet on one track (*Now's the Time to Fall in Love*); the other is a waltz, *After the Ball*. Durium began numbering at EN-0, strangely, on April 8, 1932, and every Friday would see an addition to the catalog. But before 1933 was more than a few days old, the series had ground to a permanent halt.

The use of more than one master is a frequent occurrence on Durium, and it is interesting to compare both takes of any pair on which Al Bowlly sings or Nat Gonella plays trumpet. The differences can be striking. As with Hit of the Week, the design, titles and details are etched into the central area itself, with no paper label. The silver inking makes a sharp contrast with the brown of the record.

EDISON BELL

The first Edison Bell records to appear in England did so as cylinders at the turn of the century. The Gold Moulded kind date back to 1901. It is of some interest to note that in 1904 a date—presumably of recording—appears, scratched by stylo, in the smooth wax at the end of the grooving. Thomas Edison's factory serviced the British market with these until the outbreak of war in 1914. Edison Bell discs (known thus, with large labels in dark green with gold lettering, or pale blue-green with a broad black border and black and gold lettering) first appeared in September 1909. These continued as 10½-inch records numbered from 1 until November 1912, the last known number being 490.

The firm that produced these was J. E. Hough Ltd. of Peckham, London, S.E. In July 1912 this company introduced the Winner record, starting the catalog series at 2000. For a considerable period it reissued Bell records until Winner had completely replaced them. Edison Bell Winner continued to provide a quality product at a low price—it varied from 1s. 6d. to 2s. over the years—from this point until the last independent issue in April 1933. The British Decca Record Company bought Edison Bell earlier that year. Until January 1935 it continued to issue Winner records, the last in the original series being 5692.

There was a new series of Edison Bell Winners introduced briefly by Decca in November 1933, starting at W-1. Less than two hundred issues appeared on this glossy black and gold label before it too was discontinued in January 1935. This particular species of Edison Bell Winner was devoted entirely to dance music, light popular numbers, and vocals, most of its catalog deriving from American Vocalion. The handful of British recordings in the W series have matrix numbers prefixed GB-, as they are part of the regular Decca series (q.v.). Although many of the American element are no more than straightforward dance records, they did include four very rare titles by Clarence Williams' Washboard Band, correctly credited, and one by Jimmie Noone and his Orchestra (*Dixie Lee*), for some reason issued as by Sleepy Hall and his Collegians. There were some quite interesting country-and-western sides on the black Winner label, and six by Annette Hanshaw, two with Benny Goodman in the accompanying orchestra. These were 1s., then about 20 cents.

The original Edison Bell Winners of 1912 to 1933, however, were wider in scope. They included the usual routine recordings of light popular classics, invariably churned out by military bands or small studio orchestras; and there were ballads by singers of no outstanding talent. But they also offered such

interesting items as two cello solos by Master J. Barbirolli, aged twelve; a record of *The Broken Melody*, again a cello solo, played by the composer, Auguste van Biene, a matter of ten days before he collapsed and died on the stage after playing it in a concert hall in Brighton, Sussex; a talk by the Chief Scout, Lord Baden-Powell; and one of the first records issued in England featuring Louis Armstrong: *Mandy, Make Up Your Mind*, with Fletcher Henderson's Orchestra, renamed the Regent Orchestra (as were many issues taken from American masters).

Before January 1922 all Winner records were recorded in London. In the supplement for that month were listed the first fruits of an agreement between J. E. Hough and the Starr Piano Company of Richmond, Ind., makers of Gennett records. As a result, Gennett masters were imported into England, and a large proportion of the dance records and Hawaiian items on Edison Bell Winner issued up to 1925 were of Gennett origin. They are usually recognizable by their slow-moving, close-threaded run-off, and by the matrix number in tiny but neat handwriting just inside the rim of the last recorded groove. Edison Bell allocated its own matrix numbers to imported masters, in the same series as its London recordings. These are always quoted on the labels; the correct American numbers never are.

In 1924, while still issuing Gennett products, J. E. Hough extended his American contacts to include occasional items from Emerson, several from Paramount (e.g., the Fletcher Henderson record referred to above), and even the pioneer in electric recording, Autograph. Like Thomas Edison himself, Hough was the undoubted ruler of his company. He had little time for postwar trends towards jazz and jazz-flavoured dance music. But he was shrewd enough to realise the sales potential of popular dance music played more or less in the new idiom, and even recorded such visiting American bands as the Versatile Three and Four (a pioneer Negro group), the Southern Rag-a-Jazz Band, Jack Howard's Metropolitans, and the Original Paramount Orchestra. Early in the first war, he insisted that any fit man on his staff was to "volunteer" for service in France, or be sacked. Immediately before the outbreak of hostilities he had recorded Jack Johnson, the American Negro heavyweight champion, giving a six-minute talk on how to keep fit. Hough's publicity material was quick to point out that it would be most valuable at that time and under those circumstances. (The record was announced in August 1914.) The British public did not agree. The Johnson is one of the rarest of all Winners, which are by no means uncommon. To J. E. Hough must go whatever credit lies in being the first to issue a record in England by a "jazz" band, Murray Pilcer's. Hough's own (anonymous) account of the session early in 1919 is worth repeating here:

"The leader of the great Jazz Combination, who exercise their stupendous powers in disseminating torrential tones to thrill multitudes in the Metropolis, was invited to enlarge his popularity by placing a few samples on Winners.

"He agreed, declaring he would make records that would eclipse Creation.

"Having put his cannonading party in effective positions, he divested himself of all clothing decency would permit, and fitted his feet, legs, arms and head with mediums for extracting sounds from many and various surrounding instruments.

"Then an order was given and a musical cataract commenced, increasing in volume more and more powerful and exciting until the Onlooker thought even Niagara, which is heard miles away, should in comparison be considered only a purling brook.

"When the wild-eyed leader had finished, he turned to the Onlooker, and with all the breath he could muster, shouted:-

" 'THAT—THAT IS JAZZ MUSIC!'—then he added, 'There are crowds who come up from Brighton to hear us.'

" 'Surely', replied the Onlooker, 'it is foolish to leave Brighton. They could hear you there without coming nearer!' "

The resulting records are incredibly bad. They convey nothing comparable to the vision conjured up by the above quotation from a full-page advertisement in *The Sound Wave* for March 1919.

For all his insistence on physical fitness, J. E. Hough, bearded, white-haired and bright-eyed, succumbed to a fall in the street on February 27, 1925. He was in his seventies. He had devoted the last twenty years of his life to the firm of Edison Bell. He had insisted that five attempts at recording any side were sufficient. If satisfactory results could not be obtained in five attempts, the number was to be abandoned. Whereas other companies, in America and Britain, used letters or digits to denote different takes, Edison Bell used an X in a circle for take 1, a triangle for take 2, a square for take 3, a horizontal line with a dot either side for take 4, and a circle with a horizontal line through it for take 5.

Soon after Hough died and his sons became the directors of the firm, the arrangement with Gennett also expired. Now the company looked even more to the other American sources I have mentioned. Thus the strange situation arises where something recorded for Plaza and issued on Paramount and associated labels in America was issued on both Edison Bell Winner and Imperial, a rival that drew on Banner to compete in England's cheap-record market. Paramount and a newcomer to the America market in 1930, Crown, were also contributing masters to Edison Bell's repertoire by 1931. An important pair from Paramount were the Midnight Stompers' *Tiger Rag* and *River Boat Blues,* both in fact by Devine's Wisconsin Roof Orchestra. One from Crown, as the Deauville Dance Orchestra (*Hello, Beautiful*), turned out to be by Ben Pollack's Orchestra. Titles issued on Paramount or its subsidiary Broadway, but also appearing on Banner, have a control number between 100 and about 1500 in addition to the original Banner matrix number in the 7000-9000s block. This also shows on Edison Bell Winners pressed from those masters; so they show the Banner number, the Paramount control number, and their own "matrix" number, which must have caused a certain amount of confusion for the pressing engineers.

The end of Edison Bell as an independent concern was not far away by that time, however. It came in 1933. Edison Bell provided masters for Beltona (q.v.), from 1927 to the summer of 1929, about two hundred dark blue and gold-labelled Electron records were issued, a quality product at a higher price. The label offered no American recordings. A few dubbings from Banner were issued in edited form on the eight-inch Edison Bell Radio and marketed from April 1928 to April 1932.

In its near quarter century of life, Edison Bell Winner used a variety of labels. Originally they were black, with a garish coloured picture of a jockey urging his mount to victory with a record held aloft in his left hand, his right gripping the reins. Just before the outbreak of World War I, this was changed. The jockey, lying along the neck of his horse, now held a record in each hand. The calm gentleman in the top hat by the winning post now became an excited onlooker in more casual wear. Late in 1919, the black label became bright scarlet, and all the racetrack background disappeared. Hence the jockey, even more precariously perched along his horse's neck and still clutching a record in each hand, seems to be riding alone without an audience, and at night. The label changed in the autumn of 1922 to rich chocolate brown and gold, with the same lone rider and his two precious records also in gold. After only a few months, this became red, but with the same design. After two years, the jockey retired and the trademark became a simple bell on the left side. The label stayed red, with everything printed in gold. This design remained unchanged in its stark simplicity until 1930, when it was reduced from 3½ inches to 2.35 inches. Some issues were gold-labelled, with black lettering. Decca used this colour scheme for the last hundred or so issues, but on a regular three-inch label.

There was another Edison Bell make that used American Gennett masters from January 1922, though only for a few months. This was the violet-labelled Velvet Face record. It changed to bright green in 1925 and was discontinued two years later. Starting as a 2s. 6d. record, it finished at 2s., thus keeping its price in step with its sister label. It mainly featured unusual classical works, and was remarkable for a comprehensive symposium of titles from Sir Edward Elgar's oratorio, *The Dream Of Gerontius,* a most ambitious project for a fairly small company in 1924.

The following table shows the approximate first matrix numbers recorded in each year:

1909 (c. June-July)	2000	1922	7150
1910	2400	1923	7680
1911	2600	1924	8160
1912	3000	1925	9100
1913	3400	1926	9820
1914	3900	1927	10500
1915	4500	1928	11380
1916	4990	1929	11940
1917	5310	1930	12600
1918	5670	1931	13220
1919	5970	1932	14090
1920	6430	1933	14580
1921	6820		

(Matrices 12000 through about 12180 were made on the Continent, in Bucharest, Vienna, Copenhagen, etc.)

EDISON BLUE AMBEROL and EDISON DIAMOND DISC

Thomas Alva Edison, though partially deaf and not possessed of a finely developed taste in music (his favourite song is said to have been *I'll Take You Home Again, Kathleen*), was nevertheless astute enough as a businessman to know that his favourite invention was destined for bigger things than as a mere mechanical substitute for a flesh-and-blood stenographer.

Allen Koenigsberg, in his notably interesting and minutely documented book, *Edison Cylinder Records, 1889-1912*, lists everything known to have been made during those years by the firm of Thomas A. Edison, Inc. Up to September 1912, cylinders were those known as the "two-minute wax" variety. Then, in October, the four-minute Blue Amberols made their debut. In October 1908 a coarser version of the same kind of cylinder, made of much noisier material, had made its appearance. It too played for four minutes by having its grooves cut 200 turns to the inch instead of the 100 turns of the two-minute record.

The quality of Blue Amberol has been praised and praised again ever since their first appearance. In some collecting quarters the paeans continue yet. In point of fact, they were all dubbed from discs; and though the blue and sometimes magenta plastic in which the soundtrack was moulded is smooth and the signal-to-noise ratio is low by comparison with other cylinders and indeed other discs of the time (Victor excepted), the sound itself is much inclined to the metallic. It lacks the roundness of both Victor and Columbia of the period, although it must be said that the upper frequencies are remarkable for their clarity and definition.

October 1913 saw the launching of the quarter-inch-thick Edison Diamond Disc, which had been tested and experimented on for over three years. Here again, many authorities hold these cumbersome discs up as superlative examples of the acoustic recording art. Played on contemporary Edison machines, with their specially designed soundboxes that float up and down ("hill-and-dale") over the near-microgroove track that enabled a five-minute performance to be recorded on one ten-inch side, they do offer a remarkably clear picture of what went on in front of the recording horn. To be sure, they are compressed in tonal range, giving the audible equivalent of a pinhole camera shot. As with the Blue Amberol cylinders that were dubbed from the Diamond Discs, the latter cannot compare with the far more natural sound obtainable from the average recording on a lateral-cut disc by one of the major companies. In addition, because of the infrangibility of these records, they emit a heavy rumble. They are so thick and stolidly laminated that they have the same distressing defect as a laminated Columbia or OKeh, accentuated considerably because of their thickness.

The first seven years of Edison Diamond Discs produced a number of interesting operatic items by many singers not under contract to Victor or Columbia who satisfied Edison's own strange tastes. The records had no labels. The details of the performance, as well as the trademark and numbers, were etched into the central area, almost impossible to read. In 1920, however, and until the last issue in October 1929, Edison Diamond Discs had plain white labels with black printing and a checkerboard design, and including (of course) a portrait of the inventor himself.

Although electric recording was in use by Victor, Columbia, Brunswick and other labels in 1925, it was not employed by Edison until June 1927. The year before, he had launched yet another revolutionary idea in the form of a twelve-inch long-playing record. This was a 78 rpm disc cut vertically in microgroove form but offering no music lasting longer than could be obtained on a standard lateral-cut of the time. Nor was it anywhere near as well recorded as Victor and Columbia records, even those acoustically recorded a decade or so earlier; and, of course, not by artists of the quality of Victor's and Columbia's. Instead of excellent recordings by Leopold Stokowski and the Philadelphia Symphony Orchestra, or Dr. Frederick Stock conducting the Chicago Symphony Orchestra, Edison's "long-playing" records offered—the American Symphony Orchestra, and so pallidly recorded in grooves so narrow that the diamond stylus would not track properly. The new line was discontinued after a few months.

In the late summer of 1929, Edison released the first of about eighty lateral-cut, electrically recorded black-label records. On October 19, 1929, the last Edison recording session took place in the New York studios. Thirteen days later, Thomas A. Edison, Inc. closed down its record business forever, thenceforth concentrating on radio production. As a result, these latecomers are among the rarest records of any prominent label. They were greeted with accolades in the press, barely justified. The quality of the recording is reasonable but not outstanding, the surfaces likewise. The repertoire offered nothing to excite the discerning music lover.

The Edison repertoire over the thirty-odd years of its existence was rarely anything special. There are cylinders of Sophie Tucker, Marie Dressler and other stars of the vaudeville stage; mainly on discs, a sprinkling of unusual jazz bands such as Charles A. Matson's Creole Serenaders; (Vincent) Lopez and (Billy) Hamilton's Kings of Harmony; Charlie Skeete and his Orchestra. Among the handful of regulars were the Original Memphis Five and Fletcher Henderson and his Orchestra, and a considerable number by such as the California Ramblers (labelled "The Golden Gate Orchestra," a name used for them on other makes), B. A. Rolfe and his Lucky Strike Orchestra, Oreste and his Queensland Orchestra, and the Georgia Melodians. There were many popular vocal records by the free-lance singers who filled out all the major catalogs, and a smattering of Negro blues artists (who rarely met with Edison's wholehearted approval). As noted earlier, there were records by opera singers. These included Celestina Boninsegna, Frieda Hempel, Claudia Muzio, Maggie Teyte, Giovanni Zenatello and Karl Jorn. And to Edison must go the credit for being first to record Sergei Rachmaninoff on his arrival in the United States, an exile from his revolution-torn country. The great composer-pianist made ten sides in four sessions in a week in April 1919. Afterward his records were all made for Victor.

Whatever the shortcomings of the various experiments, however erratic their commercial success, there is no denying Edison his role as a documenter of history in the earliest years of sound recording. Not content with recording famous speakers in the United States, he sent his emissary, Col. Gouraud, to Europe. There the voices of poets Alfred Tennyson and Robert Browning, musicians Sir Arthur Sullivan (speaking) and Johannes Brahms and Hans von Bülow (playing), and other celebrities such as Florence Nightingale and William Ewart Gladstone were recorded on fragile wax cylinders. Sullivan forecast with Cassandran gloom but prophetic accuracy the recording of "so much bad music." Miss Nightingale sent a conventional message to "my dear old comrades of Balaclava." Browning was apparently so overcome with the strangeness of the recording process that he forgot the words of his own poem, "How They Brought the Good News from Ghent to Aix." Gladstone, aged seventy-nine, spoke briefly but sincerely to Edison, congratulating him on "your marvellous invention," and expressing regret that old age and overstrain had taken their toll of his voice. Records are alleged to have been made of other interesting personalities, from Queen Victoria to Mark Twain, but these have yet to be found.

The following table shows the first matrix number on Edison Diamond Discs made in each year:

1910 (July 7)	100	(many in this block of numbers recorded in London and in Europe)	
1912 (Nov. 4)	2000	1922	8329
1913	2076	1923	8807
1914	2690	1924	9315
1915	3500	1925	9922
1916	4385	1926	10748
1917	5251	1927	11411
1918	5949	1927 (Nov. 1)	11999, next number 18000
1919	6539	1928	18147
1920	7084	1929	18978
1921	7713	1929 (Sept. 18)	19349 (last Diamond Disc cut)

The lateral-cut Edisons began experimentally on January 6, 1928, at N-100. The last was N-1213 on October 19, 1929. In the above Diamond Disc series, matrices 8700-8799 and 10000-10199 were recorded at Columbia Street, West Orange, N.J. All the others were made in New York, from 2000 onwards. There was also another West Orange block (1500-1585) recorded between 1920 (exact date unknown) and October 6, 1922, again apparently to some extent at least a series of experimental recordings.

ELECTRADISK

This is one of the handful of short-lived labels produced by RCA Victor in 1932-1933. Initially, Electradisk was an eight-inch record numbered exactly as was the early eight-inch Bluebird, 1800-1809. These were issued in July 1932 at 10 cents each. A month later came another short Electradisk series (2500-2509), ten-inch records with no Bluebird affiliations. Finally, between November 1932 and February 1934, a third block of Electradisks (numbered 1900 to 2177) came on the market at 20 cents each. All the records in this series were also issued on Bluebird (B-5000 series). The Bluebird catalog number was printed in parentheses under the Electradisk number on the label, which was orange with blue design and lettering. Apparently the label was produced for Woolworth's. Like most makes, major or minor, issued during the early 1930s, they are exceptionally rare.

THE ELECTRIC

Carl Kendziora, in *Record Research* for September 1964, describes this very rare label as having obvious connections with Everybody's (q.v.). The design of the gold printing on the black label; the last known catalog number of Everybody's being 1085 and the earliest of The Electric being 1086; the similarity of recorded material—all point in that direction. The last known The Electric is 1092. Popular songs and dance tunes on known examples all date their issue to the closing months of 1925. No maker's name or price is shown on the label.

There is also a "special" series starting at 1 (and possibly finishing there also). This has a strange matrix series: SAH-2 and SAH-3. It is significant that SAH-4 through SAH-7 are to be found on Everybody's 1062 and 1063. It is not known what these prefix letters stand for, or in what studio the sides were made.

Despite the label's name, all known issues are acoustic recordings. Most of them are from the Emerson-Consolidated repertoire, which did not adopt electric recording until just after the last known issue on The Electric label.

EMBASSY

This is a very rare and short-lived subsidiary label of the Paramount group. As far as is known, all its issues are from Paramount. The life span of Embassy is barely a year, sometime in 1923 to sometime in 1924.

In 1954 the British branches of F. W. Woolworth & Co. produced an Embassy label, the last make exclusively theirs. It contained no American material, and was discontinued a few years later.

EMERALD

See Rialto.

EMERSON

Victor H. Emerson joined the staff of the infant Columbia Graphophone Company in the nineties. For seventeen years he was General Manager of the Record Department. In 1916 he founded the company that bears his name to this day, and began to issue seven-inch records costing 25 cents each in April of that year, with 5½-inch issues at 10 cents each. These were advertised as "the only record that will play on Victor and Columbia machines without the use of an attachment."

At the end of the year, the Treasurer and General Manager, R. D. Wyckoff, issued a challenge to the industry: "Emerson's hat is in the ring and we are going in after it with both feet. At least 100,000 records a day is our motto for 1917."

This mighty aspiration was never achieved. With the entry of the United States into World War I, prices were raised to three records for a dollar. In January 1918 new nine-inch issues at 75 cents were announced. One year later came the first ten-inch records at 85 cents. What with the postwar inflation, by October these were $1, and a new series of mainly classical twelve-inch records was introduced at $1.50. H. L. Leeming, late of Thomas A. Edison, Inc., with which firm he had worked for twelve years, became general manager in May 1918. Over the next two years, the company signed top artists like the Six Brown Brothers' Saxophone Sextet, Eddie Cantor, Fred Hillebrand, and the Louisiana Five. It moved to 206 Fifth Avenue in February 1920, with recording studios and plating works at West 23rd Street, both in New York City. In May, studios and a factory were ready in Los Angeles.

The quality of Emerson records, regardless of size or price, was very good for its time. As we have seen, the Artists Department set its sights to provide competition for Victor and Columbia. But it was too much of a good thing. Overexpansion during the heady postwar boom of 1919-1920 led to a slump that almost engulfed Emerson, which went into the hands of a receiver in December 1920. The business of making and marketing records continued—including some by the Empress of the Blues, Bessie Smith herself, in February 1921, two years before Columbia signed her up; but the Emersons were never issued.

On May 9, 1922, a creditors' meeting was held in the chambers of Federal Judge John C. Knox in the Woolworth Building. Two business magnates from Michigan came forward with a suitable offer involving the year-old Regal Record Company. That was on May 12. But twelve days later, it was announced that the sale was off. On June 1, Benjamin Abrams, President of the Grand Talking Machine Company of Brooklyn, and Rudolph Kamarek, an independent maker of machines and accessories for the phonograph industry, formed a syndicate and offered $50,000 for Emerson and Regal. This was accepted by the creditors. Abrams announced that 50-cent Regal and 75-cent Emerson records would be produced by the reorganized company, and that most of its former officers would retain their positions. The new firm was incorporated in New York that August, with capital of $200,000. The first issues since May appeared in October. That month the offices, shipping depot and warehouse were moved to one building, 105-111 West 20th Street. Under the able guidance of the new owners, business picked up. Emerson records were reduced to 50 cents by the summer of 1923.

Meanwhile, another branch of the company, phonograph manufacturing, was busy. That autumn, new models were unveiled at prices ranging from $110 to $225. In January 1924, the enterprising company moved into the nascent radio industry with the formation of the Emerson Radio Corporation. Operating at first from the old phonograph headquarters at 206 Fifth Avenue, the radio division soon moved to 309 Sixth Avenue. In November the two companies were consolidated, with capital of $1,000,000. The incorporators of the newly merged company were Benjamin Abrams and his two brothers, who promptly sold Emerson records to the Scranton Button Company of Scranton, Pa. The Abrams brothers sensed that the world of records would soon be facing hard times (cf. Columbia's plight, and that of the Victor Talking Machine Company).

Scranton continued to produce Emerson records until 1927. From early in 1926 they were electrically recorded. But they never achieved the success or the technical excellence they enjoyed under Victor Emerson and Benjamin Abrams. Abrams had visited Europe in 1924 and had arranged for his records to be issued on a number of British labels: Edison Bell Winner, Homochord, Ideal Scala, Grafton, and their associates. Several also appeared as dubbings on the twelve-inch World Record, a strange breed whose speed started at $33\frac{1}{3}$ at the outer rim and increased steadily to 78 as it moved to the innermost part of the track. Towards the end of Emerson's chequered career, the British makes of Duophone, Goodson and Piccadilly issued several pressings from masters made by Scranton.

The Emerson label has always been striking. The design familiar to most collectors is the gold shield outlined on glossy black, with the legend "O.K. All Star Trio" or "O.K. Louisiana Five" or whatever the selected artist's identity was, in facsimile handwriting on some of them. The revamped design was more elaborate. A wide, ornate gold border surrounded a central portion largely occupied by a clef sign. There was a minimum of space for title, composer and artist details. Foreign-interest issues, notably Italian and Jewish music, were issued with bright blue labels and the same basic design. The Scranton Consolidated label was less old-fashioned but hardly less elaborate.

As might be expected, most of the issues on Emerson were of popular dance and vocal items aimed at the more discerning members of the buying public. There was a fair proportion of good jazz, and some urban blues by stalwart girl singers such as Lizzie Miles and Rosa Henderson. Eubie Blake, the ragtime pianist-composer, made some excellent solo sides in 1921, and a handful of straightforward dance titles with his orchestra. Drummer Anton Lada, late of the Louisiana Five, returned to the scene of the group's triumphs with a large dance band that offered little to interest the jazz enthusiast. The ubiquitous Fletcher Henderson and Original Memphis Five each made a few Emersons in 1924. One Henderson side, made when Louis Armstrong was in the band, was issued on Emerson as by "the California Melodie Syncopators," pressed from a Plaza master. This was *Swanee Butterfly*. In the same supplement were two sides on separate records by Charlie Johnson's Paradise Ten, today much sought-after as great rarities, although backed in each case by straight dance records by white bands, top hits that would have ensured great success—in normal times. But early 1925, just after the Scranton Button Company takeover, found Scranton drawing on other sources than Emerson for its monthly issues. The Charlie Johnsons, made by a hot Negro band, were recorded by Federal records, as were various other Emerson issues of that period.

The Emerson Radio and Phonograph Corporation of 111 Eighth Avenue, New York, went on to prosper as a leading radio and television manufacturer. Nothing apparently remains of the ledgers relating to the records produced between 1916 and 1928, whether issued as Emerson or not; but the name and the clef-sign trademark are there yet.

The following chart shows the approximate first matrix numbers made in each year for ten-inch Emerson records. The smaller issues were all made between the beginning of 1916 and the winter of 1920. The sizes are indicated by the first figure of the catalog number; e.g., the ten-inch size was issued in a 1000 or a 10000 series. The exception to this is the short-lived twelve-inch series, which was numbered 500 up, like the 5½-inch series. After electric recording was adopted in 1926, Scranton began issuing ten-inch Emerson records numbered 3000 upwards.

1918 (c. October)	4100	1925	42870
1919	4200	1926	3800
1920	4985	1926 (October)	31000
1921	41585	1927	31070
1922	42130	1928	31230
1923	42330		
1924	42540		

EMPIRE

There have been at least four distinct labels bearing the name Empire in the course of Anglo-American recorded history. The earliest was a British make, drawn from Edison Bell masters prior to 1914 but containing no American material and thus beyond the scope of this book. The latest was a British subsidiary of Piccadilly records that appeared in 1931 and remained in circulation for about a year or so. The label is dull red with black lettering, very plain in design. Here again, as far as is known, nothing American was issued on it.

The American Empire label was black and gold. It was the product of the

Empire Talking Machine Company of 429 South Wabash Avenue, Chicago. Starting in January 1920, it followed the Operaphone catalog exactly, even to using the same catalog numbers. The duplication of Operaphone continued in February, but from this point various series were used, all with three figures. Since Operaphone drew from Pathe, there is nothing on Empire that was not also on Pathe.

Although the labels proclaim the product to be "Supreme In Quality" and claim that it will "Play On All Phonographs," Empire records nevertheless are vertical-cut and in fact play only on phonographs adapted to play Pathe records. It appears that before the end of 1920 they were no longer being manufactured.

The most extraordinary Empire label had in fact no paper label at all. It was a ten-inch black celluloid flexible record ("unbreakable, non-inflammable," proclaimed the publicity sheets) manufactured by the Globe Record Co. Ltd. of 56-58 Rochester Place, Camden Town, London, N.W.1 during the spring of 1931. How long this venture lasted is not known. At most it would seem to have lived perhaps three or four months. Numbering began at 1, and in two issues had reached 70. What makes them unusual, quite apart from their shiny, label-less, flabby appearance, is that some of their material seems to have come from the defunct Dominion repertoire, some from a German make known as Phonycord (including three sides correctly credited to the great concert contralto Marian Anderson), and the up-to-date dance records from original masters or—from American Paramounts recorded in Grafton, Wisconsin. Details were etched dully into the central area in the manner of early Edison Diamond Discs and some Berliners. "The New EMPIRE Record is the result of many years of the most diligent scientific research," yelled the publicity department, "and has been placed on the market after being subjected to the most severe tests. The manufacturers are satisfied that the EMPIRE Record *has passed every known test*, and possesses virtues found in no other make of record. . . . EMPIRE RECORD, THE DISC OF THE FUTURE." Well, perhaps the disc of the next few weeks, after the issue of that proclamation. The British public must have seemed grossly ungrateful to respond so lightly to all that scientific research and those gruelling tests, especially when the records themselves cost only 1s. 6d.—about a quarter each. The makers claimed fifty Empire records could be carried in a portable machine. What they omitted to say was that a normal portable would not play one of them without a great deal of time-consuming, nerve-racking persuasion, as the needle remained rooted in whatever groove it was placed unless some kind of counterbalancing was arranged, or the Empire record was put on top of at least one ordinary black, breakable shellac record that needed no such persuasion and offered star artists aplenty.

EVERYBODY'S

This was the product of Everybodys (sic) Record Company of New York. There seem to have been some 85 issues during the spring, summer and autumn of 1925. Some were drawn from Paramount, most from Emerson-Consolidated. At least four, by Richard Hitter's Cabineers (1062 and 1063), are original, having matrix numbers in a curious SAH series (see also The Electric). The labels are black with gold lettering, bearing a close resemblance to those of The Electric (and owing not a little to the Victor design of the time, except that a crowd of people, apparently of all ages, both sexes, and various walks of life, head and shoulders only, in perspective, takes the place of the dog and phonograph). The quality of the pressing is usually quite good. But as a label, Everybody's is by no means easy to find.

FAMOUS

Famous records, with their bright blue labels and gold design vaguely suggesting a lyre but giving no indication of origin, were a product of the New York Recording Laboratories of Port Washington, Wis. from 1921 until at least early 1924. They were numbered in a 3000 series that was 1,706 numbers behind the same couplings on Paramount's popular-standard 20000 series. Thus, a pair of California Ramblers sides on Paramount 20174 are to be found in the same coupling on Famous 3168. It is not known if everything on Paramount appeared on Famous automatically, but the regularity of step in the numbering suggests that at least for a time this was so. There seems to have been another Famous group, also derived from Paramount, in a 5000 series, but these numbers bear no relationship to the parent. For example, Paramount 33079, a pair of Easter songs attributed to Ernest Davis, appeared on Famous 5013 credited to Carl Vincent. The quality of reproduction is very good, and copies that have been well treated retain adequately smooth surfaces.

FAMOUS SINGERS

This most obscure label of unknown origin made a brief appearance in the summer of 1921. The catalog does not seem to have lived up to the promise of the brand name, as the majority of its issues are by a dance band. To the best of my knowledge, no copies have been reported. My information on them is based on an advertisement in *The Talking Machine World*. There may have been only one issue of about ten records. The numbers are in a 5000 block, but the beginning and extent of them are not known.

FEDERAL

Federal records were on the market from 1920 until 1925, and appear on other makes also (e.g., Resona and Silvertone, and occasionally in England on Grafton). They have deep violet or dark blue labels, and are unusual in that they have a matrix number which varies with each take *plus* a take digit *preceding* the matrix number itself. Thus, matrix 1217 (a popular song by Charles Harrison), recorded October 27, 1921, is the third and final take of that particular number, and is prefixed 3-. The next title on the session is numbered 1-1218, the second take of which would be 2-1219, while the second take of the first title is designated 2-1216, and so on.

Straightforward dance music and popular vocals of the day seem to constitute the Federal catalog. The recording quality is quite good, the surfaces likewise, but they are inclined to wear easily. The principal catalog series begins at 5000, and about four hundred or so were issued.

FILMOPHONE

Filmophone records have something in common with Empire (q.v.) in that they were pressed in flimsy celluloid. The head office of Filmophone Flexible Records Ltd. was at 12 Oval Road, Camden Town, London, N.W.1, a little over half a mile away from the Empire headquarters. The similarity ends there, however, as Filmophones for the most part were pressed in brightly coloured translucent material. You could buy your choice of entertainment in a range of twenty colours. I once had a pair of Spanish tangos (so described) played by one Jose Gartini and his Venezulu (sic) Orchestra, in a most attractive shade of eau-de-Nil green. I have since seen Cab Calloway and his Orchestra (described as "Al Dollar and His Ten Cents") in rich red, and "Fenton's Rainbows" (which turned out to be a Perfect studio dance band) pressed in cool azure.

Whereas the Empire record cost about a quarter, Filmophones were advertised at about 45 cents. Like Empire, it was claimed for them that fifty would be easy to carry in a portable machine. But while Empire boasted that their records could be played with any needle, Filmophones had to be played with a trailer, that spatula-shaped device bent at an angle of about 45 degrees at the base of the spade. The Filmophone publicity department worked at full throttle to put over the concept of the "world's best unbreakable record—the long life record with the golden tone!" It continued: "These records are the greatest advance in the history of record-making. Owing to a secret process of manufacture it has at last been rendered possible to combine.... all the advantages of the obsolete black, bulky, breakable record—from the point of view of reproduction—with none of its disadvantages. You can bend, roll, drop, sit on, walk on, even dance on a Filmophone Flexible Record and it sustains no damage."

Exactly why anyone would want to pay about half a dollar for a brightly-coloured celluloid disc and use it as a cushion, a paving stone or some kind of missile has always escaped me. But surviving specimens show, or at least suggest, that their former owners did in fact attempt to test the validity of the manufacturers' claims. The result is that although the record did not break under such vandalism, they did become badly warped. As a result, even the fairly heavy soundboxes and pickups of 1930-1932 had the utmost difficulty remaining in the grooves, and a modern light pickup cannot be used at all. Further, even if the Filmophone record was not savaged, unless it was clamped to the turntable with some heavier material, the pressure on the outer grooves would cause the disc to climb the spindle and throw the pickup off long before the side had finished playing. "Remember it is absolutely unbreakable," continued the copywriter, "and non-inflammable, and yet costs no more than the ordinary dull, black, breakable record. You will never go back to the others."

Alas for Filmophone, the record buyers of the early thirties were generally not affluent. If they wanted to spend half a dollar on a dance tune or two, or for some conventional military band, violin soloist, Strauss waltz or "comedy vocal" (as the catalog termed romantic ballads of the day), they preferred to spend it on "ordinary dull, black, breakable records" manufactured by established firms and featuring a name artist. From one chain store or another one could buy from two to five of these "obsolete" records for the same price as one Filmophone. Heavy they may have been, and fragile, but they gave no playing trouble, needed no special attachments, and offered artists whose names usually meant something.

Just before the end, in the spring of 1932, Filmophone issued a series of Wurlitzer organ records on black celluloid, along with a curious remake of the same piece of pornography that led to Dominion's downfall two years earlier. It was still sung by Elsie Carlisle, but here under the name of Amy Brunton. It sold quite well, as did the Dominion. But it was too late to persuade the public that Filmophone records were in any way a substitute for shellac pressings.

Filmophone rates a section in this book because of the considerable number of titles it dubbed from American Perfect. Cab Calloway was represented pseudonymously with four excellent titles that sound considerably better on the original Perfect or one of its affiliates, gritty though their surfaces were in comparison with the smoother Filmophone pressings. There were several Filmophones by Bob Haring and his Orchestra and Carl Fenton and his Orchestra. It is interesting to speculate whether Filmophone 149, credited to Dell's Casino Dance Band playing *Just a Little Dance, Mam'selle*, may in fact have been transferred from the Perfect or other issue of the title by Jack Teagarden and his Orchestra. To my knowledge no copies have been reported. It is impossible to identify an American issue on Filmophone, as the original matrix numbers are suppressed and a regular Filmophone number used instead. They are in a series prefixed F. A different number was allocated for each take, starting at 1000 and continuing to about 2200.

As with most flexible records, Filmophones have no labels. The details are moulded into the central area in gold. Filmophone can claim one distinction other than bringing the first Cab Calloway records to England: a double-sided, six-minute talk on *My World's Record* by the late auto racer, Sir Malcolm Campbell. One copy is known to exist. Who would venture to guess at its value?

FLEXO

Dave Cotter of Scotts Valley, Cal., in *Record Research* of various dates but notably that of October 1972, provides us with as much as is at present known about Flexo records. As might be expected from their name, they were flexible and unbreakable. They were pressed in a wide range of bright colours. Although the specimens known to exist as commercial products (or, more frequently, as custom pressings for the artists involved, at their expense) are 78 rpm, a test pressing exists on which one side is recorded at 78, the other at 33⅓. Sizes varied from 3 to 16 inches.

These records seem to have been manufactured by the Pacific Coast Record Corporation, Ltd., incorporated on December 26, 1929 and operating from 1040 Geary Street, San Francisco, Cal. This was a most inauspicious moment to begin trading in records, even those that were unbreakable, featherweight, and thus easy to carry en masse. The bottom was fast dropping out of the record business for all companies except those with strong affiliations in radio or films, even the erstwhile giants. There can have been very few Flexo discs actually issued for public use. The corporation, headed by one Jesse J. Warner, filed for bankruptcy on May 8, 1934. Two years before, Warner had been involved in another company that produced advertising records and radio transcriptions, under the Titan label. This continued to operate from the Geary Street address until some time in the spring or summer of 1940.

The range of known Flexo matrix numbers is 124 to 1797, according to Mr. Cotter's valuable research. One of the most interesting Flexo records for the jazz buff is *Tiger Rag* and *The Talk of the Town*, by trombonist George Druck's Sweets Ballroom Orchestra, evidently recorded in 1930. This has no catalog number, so it was probably made for sale only in the ballroom foyer. Another strange Flexo is one made by Hollywood Film Enterprises, Inc., an interview with film star Ann Harding by Louella Parsons, broadcast by CBS on March 11, 1931. Other Flexos of interest as dance items feature the orchestras of Jack Coakley, musical director of the company until 1932, and Lew Reynolds, Coakley's probable successor. One ten-inch record reported by Randy Morris of North Hollywood has two Phil Baxter songs (*The One Man Band* and *Is This a Zither?*) on a Flexo with no number. It was made by the Hollywood Flexo Record Co., evidently in 1931, under the name of Dean McCluskey-Billy Grantham and their Aces of the Air. Grantham had been a banjoist nearly ten years before with Marion McKay's Orchestra in Indiana.

Many Flexo records are of indifferent quality by obviously amateur artists. But those referred to here are exceptions. The strange sizes—8¼-inch records are typical—and the garish colours make them the most eccentric-looking pressings of all. (See also New Flexo.)

GAMAGE

Messrs. A. W. Gamage, Ltd., of Holborn, London, W.C.2, have for many years been one of London's best-known department stores. In 1924, their record department sold Gamage records. Today these are extremely rare. The numbering is in a G-600 series, but there may be numbers lower and higher than this block. All the known items are from the Aco-Homochord catalogs, under the pseudonym "Gamage Dance Orchestra" for all dance items. One of these, *Chicago Blues,* is actually by Fletcher Henderson and his Orchestra from Vocalion. Its backing, *Oh! Eva,* is a London recording for Aco by Jeffries and his Rialto Orchestra. The Gamage label is very similar to Homochord (q.v.), except that the colour scheme is dark blue and white with gold lettering for the title and artist credits, instead of Homochord's olive brown and red. In place of the Homochord harpist, Gamage has an angel with half-open wings blowing a valveless, keyless horn.

GEM

A very rare label from the early years of the Depression, Gem was pressed by RCA Victor for the Crown Record Company of 10 West 20th Street, New York. Gems bear the same catalog numbers as Crown for the same couplings, although it should not be assumed that everything on Crown is automatically on Gem. (See also Crown.) It is doubtful if Gem appeared on the market at the same time as Crown. Nothing is known about the range of Gem numbers.

General

    The General Records Division of Consolidated Records, Inc., New York, produced a number of very interesting Jelly Roll Morton items in 1939 and 1940: some exquisite piano solos, some with his vocal work, and some by small bands, the last commercial records he ever made. These were in a 4000 and 1700 series. There were other, twelve-inch General issues in a 3000 series. They were aimed at the connoisseur of jazz. Beautifully recorded for the most part, they were pressed on high-grade wax initially, although wartime conditions made the maintenance of this standard impossible. Some General records have rich maroon labels with gold lettering, others a rich blue with silver lettering. The matrix numbers extend from R-2000 to R-5000. So wide a range for so few issues of any sort suggests that many were private recordings or advertising material.

GENNETT

The Starr Piano Company of Richmond, Ind. had been in the instrument business for many years before it decided to launch into the record business. The Gennett brothers, Fred, Harry and Clarence, were the principal officers in the firm at the time, 1917. Thus did an important label get its name.

The initial issue appeared in October 1917, a vertical-cut disc with 150 "lines" to the inch that enabled it to play for up to five minutes. There were two recording studios. One was in a room in the home office in Richmond, close to the railroad track. This of course created problems every time a heavy locomotive thundered past. The other studio was in the New York branch offices at 9-11 East 37th Street.

Gennett catalogs and supplements for the years 1917 and 1918 reveal a very energetic new label, catering to all possible tastes impartially. The numbering of the records is interesting. The price in cents forms the first two or three digits of the catalog number. Thus, popular vocal and dance records in a 6500 series cost 65 cents, others in a 7500 series 75 cents, still more in an 8500 series 85 cents. Classics, some of them unusual and interesting material sold for $1.00 each in a 10000 series. And so on. As war prices forced up the cost of raw materials and hence the retail price of the records, the serial numbers became confused. Thus the 10000 and new 11000 series both sold at $1.10, the 7500s and 8500s at 85 cents.

After the Armistice in 1918, the vertical-cut discs were gradually abandoned and a lateral-cut that conformed to the established makes was introduced in April 1919. The green-labelled 10000 series was retained at $1.00, lone survivor of the old regime, and reduced to 90 cents in 1921. The popular series that replaced the 7500-8500 category was numbered 4501 upwards and sold for 85 cents, falling to 75 cents in 1921. There was a twelve-inch lateral-cut series numbered 2501 upwards. This was launched at $1.50 but reduced to $1.40 in line with the others. The popular series, regardless of size or type of cut usually have blue labels. Originally this was quite a plain design, with the name Gennett in the familiar ornate lettering across the top half. Soon it was changed to a more decorative and distinctive pattern, a gold hexagon with an outer ring, the segments filled in with heraldic leaflike shapes. This was maintained until the coming of electric recording and the black and gold Electrobeam Gennett in a series that started at 6001 in February 1927. This reached 7324 in December 1930, at which point the company decided, in view of the chill winds of Depression, to dispense with its principal label and maintain only the lower-priced Champion (q.v.). (There was also a red Gennett, numbered 3001 to 3412, between May 1925 and January 1927, using exactly the same design as the blue and, to a great extent, the same repertoire.)

There seems little to merit special comment on the vertical-cut issues, apart perhaps from one (8512) which featured a couple of saxophone solos by Duane Sawyer, who "has filled engagements with Raymond's Blackstone Orchestra of Chicago and with the orchestra at the Detroit Athletic Club." The interesting point about this is that the piano accompanist was a nineteen-year-old immigrant from France, Jean Goldkette, whose first records as a bandleader—on Victor, in 1924—were made in the Detroit Athletic Club itself.

By contrast, the successors on lateral-cut records include some of the most famous jazz records of all time. By the mid-twenties, Gennett seems to have abandoned all attempts to compete with Victor and Columbia in serious music—where, in truth, their efforts never presented any real challenge. But throughout the twenties, Gennett produced a catalog of records of such abiding interest to jazz enthusiasts as to make its very name a byword among them. Beginning in 1919, we find Jimmy Durante—later to become world-famous as a film comedian—and the Original New Orleans Jazz Band recording for Gennett on their first issue of laterals. In 1921 came the first of two long series of records by Ladd's Black Aces, illustrated in the catalog as five Negroes with the instruments heard on the records, but in fact a Sam Lanin band. Bailey's Lucky Seven, another Lanin group, often produced interesting jazz on Gennett. And from 1923 to the end, Gennett regaled the pioneer collectors of jazz with the first recordings ever made by such luminaries as King Oliver, Louis Armstrong, Johnny Dodds, Bix Beiderbecke, the New Orleans Rhythm Kings, Hoagy Carmichael, and the first solo piano records by Jelly Roll Morton. The later Electrobeam Gennett label offered jazz classics by the State Street Ramblers, Alex Jackson's Plantation Orchestra, Jelly James and his Fewsicians, Brad Gowans' Rhapsody Makers, and many blues records with interesting accompaniments. Burl Ives, the great folk artist, and the famous Mills Brothers also made their recording debuts for Gennett, but their efforts were never issued.

Having a studio in Richmond, Ind. meant that artists based in Chicago were within reasonably easy reach. Many first-class Midwest dance bands like those of Art Payne, Curt Hitch, Art Landry, Eddie Mitchell, Henry Thies and Emil Seidel were duly offered contracts. Nor did the New York studios overlook jazz. When Naylor's Seven Aces, a band of mostly New Orleans white musicians under the direction of Oliver Naylor, arrived in New York early in 1924, they were signed and made many excellent records. The ubiquitous California Ramblers, thinly disguised as The Vagabonds, made a host of Gennett records in New York. There were, needless to say, many records made in both studios by artists who lived by their free-lance recording dates and included Gennett in their regular studio.

Gennett also recorded such genuine country artists as violinist William B. Houchens. In the spring of 1926 an expedition to the Grand Canyon recorded twelve sides of tribal songs and dances by the Walpi Tribe of the Hopi Indians. A year later, Starr provided recording facilities for the Black Patti label (q.v.), and in 1928 it recorded some magnificent sides for the QRS Company (q.v.) in its new studios in Long Island City, New York—all by jazz, blues or country-style artists. The Richmond studios, long the scene of private recording sessions, in 1929 was the scene of many sessions by blues and jazz artists for Paramount (q.v.). Many of these later electric recordings were made by the Radio Corporation of America, not then in control of Victor, a new contract between Gennett and RCA Photophone having gone into effect on July 1, 1928.

Gennett had other subsidiary labels besides Champion, among them Buddy, Superior and Supertone (q.v. all). In England its products can be found on Aco, Beltona, Coliseum, Edison Bell Winner, Guardsman, Homochord, Scala, Sterno, Tower and Vocalion. From 1919 to 1921, and from 1925 to 1928, Starr seems to have had an open arrangement to supply masters to all of these (except Edison Bell Winner, with which it had a contract from 1921 to 1925). Very few indeed of the choice jazz history-makers appeared in England, but a large number of dance bands and popular vocalists did, mostly under pseudonyms.

The recording quality on Gennett is usually only fair, but the RCA Photophones show a marked improvement. Surfaces generally are adequate, but rather easily worn. Hence the terrible distortion on the English Brunswick dubbings in the 1936-1937 album sets of *Swing Music* and *Twenty-One Years of Swing Music*, many of which are from Gennett pressings.

Although the last conventional commercial Gennett records appeared in December 1930, for many years afterwards it was possible to buy its sets of sound-effects records specially prepared for use in theatres, on radio stations, and the like.

The following chart shows the first matrix number made in New York and Richmond in each year, lateral-cut records only:

	New York	Richmond (including Chicago, Birmingham, St. Paul, Los Angeles, New Orleans, etc.)
1919		6000 (approximately)
1920		7200 (approximately; most of 6000 block not used)

1921	7420	11000 (August 20)
1922	7720	11039
1923	8167	11273
1924	8689	11716
1925	9258	12114
1926	9926	12452
1926 (February 23)	X-1	
1927	GEX-430	12589
1928	GEX-1037	13335
1928 (RCA July 1)	GEX-2000	14000
1929	GEX-2157	14633
1930	GEX-2556	16051
1931	GEX-2864	17404
1932	GEX-2898	18295
1932 (June 29; last in series)	GEX-2953	
1933		18958
1934		19447

The last number in the Richmond series, 19997, was recorded on November 9, 1940. The last record issued commercially from this series was Champion 16832, recorded October 25, 1934 (matrix 19737).

It is worth noting, in addition, that the 9000 series of Starr records in Canada began life in April 1919 in the United States as a more expensive version of the 4500 popular series, which it duplicated both as regards artists and appearance. It was priced at $1, and was discontinued as an American issue in 1921 but maintained in Canada, drawing on Gennett under its new Starr identity.

GLOBE

Globe records were produced first by Arto (q.v.). They are numbered the same as Arto for the same couplings, but with the first digit of the four a 7 instead of 9. After Arto discontinued records in 1922, Globe continued for a time, drawing on Grey Gull material and using the same or similar numbers. The Arto-type Globes seem also to have had a K-1 series that reached about 100. These have black and gold labels very much like the Arto design, while the Grey Gull successors are reddish brown and gold.

Since all Globe issues of both kinds are derivative, there is nothing to be said about them that has not already been mentioned under Arto (or their successors, Bell, which supplied some of the last pre-Grey Gull Globe catalog) or Grey Gull. Cheap records designed for the undiscriminating popular-music public, for sale in chain stores, they are inclined to have rather rough surfaces. Clean copies, however, generally reproduce quite well.

GOLDEN

A wealthy businessman named Theophilus Fitz started Golden records from his laboratory at 1044 South Hope Street, Los Angeles, Cal. in the late autumn of 1922. He claimed in his publicity that it was the first label from the Pacific coast—despite the fact that Andrae Nordskog had already been recording there for about a year by that time. Fitz and his Golden label faded into oblivion after about a year. Golden's chief claim to fame is that it recorded the first Jimmy Joy band, later to record for OKeh and Brunswick. Doubtless Golden made many other records for the use of, and at the expense of, the artists taking part. The labels are black with ornate gold design and lettering, and the surface quite good. The recording quality is remarkable in view of the almost amateur status of the enterprise. Pressing was done by the Starr Piano Company of Richmond, Ind. There are no catalog numbers. The matrix numbers are in a three-digit range prefixed G.

GOODSON

This was a British record, flexible and unbreakable. It appeared on the market in the autumn of 1928, and was thus ahead of its competitors in this category by some considerable time. By the end of 1931, it had vanished.

Produced by the Goodson Record Company, Ltd., of 12 Old Burlington Street, London, W.1, these "non-flam, featherweight" records that cost 1s. 9d (about 30 cents) presented a most unusual sight. They were the colour of cream and had no labels. The title and artist credits were printed in blue four times *on the actual playing surface* at right angles to each other. Underneath these in each case was the title on the other side. The trade-mark, also printed at least partly on the grooves, was a hand holding a Goodson record and bending it, surrounded by the legend "Featherweight—Pliable—Unbreakable." The advice to "Fit a used needle—greater purity of tone is thus obtained" also appears on each side, and those who ignored it did so to their cost. The consequence of playing a Goodson record with a new steel needle was to grind part of the material out of the grooves in a fine powder, thereby rendering the record virtually unplayable.

The publicity accompanying Goodson records was less flamboyant than that of, say, Filmophone (q.v.), but it claimed that sixty of them could be carried in a portable machine (Filmophone quoted fifty). Goodson records lack the smooth surfaces of other pliable makes, despite the material in which they were pressed: Rhodoid, according to the reading matter on the grooves. Rhodoid was covered by British and overseas patents.

The Goodson repertoire compares favourably with that of their successors in the same category. At first, their American source was the Emerson-Scranton catalog. After a few issues (and reissues, in some cases), the Grey Gull-Van Dyke-Radiex complex began suppling masters, as they did to Dominion and Piccadilly (q.v. both). There is evidence that some masters, not necessarily American, were used for Goodson and Dominion, certainly for Goodson and Filmophone. On Goodson A-269 *and* Filmophone 113 can be found the voice of Guido Volpi, a tenor singing *L'anima stanca* from *Adriana Lecouvreur*—not at all the kind of music normally associated with any record costing so little. Signor

Volpi is also a feature of the Dominion blue-label B series ("classical"), and on Dominion B-18 *and* Goodson A-262 he sings *Dai campi, dai prati* from *Mefistofele*. There are several other examples of masters recorded by Dominion being used on Filmophone and/or Goodson and/or Dominion itself: mostly "classical," and quite well performed and recorded.

The Grey Gull source seems to have dried up during the summer of 1930. Nothing loth, Goodson began issuing records pressed from American QRS masters. These, and some English recordings from Dominion (lately extinct) and Filmophone, and from pre-1914(!) Continental sources, made up the last few monthly supplements until Goodson withdrew from the market.

Most of the collectors' items on Goodson are in the nature of jazz or dance records, among them Cliff Jackson's Krazy Kats' *The Terror;* a strange version of *St. James' Infirmary* by the California Ramblers, described as the Bay State Broadcasters on Goodson; and an uninhibited version of *Painting the Clouds with Sunshine* by the Grey Gull studio band under the name of the Manhattan Syncopators. (Cliff Jackson's band was renamed Marvin Smolev and his Syncopators.) All these are from Grey Gull. The Emerson contributions consist largely of rather uproarious performances by Fred Hall and his Orchestra. The QRS titles are so rare that only a very few have been reported; thus, little is known of how interesting they may be musically.

The earliest of all Goodson records are without catalog numbers. These and the other Emerson-recorded sides have matrix numbers in the 31000s. Grey Gull takes over after about the first two dozen numbered issues (they begin at 101, and 128 is a Grey Gull coupling) with matrix numbers between about 3400 and 4100. Shortly before the last Grey Gull was issued came the first QRS, matrix numbered in the early 2000s. Most if not all of the Goodson 300s are original London-recorded sides. They do not seem to get beyond about 340, probably about March or April 1931. These have matrix numbers that start at S-1 and reach about S-150.

A number of Goodson records were issued as early advertising gimmicks for a nationwide chain of drugstores, a make of lamp, and other merchandise. Early in 1928 a seven-inch Goodson, evidently pressed from Emerson's Marathon record, appeared in a 7000 series and included different takes from the same titles on the regular ten-inch series. There was also a record issued in 1931 that looked like a Goodson and featured the voice of Pope Pius XI broadcasting from the Vatican on February 12 of that year.

GRAFTON

Grafton records were the subsidiary of the Scala Record Company in England from about September 1923 until about December 1927. Numbering began at 9000. In slightly over four years only some three hundred issues appeared, initially on a bright green label without decoration but with all printing in gold. This changed after about twenty or thirty issues to a rich red with exactly the same design, this remaining unaltered for the rest of the label's life.

Most of the output was dance music and popular vocals. The first hundred issues apart, the origin was American and British Pathe. Those of American origin bore the 70000 or 105000-107000 Pathe matrix series. Those recorded in London are in a 90000 series. The first hundred or so were derived from American Vocalion, Emerson and Federal, in that order, mainly Emerson. The Vocalions have matrix numbers around 10300 to 10800. The Emersons are in the 42000 block. The few Federals are readily identifiable by their take-digit preceding the matrix number, in the 2000s.

The rarest and perhaps most desirable Grafton issue is *The Meanest Blues* (9074) by the Bar Harbour Orchestra: actually the Original Memphis Five, from Emerson. The same band, as Gavin's Grafton Band, appears on 9013 (*Loose Feet*) and on 9020 as Black's Jazz Band (*Runnin' Wild*). A handful of records by Harry Reser, the California Ramblers, the Red Heads (*Poor Papa*, 9217, as the Windsor Orchestra) and other semihot dance records make up the Graftons likely to be of interest to a collector. Surfaces usually are smooth, in particular the Pathe-derived titles.

GRAMOPHONE AND TYPEWRITER

See His Master's Voice.

GREY GULL

The story of Grey Gull records, even without allusions to its affiliates Madison, Radiex, Supreme and Van Dyke, and the overseas labels which drew on its repertoire for their own American dance music and popular vocalists, is a complicated tangle. A maze of pseudonyms and anonymity obscure the position further. As Carl Kendziora commented in *Record Research* (April 1967) "Grey Gull used numbers like there was no tomorrow!"

This is not an overstatement. For a firm operating on a shoestring—their repertoire, general appearance and performance certainly suggest this—they introduced about a dozen different series in as many years, all offering much the same kind of music: popular songs, dance music, some out-and-out jazz, and an occasional instrumental solo or small group.

The first reference to Grey Gull Records I can trace is in May 1919. The firm, then based at 693 Tremont Street, Boston, Mass., announced that after fourteen months of laboratory research, a record in both vertical- and lateral-cut forms had been perfected. A little over a year later, in July 1920, the company announced with what looks now like a curious turn of phrase, "The Queer New Record That Plays So Long." This was a foreshadow of the principle of extended-play. With a track considerably narrower than the then standard width, Grey Gull records, with two separate tracks on each side, played for something slightly under 5½ minutes a side, thereby upholding the makers' claim of "nearly eleven minutes of music on one 10-inch record."

By now the headquarters had been moved to 295 Huntington Avenue, Boston. It is believed to have remained there until the company went out of business in the late summer of 1930. The "queer new records" were undoubtedly ahead of their time, so much so that most customers found them too advanced. Or it may be that their price tag of $1 was too high, even for two extra performances. They disappeared sometime in 1921. Grey Gull then proceeded to issue popular records in volume, at a more acceptable price, for the next nine years.

The earliest and rarest Grey Gull records have distinguished-looking labels in orange, white and blue for the laterals. They sported the same design in light green, white and black for the verticals. The "extended-play" issues are coloured in two shades of olive green, one slightly deeper than the other, and black, again with the same basic design. By 1922 these attractive, unusual designs and colour-schemes had given way to a rather dull, dusty brown, varied with a much brighter, glossier maroon. The earlier issues had been numbered in brief series starting at H-1000, H-2000 and H-4000. Their conventional two-titled lateral-cut successors started their numbers at 1000 and continued them until the 1800s. There ware also 2000, 4000, 7000, 8000 and 9000 series more or less contemporaneous with the 1000s, but none as long-lived.

Between 1922 and 1926, Grey Gull seem to have relied extensively on other companies for their masters, probably leasing from at least three. The original matrix numbers were largely disguised and a code letter denoting the origin added as a prefix. Thus Grey Gulls of the latter acoustic era with X series "matrix numbers" are of Emerson origin. A prefix Y shows the title to be from Paramount. Material from the Plaza group (Banner, Domino, Regal, etc.) is prefixed Z.

In June or early July 1926, Grey Gull began electric recording in a studio at 122 Fifth Avenue, New York City. It continued the matrix series probably begun at 500 in 1921, when the "queer new records" were discontinued. This was maintained until the last known recording, slightly above 4100, about July or August 1930. The quality of the reproduction is not outstanding, although most electrically recorded Grey Gulls are loud and sharply defined. Against this, many of them have a tendency to blast during ensemble passages.

The numbering eccentricities are only part of the Grey Gull conundrum. During the electric era, at least, and possibly earlier, it was customary for a Tin Pan Alley success to be offered on one side of the record, with an unimportant song on the B side. This fill-in song might appear two or three times in this humble capacity, not only with a different artist credit each time, but on an affiliated label under a different title. For example, what Grey Gull, Madison, Radiex, and Van Dyke 5008 call *That Wicked Stomp* is known as *Just You, Honey* on Van Dyke 71798. When it appeared on Goodson in England, it was renamed *Waiting for You*. Most Grey Gull dance records of the electric era are by studio bands, usually headed by and prominently featuring trumpeter Mike Mosiello, one of the unsung heroes of his time, and Andy Sannella, who was as much at home playing clarinet or alto saxophone with concert platform technique as he was at producing lively, truly hot jazz improvisations. He also played steel guitar on many Grey Gull sides. These bands sometimes employed artists of the stature of trombonist Tommy Dorsey. Another frequent member of the coterie was piano-accordionist Charles Magnante. The names accorded the band are strictly 1920s romance: the Atlanta Merrymakers, the Wolverine Pepperpots, the Memphis Jazzers, the White Way Players, even Ginger Ale and his Sparklers. Occasionally, as if to sober up after a wild party, Grey Gull nodded in the direction of truth and called the houseband Mike Mosiello and his Radio Stars. Although, as I have said, the recording quality was inclined to be rough, somehow it suited the music. There is an uninhibited character about such numbers as *Painting the Clouds with Sunshine*, as I mentioned under Goodson. One session for Grey Gull in November 1929 (by Mike Mosiello, Andy Sannella, a second alto saxophonist doubling clarinet, and piano) produced four abandoned, superb examples of quartet jazz, all composed by Negro pianist Porter Grainger. One of these, *In Harlem's Araby,* was issued in England on both Metropole and Piccadilly, the former as the Bohemian Band, the latter as the White Star Syncopators. So fine is Mosiello's trumpet work, open and muted, that it was once thought to be by Joe "King" Oliver himself. And there are other instances on this and other dates of truly hot trumpet work.

There were several very interesting electrically recorded Grey Gull sessions by such Negro bands as Clarence Williams', Cliff Jackson's, Wilbur Sweatman's, the Five Hot Chocolates (probably directed by J. C. Johnson, pianist-composer of such numbers as *Louisiana, Dusky Stevedore* and *Empty Bed Blues*) and the Wabash Trio. These and most other Grey Gull titles appeared on the affiliates as well as on the parent. Although the majority were credited to some fancy-named artist or band, the Grey Gull issues were, as I mentioned, anonymous. A classic example of this is Clarence Williams' beautiful big-band recording of *Baby, Won't You Please Come Home?*, issued in the summer of 1929 on Grey Gull 1724. Even the catalog numbers of the affiliate issues tally with those of the parent label in many cases, or are the same with an extra digit added in front. Thus, Grey Gull 1816 is on Van Dyke 81816, and Grey Gull 1805 appears on Van Dyke 71805. Grey Gull and Madison 1718 are the same. But on Radiex the number is 1763, and on Van Dyke it is 7801 *and* 77038!

There was evidently a lively overseas department in Grey Gull. Its masters appear in England on Dominion, Metropole, Piccadilly and Goodson (all q.v.). It is possible to find the same master used on all these, sometimes without even a change of artist credit. This is the case with the only name band to record for Grey Gull, Vincent Lopez and his Orchestra.

During the mid-1930s, large numbers of Grey Gull and Van Dyke records, sometimes Radiex too, appeared on the counters of British chain stores, the equivalent of America's "five-and-tens." The price for them was—just three pence, or about a nickel. To this day, these labels are second only to Victor in the frequency with which American makes show up in British junkshops. Doubtless some cut-price British distributor had bought up all the remaining stocks for a cent or two when Grey Gull folded its wings.

This chart shows the approximate first matrix number used in each year on Grey Gull and its associated labels, from 1921 to 1930. Prior to this another series was in use, but the only exact date known or able to be estimated is for 1183, a side by Charles Harrison recorded under the direction of Ed Kirkeby on February 25, 1921. (Thanks to Mr. Kirkeby and Perry Armagnac for passing this information on to me.)

1921 (c. August)	500	1926	1870
1922	545	1927	2240
1923	750	1928	2756
1924	1110	1929	3272
1925	1470	1930	3811

The 3000 series found on Grey Gull and other labels during the 1924-1926 period are from the Emerson-Scranton master file (q.v.).

GUARDSMAN

This was the name to which the British Invicta label was changed in 1914. For the first five or six years after this, there were no issues on Guardsman that were not recorded in London. Then in April 1920 came the first (vocal) titles from the Gennett catalog in America. In May some Gennett dance records followed. Many of these were given their correct artists' credits: Sam Ash, Arthur Hall, Harry Raderman's Orchestra, Yerkes' Saxophone Orchestra, Billy Murray, Billy De Rex, and many more. The Invicta numbers had begun at 1 in 1911. By the time the American issues began, Guardsman had reached 996. They continued to appear monthly until about the end of 1927 or early 1928, by which time the numbers had reached over 2100.

For most of their life, Guardsman records were distributed by the London wholesale record distributors, Messrs. Lugton's, Ltd. of Tottenham Court Road. They were manufactured by Vocalion from Aco masters and such American affiliates as Vocalion used; hence Gennett early on, and again for the last 300 issues or so. The earliest Gennetts have their matrix numbers removed. The later ones show them on the label and often indented into it. Between 1922 and 1925, American Vocalion masters were used, of course, and they yielded the most remarkable set of records ever to reach the British market up to that time.

That distinction belonged to the Guardsman 7000 "race" record. It bore the same handsome if ornate label in cream, black and gold as all the others, and sold at the same price, 1s. 6d. (about 30 cents). The group consists of nineteen records from the American Vocalion catalog. Of the thirty-eight sides, thirteen are by Fletcher Henderson and his Orchestra, nine by the Tennessee Tooters, and the rest divided between three blues singers, a hot dance band called The Ambassadors, four titles by the Mound City Blue Blowers, and two sides by a genuine Louisville jug band. All these are extremely fine, and most are rare to the point of being barely heard of. For more than half a century, jazz collectors have been wondering whose idea it was to make such choice fare available to so small a market, and why. Only one record is of minor interest, a vaudevillian duet by Gene Austin and Roy Bergere, the only one issued under the correct names of the artists.

Before 1920, and for a short time thereafter, there were Guardsman records by name artists such as H. M. Scots and Irish Guards Bands, the Honourable Artillery Company Band, J. H. Squire's "Karsino" Orchestra (from a celebrated pleasure centre on an island in the Thames), banjoist Olly Oakley, and concert celebrities Ethel Toms, Robert Carr and Edward Halland. With the disappearance of the greenish-stone coloured label with the dark green print and the coming of the much smarter cream-black-gold design, such items disappeared. The last thousand or so Guardsman issues are nearly all popular dance and vocal records, with much to interest the jazz enthusiast, along with light hardy perennials from the vaudeville stage. Recording is adequate, and Vocalion's unusually good. Surfaces incline to be gritty. (See also Aco.)

HARMOGRAPH

The story of Harmograph ("The Human Echo," as it was subtitled on its bright blue labels with gold printing embodying a laurel-crowned three-stringed lyre) was told in the August 1949 issue of the late and lamented *Playback* magazine by John Randolph of St. Louis, Mo., where the Harmograph Talking Machine Company had its headquarters at 108 Pine Street. The name of this firm was originally the Harmograph Record Company, and it was copyrighted in the autumn of 1921 by the largest wholesale hardware dealers in St. Louis, the Shapleigh Hardware Company. This firm had been making phonographs since 1916. Through its Harmograph subsidiary, it produced records from 1922 until 1925.

The first year of Harmograph issues saw the launching of the label using Cameo masters. These were obtained from a New York wholesale dealer in masters, Earl W. Jones, who ran Standard Records. He sent out test pressings for approval to his customers, who could then choose as many or as few as they required. They were then pressed with the client's own label, and sold accordingly. So it was with Harmograph. It is thought that the first issue was numbered 700 or 701.

After about a year, Shapleigh abandoned the contract with Standard Records and began ordering its records from a Chicago wholesaler named Foerster. He dealt in Paramount and Pathe records. For at least another year, Paramount masters appeared on Harmograph in numbers from 763 to 937. As John Randolph points out, a strange feature of these is that the blue singers, such as Ida Cox, Alberta Hunter, Ethel Waters and Ma Rainey, were given pseudonyms— except for one by Ida Cox which slipped out under her real name in error, and nearly ruptured relations between Shapleigh and Paramount. On the other hand, such bands as King Oliver's, Jelly Roll Morton's, Fletcher Henderson's and Perry Bradford's appear in their correct identities.

The styling of the Paramount-derived labels is akin to that of Paramount itself, both as to shade of blue and typography. The Cameo era of Harmograph saw labels of a dark powder-blue, with the brand and company name in white and the title and artist credit in black on a pale blue panel bordered in gold. With the change to Pathe masters, which extended to Harmograph 1083 as far as can be traced at present, the label colour and design remained as for Paramount, but the typography was Pathe's. In the latter section of the Harmograph popular catalog are at least two blues items from Plaza-Banner, 925 and 983. The latter, unaccountably, has a label of regular Harmograph design, but on red with gold lettering.

There were also at least three other types of Harmograph: a 2500 series ranging from 2501 to 2578 at least, devoted mainly to sacred music and opera (with two maverick couplings by blues singer Gladys Bryant on 2539 and 2540); a 4000 series, beginning probably at 4001 and possibly not extending beyond it, devoted to German music; and a 300 series of light classics. All these stem from Paramount.

As might be expected, Harmograph is an extremely rare label outside St. Louis. The recording quality is of course as for Cameo, Paramount and Pathe. The pressing is usually of a high standard. For the jazz and/or blues collector, Harmograph is a hallowed name, especially its 160 or so Paramount derivatives.

HARMONY

In the first decade of the century, there were several phonograph makers whose models had large spindles, not unlike those on the RCA Victor single-speed 45 rpm attachment of 1949. To provide records for these, one firm, the Standard Talking Machine Company of Chicago, made an arrangement with Columbia to purchase surplus discs, give them larger holes and a new label without artist credit, and sell them. Other phonograph makers followed, among them the Harmony Talking Machine Company of 618 South Dearborn Street, Chicago, Ill.

As with its competitors, Harmony attached its own black and silver label to existing Columbia records, quoting Columbia catalog and matrix numbers thereon—everything, in fact, except the artist's name. When competition heated up, as it was bound to, the agreement with Columbia over the anonymity of its artists was broken by the large mail-order companies moving in on a booming record market. Smaller operators like Harmony could not compete with Montgomery Ward and Sears, Roebuck. In a year or so, Harmony went bankrupt.

There was another Harmony label at that time. It was produced by the Great Northern Manufacturing Company of 147-153 Fifth Avenue, Chicago. As these were also Columbia products, it seems likely that Great Northern was one of the "big boys" who helped drive Harmony out of business, after which Great Northern presumably maintained the Harmony label for a time.

The best-known and longest-lived Harmony label was a genuine Columbia product. It was designed for those who found 75 cents, the cost of a popular Columbia, too much to pay for a dance or vocal record. Harmony, with a plain maroon label printed in gold, was launched as a 50-cent label in September 1925, the numbering starting at 1-H. The matrix numbers were interlocked with Columbia's (q.v.), and the label flourished until June 1932. By then, the majority of people could not afford dance records, be they ever so cheap. Like many a luxury, Harmony records could not survive the Depression.

A strange point about Harmony records is that they were all made acoustically until 1929, when over 900 of the total of over 1400 had been issued. This, from a company that had pioneered the use of Western Electric's recording system! Nor is the quality of the recording notable. It has a curiously constricted, "boxy" sound quite unlike the mellow, warm sound that always characterized Columbia's acoustic issues. To anyone who has ever listened to a selection of Harmony records of any calibre made during those first three to four years, the sound is unique, unmistakable. When we consider how superb is the sound, recorded in the same studios, on a Columbia record of the same period, it is frustrating indeed. So much of the beauty of the music produced by the great bands recording for Harmony is lost irrevocably. When electric recording was finally adopted during the summer of 1929, the difference is shattering. It is as if, having been used to hearing a voice on a telephone, we suddenly meet the owner in person and hear him speak. The ballyhoo about how marvellous electric (or, as Columbia termed it, "Vivatonal") recording was seems to have made little impression on most buyers of popular music, however. They flocked to buy Harmony records, and its sister labels, Diva and Velvet Tone (q.v. both) regardless of the method of recording.

Although a low-priced label of the 1920s, Harmony featured top names. To be sure, there were pseudonyms aplenty. Sam Lanin assumed the cloak of the Broadway Bell-Hops. Ben Selvin, Columbia's popular music director, became the Manhattan Dance Makers. Fred Rich was dubbed The Astorites, after the hotel where his band played. Fletcher Henderson became The Dixie Stompers. Clarence Williams' Dixie Washboard Band appeared as the Blue Grass Footwarmers. Following the popularity of Whispering Jack Smith on Victor came a still unidentified performer in much the same style known as Confidential Charlie. A teenage girl with a winning way named Gay Ellis turned out to be Annette Hanshaw; and when doing her lifelike impressions of Helen Kane, she was Dot Dare.

Long years after the demise of Harmony records, in 1949, the name was revived briefly by Columbia for a series of about a hundred reissues of original Harmony material, and anything else to which CBS had rights. It had a puce label designed exactly like the old Harmony, but used the Columbia typography of the time. There was also a cutrate Harmony LP line in the fifties and early sixties.

HERSCHEL GOLD SEAL

Herschel Gold Seal records are among the rarest of any ever issued in the United States. They appeared in 1926-1927, all pressed from Gennett masters for the Northwest Phonograph and Supply Company of St. Paul and Minneapolis, Minn. The president and owner of this company was Harry Bernstein, who also distributed Gennett and other major labels during the 1920s throughout the Northwest.

There was apparently some legal trouble that ground the project to a halt after only twenty-one issues (numbered 2001-2021) had appeared. According to researcher Henry Henriksen of Minneapolis in *Record Research* for January

1975, unsold stock amounting to some 15,000 discs were stored in the Furniture Exposition Mart, 3338-3342 University Avenue, Minneapolis by owner Charles Bernstein, son of Harry. After the latter died in 1945, the staff and relations of the family helped themselves to these records, and about two-thirds of them were thrown out.

The twenty-one issues were mostly dance records by Willie Creager, Harry Pollock, and Elmer Grosso and the Royal Troubadours. There were semi-jazz items by Clesi's Aeoleans, and Johnny Sylvester's Orchestra; a piano "novelty" by Sidney Williams backing a blues by Slim Johnson ("The Blues Crooner"); and the usual complement of popular vocals by Vaughn De Leath, the Radio Franks, Vernon Dalhart and others. The label design is based on that of Electrobeam Gennett, even to the black and gold colour scheme.

HERWIN

John Randolph of St. Louis, Mo. thoroughly researched the story of Herwin records and presented his findings in *Playback*, August 1949. He discovered that the name derives from the brothers *Her*bert and Ed*win* Schiele, at the time of interviewing them as chief officers of the Artophone Corporation, wholesale dealers in electrical appliances. Herbert Schiele said that Herwin records were on sale from 1924 until 1930, when the subsidiary company was sold out to the Wisconsin Chair Company. The latter hoped to use the assets for the benefit of Paramount records. The latter had supplied a considerable number of masters used for pressing Herwin records in happier times, as had the Starr Piano Company of Richmond, Ind.

Many Herwin records are of great interest to jazz and blues collectors. Despite Mr. Schiele's claim that in good times annual sales topped 600,000 records, and then only by mail order to the Midwest and South, Herwin records of any kind are extremely rare. They have black labels, printed in Paramount or Gennett typography, with a minimum of design. One of the most interesting issues is 92019, on which what is called the Birmingham Bluetette play *Back Home Blues* (as on Paramount 12279 by Jones' Paramount Charleston Four, and entitled *Homeward Bound Blues*) and *Old Man Blues*. The latter seems to be the only issue of this performance anywhere. The next matrix number is for a Jimmy Blythe band with Freddie Keppard and Johnny Dodds, names to conjure with indeed; but neither are present on this one. It is, nevertheless, a good band recording in Chicago.

HIS MASTER'S VOICE

"The world's most famous trademark," a fox terrier gazing quizzically down the horn of a Berliner gramophone, was painted by the late Francis Barraud, probably late in 1898. He registered his copyright for the picture on February 11, 1899. The legend is that it originally showed the dog listening to an Edison cylinder phonograph; that the picture was offered to the London branch of Edison's company and rejected by it; and that Barraud substituted a Berliner disc machine and after some months sold the altered painting to the Gramophone Company. The story is probably wrong only in one detail, that it was Edison to which the original was offered. The fact remains that the final version, examined carefully in good light, shows the ghostly outline of a phonograph with cylinder and horn under the position of the Berliner machine.

The story is told in fascinating detail in Leonard Petts's book, *The Story of Nipper and the 'His Master's Voice' Picture,* published in 1973 by Ernie Bayly for the Talking Machine Review International. Despite the date of purchase by the Company, October 17, 1899, the picture was not used on records issued in Britain until February 1909, and then only on the "popular" black-label issues. It was applied to the Red and other Celebrity series from January 1, 1910. The picture and its famous caption was registered as the Gramophone Company's trademark on July 22, 1910. An unsuccessful attempt to register the word "Gramophone" as a trademark also led to the substitution of His Master's Voice as the make of record from October 20, 1910. The existing terms, Gramophone Concert Record for ten-inch and Gramophone Monarch Record for twelve-inch discs, were thenceforth discontinued.

They had described the products of the Gramophone and Typewriter Ltd., and sister companies, since the introduction of ten-inch records in the autumn of 1901 and of twelve-inch in March 1903. (The seven-inch size, bearing for the most part black labels designed exactly like their larger brethren, were described simply as Gramophone Record. They were discontinued after February 1906.) The first ten-inch and seven-inch records with labels had smooth blank backs. The labels themselves were flush with the record surface, as became the industry norm in January 1927. In the summer of 1902, labels were pressed on a raised "platform" that brought them level with the raised rim of the records themselves. This was soon abandoned. It was found that the labels fast got a scuffed look, particularly the newly introduced Red Label Celebrity issues, which carried a price tag of 10s.—$2.50 or so in those days—for the ten-inch and half as much again for the twelve. Such luxuries could not be allowed to look worn, so the labels were sunk into the records and surrounded by a raised ring to protect them. The ring eventually disappeared, but the labels remained sunken.

Pressings made in 1902 and until single-sided issues were discontinued in 1924 bear the "Angel" trademark on the blank side, and until 1908, the legend "Reproduced in Hanover," the German city where Emile Berliner's brother Joseph directed the first disc factory in Europe. The huge Gramophone Company factory in Hayes, Middlesex, now a London suburb, was opened in 1908 at a ceremony graced by the presence of operatic soprano Luisa Tetrazzini.

William Barry Owen, Managing Director of the Gramophone Company, was convinced that the enormous success of the new invention was no more than a bubble that would burst unless something was brought in to sustain it. The company decided therefore to promote the Lambert typewriter. In December 1900 the words "and Typewriter" were officially inserted into the registered

name of the business. Contrary to Owen's forebodings, it was the typewriter that proved a flop. With operatic celebrities of the calibre of Nellie Melba (even if she did insist on a special label—pale lilac—and a special sleeve for her records, as well as a fee that brought their price up to £1); Adelina Patti, also with her own label and sleeve; Francesco Tamagno, content with a red label, but with a tag giving an individual number to each copy; Emma Calvé, the embodiment of the tempestuous *Carmen*, who threw herself wholeheartedly into the part even in front of a recording horn (once she had overcome her distrust of making records); Pol Plançon, the magnificent French bass, tall and bearded, looking the very image of the Mephistophelean part he sang so superbly; the new tenor from Naples who had conquered Milan and London and went on to conquer New York, Enrico Caruso—with these and countless others of similar stature all recording exclusively for Gramophone, how could the company fail? Obviously it could not be sustained by the sales of single-sided records giving at most four minutes of music for £1, which was a week's wages for a large part of the population at the time. But for those whose tastes and resources did not run to great singers on red or fancy-coloured labels and fancier prices, there were excellent reproductions of H. M. Coldstream Guards' Band playing everything from light concert pieces and marches to the best-known melodies from operas, musical comedies and operettas. There were English-speaking singers, artists such as the Australian Peter Dawson, the Irish tenor John McCormack, the Scottish baritone Andrew Black, the Welsh lyric tenor Ben Davies, and English singers like Robert Radford, John Harrison, Perceval Allen, and a teenage girl named Maggie Teyte, who was generally thought of as having a great future. All these recorded on the black G & T label, as it is usually known among collectors now. All these and hundreds more: music-hall stars Marie and Alice Lloyd, Vesta Victoria, Gus Elen, Harry Lauder, Albert Whelan, Dan Leno; and a wide selection of instrumental soloists playing everything from handbells to cornets, including (and this on the less expensive black label) concert pianists of the stature of Ilona Eibenschütz. A pupil of Johannes Brahms himself, she made some superb recordings in London in 1903.

A seemingly indissoluble link with Eldridge R. Johnson's Victor Talking Machine Company had been forged even before that company came into being. As a result, the monthly supplements from the beginning of the century had their quota of American recordings from Victor masters: opera and military bands, concert artists and banjoists, popular singers, sets of minstrel turns, it was all there. Thus the name of the English branch reverted to the Gramophone Company Ltd. and Sister Companies. This was in 1908. As we have seen, the last three words were dropped following the registration of "His Master's Voice" in 1910.

Victor introduced double-sided records in October 1908, but only for popular artists. The Red Seal operatic celebrities remained single-sided until 1924. HMV did not launch double-sided issues until September 1912; and for several years after that, many artists of the theatrical and music-hall stage continued to appear as singles. Until that date, the system of allocating catalog numbers according to sex, language or nationality, and kind of music, adopted from the beginning with Berliners, was applied fairly consistently. (It seems strange that Enrico Caruso singing *For You Alone* should be described as "English tenor" rather than "Tenor in English" which was the later description on the label. And for Arthur Pryor to be classified as "American Trombone" seems odd indeed.)

The practice of giving each title issued a "single-sided" type of number continued until the autumn of 1934. This number was shown on the labels while the matrix number was not. Many beginners were thus led to assume that the number was the matrix serial.

The first double-sided issues had what were officially described as plum labels from the beginning of their career to the end in February 1958. In that time they spanned from B-100 to B-10968, the ten-inch series covering every kind of music from military bands (the first two dozen were all by the Coldstream Guards' Band) to swing music, from oratorio to comedy sketches; and from C-100 to C-4280, covering the same spectrum of recorded sound. The exact shade of label varied considerably in the 45½ years, from a genuine plum to rose pink, sandy brown, dark chocolate and deep tan. The first issues showed Francis Barraud's masterpiece in something approaching natural colour, which improved to give a more "real" appearance. For the last year of World War I and the first year thereafter, a black-and-white photographic reproduction replaced this. The natural colour returned at the end of 1919 and remained, with varying shades of background, until immediately prior to World War II, when the trademark was shown in soft shades of olive green. This continued to the end of 78 rpm issues.

Under the trademark is shown an oblong panel of varying tints—green, pale blue, but mostly buff or cream, and finally white—all bearing the catalog number. This panel vanished at the end of 1917 in favour of an even more distinguished design involving a pair of white triangular inserts at the foot of the label, one on each side of the copyright stamp that showed, in accordance with the provisions of the Copyright Act of 1911, how much in royalty had been paid to the publisher of the recorded work. These inserts give the description of the performance, the would-have-been single-sided number to the left, and the catalog number to the right. This design was used for all classes of records—black-labelled D (12-inch) and E (10-inch), red DA (10-inch) and DB (12-inch)—until the spring of 1926, except that the white filling of the panel applied to the "plum" B and C series only, and not even to these after December 1924. The position of the copyright stamp, or a facsimile of it, and the details flanking it, remained as before until 1933, in the summer of which year the design was again altered to its final form, with the description to the left and the catalog number to the right of the spindle hole.

The black-label issues began at D-1 in February 1918 and E-1 in February 1920. They are in many ways the most interesting of all the HMV double-sided series, as they feature not only musical comedy and light opera stars in their original rôles, but also records of immeasurable historical importance by politicians and statesmen. Winston Churchill discusses the Budget of 1909 and the aftermath of World War I in 1918 on D-379 and D-380. Sir Edward Elgar conducts his *Carillon*, while the great actor Henry Ainley speaks a poem in tribute to the Belgian resistance of 1914. Presidents Taft, Wilson and Harding all have at least one record each covering topics of importance to the United States before and after World War I. There are complete operas and symphonies, Gilbert and Sullivan in both acoustic and electric form, and various stars of music hall and vaudeville. The only form of entertainment not to be found on D and E records is dance music. The last of these series to be issued are D-2072 (May 1932) and E-610 (November 1935).

The red-label double-sided records did not begin until 1924. The first few hundred of both ten-inch DA and twelve-inch DB consist of couplings of existing single-siders, mostly by top-flight operatic singers of all kinds and both sexes in many languages. Where single-sided records had cost 15s. each in the G & T days, now two of them back to back cost slightly more than half that sum. Among the first announced was DB-111, which coupled the two famous tenor arias from Leoncavallo's *I Pagliacci*, *Vesti la giubba* (originally a single-sided 052159) and *No, Pagliaccio non son* (formerly 2-052034), and DA-103, bracketing the famous Neapolitan songs *'A vucchella* and *'O sole mio*. These sold in such incredible numbers as to invite the comment from one critic: "If Enrico Caruso had never made any other records than these, he'd have been a wealthy man from the royalties on them." Both the DA and DB series include large numbers of Caruso records, very nearly all he ever made for the Gramophone Company and Victor that had been issued in single-sided form. Many fine examples of the recording engineer's art in the early days (usually the brothers Fred and Will Gaisberg) appeared on these familiar red labels.

With the coming of electric recording came magnificent records by Vladimir de Pachmann, playing Chopin as only he could, frequently with (now) intelligible comments as he played; readings of chamber music by Mozart, Beethoven and Schubert by the Flonzaley Quartet or the famous Alfred Cortôt-Pablo Casals-Jacques Thibaud trio playing Haydn, Schumann and Mendelssohn—and more Beethoven and Schubert. The great symphony orchestras that had been a feature of the D series now began appearing on DB. Leopold Stokowski and the Philadelphia Symphony Orchestra was the best-known and probably the most prolific. Then in the 1930s came Arturo Toscanini and the New York Philharmonic, Wilhelm Fürtwängler and the Berlin Philharmonic, Eugene Ormandy and the Minneapolis Symphony; and, of course, more singers, some with their voices matured to perfection in time for electric recording to do them full justice (Tito Schipa, Beniamino Gigli, Jussi Björling, Rosa Ponselle), and some new artists too young to have made an acoustic record (Tito Gobbi, Giuseppe di Stefano, Victoria de los Angeles, Kirsten Flagstad).

There were other categories of HMV records with distinguishing labels. There had been a single-sided violet label for artists whose eminence was felt to be somewhere between black and red. When everything became double-sided, the operatic duets, trios and choruses (including top names—the various recordings Caruso made of the *Rigoletto* Quartet and the Sextet from *Lucia di Lammermoor*, for example, each with a different cast) were coupled and given a special series with its own tint (buff, pale green, pale blue, and the most expensive, white) and its own prefix code. None of these lasted very long.

The record world was shaken early in 1931 when it was announced that a merger had been arranged between HMV on the one hand and Columbia and Parlophone on the other: a union of the main record companies in Britain. A pleasant surprise followed early in 1935 when a 1s. 6d. popular record on all three labels was presented to the public. Now first-class popular artists in the dance band, vocal and instrumental world, including some hot jazz, would be available at little more than half the cost up to that point. The HMV series was prefixed BD, and BD-100 went on sale in February 1935. After a year this three-figure series became devoted to any artists except dance bands, which were given their own BD-5000 series. Both sets lasted until September 1955.

As a barometer of changing public taste, the B (and to a lesser extent, the C) series, with their quiet, tasteful "plum" labels, are without parallel in the history of HMV. As I mentioned earlier, they began with many military band couplings. These were quickly augmented by records of light orchestras, and eventually by ballads, comic songs, and instrumental novelties (including one by the famous Six Brown Brothers, *That Moaning Saxophone Rag* (B-526), described on some copies as "English Xylophone Sextette," which is wrong on all counts as they were American, saxophone players, and all men, thus a sextet). Some of the less highly paid musical comedy cast members appeared on plums, while their more expensive colleagues continued on single-sided black labels. It was on two separate C issues that the first records of Beethoven's *Kreutzer* Sonata for violin and piano was published.

In June 1919, on a special issue devoted to the latest revues, three records of importance were announced. B-1024 gave us one side (*On the Level You're a Little Devil*) by a new French comedian named Maurice Chevalier, then appearing in *Hullo, America* at the Palace Theatre. On B-1021 and B-1022 there were four sides by the Original Dixieland Jazz Band recorded for Victor twelve to fifteen months before. Although HMV had access to ten other sides by the band, then appearing to great acclaim in various London night spots, the company declined to venture further with this incredible new music. Nevertheless, over the years some fine examples of other genuine forms of jazz did get issued on HMV. And of course its dance bands, from local talent such as Jack Hylton, Ambrose, Carroll Gibbons, Ray Noble, and the various Savoy Hotel bands, to exotic names from the Victor catalog, fairly flooded out in a stream of plums.

However, even through the Roaring Twenties, or the Dancing Years, or whatever they may be called, dance records did not account for the majority of plum labels on HMV. Public taste still hankered after the Band of the Coldstream Guards, and that of the Royal Air Force. There was still a great deal of interest in the superb records made by Sousa's Band for Victor, many of them appearing on HMV. In less rumbustious vein, there was cafe music month after month by de Groot and the Piccadilly Orchestra. On the vocal side, there was everything from the bass voices of Peter Dawson singing anything and Paul Robeson singing spirituals and such pop songs as were deemed suitable (several were barely so) to the outlandish humour of Lancashire-born Gracie Fields and the gentle seduction of Jack Smith. The most popular vocal plum was by none of these, however. It was not by the million-notcher Gene' Austin, nor the sensational vocal quintet The Revellers, popular though they were. It was the voice of a young schoolboy named Ernest Lough, principal chorister of the City Temple Choir, assisted by his contemporaries and older colleagues of the Choir. With choirmaster Dr. George Thalben-Ball at the organ, they sang Mendelssohn's *Hear My Prayer* and *O for the Wings of a Dove*. It was recorded late one Saturday afternoon, so legend has it, after several breakdowns caused by several of the younger choir members, who had lunched not wisely but too well on confections that overwhelmed their singing. The record was issued in June 1927 on HMV C-1329, and sold by the million all over the world during the next forty years.

Of the big instrumental sellers, few could match Reginald Foort at the organ of the New Gallery Cinema in Regent Street, London, playing two very popular pieces by Albert W. Ketelbey, *In a Monastery Garden* and *In a Persian Market*. This also sold on a worldwide scale in vast numbers. The most successful novelty record was not the sounds of various animals in the London Zoo (it was a flop), but one of some nightingales recorded in the country garden of the great cellist, Beatrice Harrison, who accompanied them on several titles. At one point on one of them, a dog can be heard barking—perhaps in protest that what was being recorded was not its master's voice. Fifteen years later, the HMV engineers set up their microphones in a Sussex wood on a May night to record a new generation of nightingales. They had chosen the night that Bomber Command had selected to wreak revenge on Mannheim for the London, Coventry and Portsmouth raids. The flight path lay directly over the microphones. The contrast between the ethereal sound of the birds' voices and the ominous thunder of the bombers is something unique in the history of commercial recording.

It was HMV that preserved something of the sound of the battlefront of World War I. Just a month before the Armistice of November 11, 1918, the company sent one of its senior recording engineers, Will Gaisberg, and a team of assistants to France to record the actual sound of the Royal Garrison Artillery bombarding the enemy with gas shells prior to the capture of Lille. This, suitably edited, was issued three months after the cessation of hostilities, a grim single-sided reminder of the war to end all wars. Within a month of the visit to France, Will Gaisberg was dead, a victim of the influenza epidemic that claimed more victims, it was said, in six months than the war had in four years.

His Master's Voice, or at least the Gramophone Company, has always meant all things to all people. Whatever the public wanted to hear—Commander Robert Peary talking about his expedition to the North Pole; Commander Shackleton discussing his voyage to the South Pole; some pygmies from the Congo brought to London in 1905 and recorded singing and laughing; the memoirs of a prisoner whose sentence was quashed; an Italian journalist who had dined with Kaiser Wilhelm II; Sir Arthur Conan Doyle talking about Sherlock Holmes a few weeks before Doyle died—or whether they just wanted entertainment from the world's top artists, it was there on HMV.

The first studios were in a basement at 31 Maiden Lane, behind The Strand, London, W.C.2. It was not the kind of venue to inspire confidence, much less art, in a temperamental prima donna or a sensitive concert pianist or violinist. In the summer of 1902 the premises were moved to 21 City Road, London, E.C.1. There the studios and offices were combined until everything but the studios were moved to Hayes in 1908. Experimental recording began at Hayes almost at once, and on June 6, 1914, the last commercial recordings were made at City Road.

The main studio in Hayes was on the second floor of a large office block on Blyth Road. It remained the principal location for British recordings until 1931. On March 15, 1921, a new system of acoustic recording was adopted throughout Europe, and the matrix serials were universally changed and brought into line. This lasted for just over four years. Then, another breakthrough. The star of Noel Coward's revue, *On with the Dance*, produced by C. B. Cochran at the London Pavilion, was the vivacious French girl, Alice Delysia. On June 24, 1925, she visited Hayes in the morning and made two sides from the show including *Poor Little Rich Girl*. That afternoon Jack Hylton and his Orchestra recorded *Ah-Ha!* and two other numbers. All five were recorded into a microphone. One of them, *Feelin' Kind o' Blue*, was issued on B-2072. The electric recording era had begun.

Within a couple of years, records had been made in many of the finest concert halls, churches and cathedrals in the country. A new block of studios was acquired in Queen's Hall, London, W.1. Gradually this and Kingsway Hall superseded the Hayes complex. On November 12, 1931, in a formal ceremony attended by Sir Landon Ronald (who had joined the Company as an accompanist and entrepreneur in 1900), George Bernard Shaw and other guests, new studios were opened in a converted Victorian mansion in St. John's Wood, London, N.W.1 with a recording of Sir Edward Elgar conducting the London Symphony Orchestra playing his *Falstaff* music. The building is the home of EMI studios to this day, the first studios in England built specially for recording.

The following chart gives the first matrix number in each set in use on the first day of every year from the beginning of ten-inch records in 1901. It includes twelve-inch records distinguishing among those made in various locations when field recordings became feasible on a grand scale at the introduction of electric recording.

Recordings made at 31 Maiden Lane, later 21 City Road, London				*Hayes experimentals*	
	10-inch	10-inch	12-inch	10-inch	12-inch
1901 (April)	1				
1902	c.1295				
1903	3200		1		
1904	4770		c.300		
1905	6431	1600	c.420		
1906 (May 23)	8146	3254	c.730		
1907	9619	c.5130	c.1750		
1908		c.7700	c.2200 (October 8)	HO-1	
1909		9378	2772		
1910		11148	3965		
1911		13026	4735		
1912		14705	5848(October 12)	HO-179 (January)	HO-100
1913		16195	6947	HO-256	HO-377
1914		17354	7721	HO-793	HO-542

(The two columns of ten-inch numbers refer to Fred and Will Gaisberg's recordings respectively. After about 1907 other recordists shared Will's numbers with Fred.)

Recordings made in Hayes, Middlesex

	Old Series		*New Series* (previously experimental)	
	10-inch	12-inch	10-inch	12-inch
1915	18765	8228	HO-1123	HO-620
1916	19803	8498	HO-2298	HO-1403
1917	20578	8703	HO-3377	HO-2430
1918	20994	NONE	HO-3884	HO-3028
1919	21408	8717	HO-4544	HO-3539
1920	c.21900		HO-5489	HO-4209
1921	c.22250		HO-6019	HO-4690

(Until January 1, 1920, each take was allocated a different matrix number. From that date, takes I, II, III, IV, etc. were used.)

Recordings made in Hayes, Middlesex	Small Queen's Hall	Other locations
1921 (March 15) Bb-/Cc-1		
1922 847		
1923 2320		
1924 4030		
1925 5517		(November) BR/CR-1
1926 7596	(September 10) 9200	118
1927 10023	9577	c.960
1928 12300	12200	c.1650
1929 15315	15492	c.2260
1930 18258	18516	c.2700
1931 OB-/2B-1	201	OBR-/CR-1

From March 15, 1921, no distinction in numbering was made between sizes. Only the prefix changed.

Recordings made in St. John's Wood, London	
1932	OB-/2B-2080
1933	4600
1934	5840
1934 (August 24)	OEA-/2EA-1
1935	715
1936	2662
1937	4183
1938	5150
1939	7268
1940	8363
1941	c.9000
1942	c.9600

See also Zonophone.

HIT OF THE WEEK

In *Record Research* for January-February 1960, famed discographer Howard J. Waters contributed a long article, occupying the entire reading section of the issue, on Hit of the Week records. Without it, I frankly admit I could not have compiled this chapter.

These flexible records were made of Durium (and are thus connected with the British make of that name, q.v.). Durium is a heat-resistant synthetic resin pressed on a fibrous base ten inches in diameter. The company that produced them initially in February 1930 was the Durium Products Corporation of 460 West 34th Street, New York City. It had recording studios in the old McGraw-Hill Building on West 42nd Street, near Ninth Avenue. To Dr. Hal T. Beans, a Columbia University professor of chemistry, belongs the credit for the invention of the material. The marketing idea was that a light-weight, indestructible long-playing record, featuring one carefully chosen hit song played and/or sung by a well known artist, could be sold on newsstands all over the United States at 15 cents a copy—and offer serious competition to the Big Three, Victor, Columbia and Brunswick, whose popular double-sided solid-stock or laminated discs sold at five times as much.

Arrangements were made to record prominent dance bands such as Ben Pollack's, Bert Lown's, Don Voorhees', and even Duke Ellington's. (He was a Victor artist in his own name but recorded widely on other labels: on Brunswick as The Jungle Band, on Columbia as Joe Turner and his Memphis Men, on OKeh as The Harlem Footwarmers. He used various flamboyant pseudonyms on Banner and its affiliates. On Hit of the Week he was given the name of the Harlem Hot Chocolates to add to his collection.) Wandering minstrel Vincent Lopez, fresh from a handful of sides for Banner and Grey Gull, now turned his talents to Hit of the Week, along with Phil Spitalny, Ted Fiorito, Sam Lanin and Harry Reser, the first two being Victor artists and the others free-lance.

For some months into 1930, it seemed that Hit of the Week had made the biggest hit in the record industry since electric recording five years before. *Variety*, in its issue for June 18, 1930, bemoaned the depressed state of the record market but called the new label "a ray of sunshine." Pressing orders, even during the normally slack summer months, reached half a million copies of each issue. Then came the fall—in weekly sales of Hit of the Week. They dropped to about 350,000 by November. The following March, publishers and songwriters failed to receive royalty statements or payments for the last quarter of 1930, and began bringing lawsuits against Durium. An auditor's report gave the exact total of royalties due as $141,410.39.

On March 19, 1931, New York Supreme Court Justice Coleman appointed the Irving Trust Company as receiver in equity for Durium. By agreement with the latter's directors, Durium continued to produce records in an attempt to liquidate the claims of creditors, mainly the publishers and the composers they represented. On May 12, Irving Trust appealed to the Court for an order to show cause why Durium should not be sold, at the request of these publishers. Durium's stockholders opposed the appeal, but in June the company was sold to the Irwin-Wasey Advertising Agency.

On August 13, Hit of the Week appeared in a new format. It now boasted two full-length numbers on its one side, but still sold on newsstands for 15 cents. The records played for five minutes. The old numbering, from 1019 to 1157, though retained as the matrix serial it had always been, now changed as a catalog reference to a complicated code system with a letter of the alphabet denoting the month of issue, starting at J. There was a separate number for each track. Thus, M-3-4 was issued in December 1931.

Artists of the standing of Eddie Cantor, Morton Downey, Nick Lucas, Rudy Vallee and Gene Austin, all lately regular Victor or Brunswick artists, began recording for Hit of the Week. The "house" orchestra was under the direction of Phil Spitalny. They did not arrest the declining Durium fortunes, however. RCA Victor announced its new unbreakable long-playing record that gave three or four times as much music on one side as Hit of the Week, and rumours were rife that Victor was negotiating with Woolworth's to put out a ten-cent and twenty-cent popular dance record, shellac-made but double-sided and quite durable. It was the end of the road for Hit of the Week. With its weekly distribution down to 60,000, about a tenth of what it had been two years or so earlier, the situation became hopeless. After June 23, 1932, Hit of the Week vanished forever, although Durium continued to produce advertising records.

The surfaces of Hit of the Week are very good for the price, and the recording quality is as a rule excellent. There is a tendency to rumble, common to all laminated pressings, but the records gave value for money. Like its British opposite number (known as Durium, q.v.), and other flexible, unbreakable makes that flooded the British market about the same time, Hit of the Weeks warp easily. They usually have to be clamped to the turntable by means of a clothespin or some similar device, to keep them from riding up and throwing the pickup arm off the record. For best results, I suggest pasting the record to a conventional shellac 78 of no value. This assures a surface flat enough for satisfactory playing, and is permanent.

HOLLYWOOD

As might be expected, this was the product of a California studio that evidently had some connection with other West Coast labels in the mid-1920s. The same titles from the same masters occur on all of them. A very rare label, Hollywood issued its repertoire sometimes without catalog numbers but otherwise in a 1000 series. It is best remembered now for at least eight sides by Fred Elizalde and his Cinderella Roof Orchestra in the summer of 1926. There were also sides by other bands of considerable interest, such as Steve White's Danceland Orchestra and Carlyle Stevenson's El Patio Orchestra, which probably appeared simultaneously on Sunset. Enthusiasts for Negro jazz value the collection of sides made apparently in 1924 by Harvey Brooks's Quality Four.

The dark blue label, with its ornate decoration and printing in gold, is outstanding. Recording is reasonably good acoustic for the most part, though it is thought that some of the latter issues are electric. The surfaces as a rule are quite smooth. The label seems to have disappeared about 1927.

HOMESTEAD

A very rare label from the Plaza Music Company's repertoire, made for and distributed by the Chicago Mail Order Company (no address given) during the mid-1920s. The original matrix numbers are not shown on the label or the wax, but are supplanted by a control number in the same way as is found on Oriole and affiliated labels. The typography is the same as Oriole's of the period. The numbering is in a 16000 block.

HOMOCHORD

The original Homochord label, of German origin, flourished in England during the four or five years preceding the outbreak of World War I. All its issues came from European-recorded masters, none of them of outstanding interest apart from the obvious music-hall artists featured prominently. In October 1921, it was announced in the gramophone trade magazines that a new Homochord record was in production, and the first release would cover no fewer than a hundred items. These duly appeared, beginning the ten-inch numbering at H-100 and the twelve-inch at HD-2000.

The head office of British Homophone, which did its own manufacturing, was at 19 City Road, London, E.C.1. For the next fourteen years this company produced Homochord and other records for less affluent gramophone owners. At the outset, the company relied on English and American Vocalion for its catalog, and also to some extent Gennett. The original matrix numbers of both Vocalion companies were shown in the wax and on the labels, but with a figure 3 after each one. There is no known reason for this, unless it was an attempt to cover up the use of the same masters on other makes with Vocalion connections, such as Aco, Beltona, Coliseum, Guardsman, etc.

In 1922 Homophone evidently opened a recording studio, probably in its headquarters in City Road, and began making records not issued on other makes, while still using American items that were. The English Vocalion sides have 0 prefixes. The Homochord sides are in an L-00100 series, with the vaguely coded recording date handwritten like a second serial in the smooth wax just outside the rim of the label. Thus, a side made on September 19, 1923 will be marked 19923. There was also an S series that included a curious recording of the sound of Bow Bells, recorded acoustically in the vicinity of the bell tower of St. Mary-le-Bow Church, Cheapside.

In June 1924, the H- series became the clue to the sides recorded by American Vocalion and English Aco (q.v.). That same month Homochord began issuing titles from the American and English Pathe catalog. It used the same numbering system as before but added a C- prefix. Thus it is possible to find two Homochords with the same set of numbers but with differing prefix letters. The vocal artists received new pseudonyms, not the ones used for their work on other labels. Dance bands on the H- series were almost always described as "Homochord Dance Orchestra" if from Vocalion, though there were a few exotic inventions early on such as the Alabama Specialty Orchestra (at least one side so labelled was from English Vocalion, recorded in London by British musicians!) and the Mississippi Coons, who were a rough but exciting Dixieland jazz band directed by the ubiquitous Harry A. Yerkes. Other British bands were usually described as "Selwyn's Dance Orchestra" or "The Famous Broadway Band under the direction of Charles Starr." When Pathe material was introduced, most of the dance bands were lumped together as "Eldon's Dance Orchestra," whether they were Fletcher Henderson's Orchestra or Nathan Glantz's, the Original Memphis Five or the California Ramblers. This was a time when all that mattered was the tune to set young listeners dancing. Whose band they heard, and where it came from, mattered not in the slightest.

These two types of Homochord were pressed by the English branch of the American parent company in each case. The Vocalion H- prefixes came from the Aeolian Company's factory in Hayes, Middlesex, and the C- prefixes from Pathe Freres in Stonebridge Park, London.

After American Vocalion merged with Brunswick in the United States, the supply of masters to Homochord and its English Vocalion associates ceased. British Homophone signed a two-year contract with, of all firms, the Gramophone Company of Hayes, Middlesex, for providing studio facilities and pressing plant. The quality of Homochord records, hitherto rather gritty and indifferently recorded, improved immediately. The EMI files give no clue as to the artists employed, but those with keen ears can identify habitues of the recording studios of the time (1926-1928), most of them appearing on Zonophone under their real names. At least two strange issues appeared on the new Hayes pressings: two saxophone solos by Clyde Doerr, and two pipe-organ solos by Mark Andrews, both from Victor and bearing Victor matrix numbers. The organist is heard playing hymns, but not as Mark Andrews. He is dignified with the name "Professor Frederick Retter." The numerical sequence was maintained, but now prefixed D-. What other Victor masters were used on Homochord?

This continued for some four hundred issues, until the summer of 1928. From this date until the demise of Homochord in 1935, all issues were pressed in the Tunbridge Wells factory in Kent. All British recordings, many of them were also issued on Sterno and are outside the scope of this book.

The Homochord label changed very little over the years. It was based on the black and gold design of pre-1914. The basic colour is a rather dull olive brown, with an outer ring of leaves in red. The make appears in heavy gold block in an arc round the top of a picture of an apparently naked girl (visible from the waist up) playing a harp in a bush that could be a laurel, from which protrudes a horn. Doubtless the horn was intended to be part of a Berliner type of gramophone, but it could equally be an alto horn or something of the kind. The portrait is depicted in gold and black on a bright red background. The lower half of the label assures "Clear and perfect reproduction. British manufacture." The price varied little during the life of this label, most of the H-C-D complex being 2s. 6d. (50 cents or so), the twelve-inch 4s. There was a P- series that cost 3s. for ten-inch discs and 4s. 6d. for twelve-inch. The last Homochords, in an HR- series, were only 1s.

HOT RECORD SOCIETY

Formed in 1937 to make available to collectors some of the jazz classics of the 1920s (even though collecting the originals was at that time simpler than it has since become), the Hot Record Society did in fact produce some remarkable records over the next three years. With the assistance of the American Record Corporation and Decca Records, which gave permission for its masters to be used, or made new ones by dubbing from clean copies, HRS issued a variety of first-class jazz items. Nor did the programme stop there. HRS hired General's studios to record the Muggsy Spanier-Sidney Bechet Big Four for two sessions of twelve-inch classics of jazz. HRS leased the ARC studios eighteen months before this, in August 1938, for a jam session where veterans of the Chicago and Harlem schools of jazz mingled with those from New Orleans to produce some lively improvised music. Operating from 827 Seventh Avenue, New York, the Society published *The Rag,* a small magazine that ranks as one of the first of its kind anywhere, a periodical devoted to those who loved jazz in its purist sense, who were weary of the commercial debasement of their music under the overworked name of Swing.

Originally, HRS labels were cream with black lettering and no decoration. Before the project was abandoned completely, the labels had become dead white with a red upper half on which the full name of the Society stood out in white ornate lettering. The transfers of those titles for which no master was available were done with incredible naturalness, which would—and did—shame many later attempts on LP, even those by large firms. The HRS surfaces were impeccable. The records are on the scarce side. The ten-inch issues sold for $1, the twelve-inch for $1.50—at a time when most popular and jazz records were selling for 35-75 cents.

HUDSON

The J. L. Hudson Company, a major department store in Detroit, Mich. entered the record market briefly in 1924. It drew on Emerson's latter-day masters and pressed at the Bridgeport Die and Machine Company. As this company apparently went bankrupt in the summer of 1925, it is reasonable to assume that Hudson records were discontinued around that date.

The records have dark blue labels with all lettering and ornamentation in gold. The company monogram is in blue on a white circle at the top. The catalog numbers are those allocated to the same couplings on Broadway, Lyratone, Puritan and Triangle, around the 11300-11400 mark, and on Pennington with the first digit omitted. Carl Kendziora suggests logically that whatever J. L. Hudson chose to promote in its stores would be pressed to its order by B. D. M. Thus it cannot be assumed that all these Emerson-originated labels carry identical issues. Little is known about the extent of the Hudson repertoire. It offers interesting scope for researching jazz and near jazz items among the more conventional dance and popular vocal issues that probably comprise the bulk of it.

There was also another Hudson label, produced in Britain in 1934 and for about two years afterwards. Its chief interest lies in the fact that a seventeen-year-old girl singer named Vera Lynn made her first records for Hudson with Howard Baker and his Orchestra. There are no American recordings included in its catalog. The usual label is reddish-brown with a white segment showing the title and artist credit in the same colour as the surround, with the name in gold above.

HY-TONE

    This is another label affiliated with Arto. It made its brief appearance on the American market probably in the summer or early autumn of 1920, disappearing about two years later, or perhaps somewhat less. The label, a glossy black with gold design and lettering, credits manufacture to the Indestructible Phonograph Record Co., no address shown, and claims that the record "plays on any standard phonograph." The name Hy-Tone is printed in large capitals on a treble stave decorated—one cannot use any other term—with crochets and quavers flung at it haphazardly. The catalog series is as for Arto, except that the 9000 series becomes K-1 upwards. E.g., Arto 9097 becomes Hy-Tone K-97. Matrix numbers are rarely visible. When they do appear, it is in reverse, handwritten under the Arto catalog number heavily indented inside the concentric ring set about one-tenth of an inch beyond the last turn of the recorded groove. Recording is satisfactory, and surfaces adequate.

IDEAL SCALA

This British label first appeared in 1923. The numbering started at 7000 or 7001. Although it continued on the market until the end of 1927, in over four years only just over two hundred records were released. These were drawn from Pathe (American recordings have 69000-70000 and 105000-107000 serials), Federal (with the take digit *preceding* the matrix number in the 2000s) and Emerson (41000-42000s). The records probably sold at 1s. 6d., or about a quarter. Not surprisingly, they offer nothing of outstanding merit. For the collector of jazz-orientated dance music, however, there are a few sides by such as the Synco Jazz Band and the California Ramblers, usually labelled "Astoria Orchestra" or "Paul Allen's Orchestra," names applied with equal favour to straight dance bands. London recordings for Pathe have matrix numbers in a 90000 block.

The records were apparently issued by the Scala Record Company but pressed mainly by Pathe. They bear the processing date in reversed handwriting in the smooth central area in the manner of Pathe. The surfaces are generally very smooth, but there is a tendency for the labels to be pressed off centre. The labels are pale blue with dark blue printing and design, showing the famous Milan opera house to the left of the upper half.

IMPERIAL

The Crystalate Gramophone Record Manufacturing Company, Ltd., of Tonbridge, Kent, England, began producing Imperial records in 1920. Prior to this, their factory had manufactured various other pre-1914 labels that had no American links.

Until the summer of 1923, Imperial issues were all of British recordings, with a few European items here and there. The labels of these early releases, and those issued up to the summer of 1926, are bright blue with all printing in gold. The title and artist credits are shown between the open drapes of a pair of curtains surmounted by a crown. From 1926 until 1930, the crown remained, placed centrally above the word IMPERIAL in an arc printed in gold on a violet background, bordered in pale mauve and with a semicircular panel of the same tint printed in violet. From 1930 to the end of 1931 the design remained unchanged, but with the violet now very dark blue and the mauve bright scarlet. The panel, hitherto shaped eccentrically, now became concentric with the rim of the label. It was now one of the most attractive and dignified of all British labels. (The quality of recording, hitherto done in studios at 63 Farringdon Road, London, E.C.1, improved considerably when new studios in Broadhurst Gardens, West Hampstead, London, N.W.3 were opened in 1929.)

The catalog numbers ran from 800 to 2953. The last Imperial record was issued in February 1934. Throughout the years from 1923 to the end, American masters were drawn from Banner, both as a Plaza label and later as a member of the American Record Corporation. Not all Banner masters bear the original matrix numbers, by any means. They run in a 5000-13000 series, but the number on Imperial labels in a series from 100 to something over 2000 is a control number of Crystalate's devising. The American Crown label, with matrix numbers between 1000 and 1500, also supplied several masters to Imperial, issued on Imperial between 2400 and 2600. (See Banner and Crown for dating charts.)

The Imperial catalog, as would be expected from a record costing 1s. 6d. or 1s. 3d. (about 20 to 25 cents), is aimed at the popular market. The well tried light classics abound, particularly earlier, along with "cover" recordings of music-hall songs done in imitation of the originals; banjo, bell, cornet and xylophone solos; standard and popular ballads; and, of course, dance music. Later came a few Wurlitzer organ records from America by George Epstein (so named), Leo Le Sieur and Harry Chrysler; numerous crisply clear vocals by the omnipresent Irving Kaufman; and, from the British side, records by A. Mantovani (violinist) and one Gandino and his Orchestra, who turned out to be the alter ego of Mantovani himself.

Among the dance bands can be found several by Fletcher Henderson, some featuring Louis Armstrong. Imperial 1420, this band's recording of *Alabamy Bound* issued in May 1925, contains the first solo by the great jazz trumpeter ever issued in England. The Original Memphis Five, the Kansas City Five (cloaked as the Six Black Diamonds), the California Ramblers, Jack Pettis and his Band, and many others of interest turn up on Imperial, usually under their real names but sometimes following pseudonyms allocated to them by Banner. Imperials were cheap yet offered clear, if rather bass-deficient recordings. They sold well in chain stores and regular record stores alike, and many of them still turn up today.

Imperial issues of Hebrew music, religious and secular alike, including some by the great Cantor Sirota, brought forth paeans of praise from the critics at the time. So did the operatic excerpts and Neapolitan songs by Luigi Cilla. To please Scottish, Irish and Welsh purchasers, there were many records by genuine artists singing and playing interesting folk music.

This chart shows the first matrix number recorded by Imperial, exactly or approximately, in each year:

Year	Matrix	Year	Matrix
1920	c. 2800	1928	4769
1921	c. 3000	1929	5078
1922	c. 3160	1930	c. 5345
1923	3307	1931	c. 5570
1924	3515	1932	c. 5980
1925	3730	1933	c. 6300
1926	3954	1934	c. 6550
1927	4580		

In the middle of the first decade of the century, there was an Imperial record manufactured in the United States, single-sided and numbered in the 40000s. It bore a white label with curtain design in purple and gold, not unlike the earliest British Imperial of some fifteen years later. Matrix numbers are in a 7000-8000 block, suffixed D. The general appearance of the discs is not unlike that of Victor's records of the same period, even to the conditions-of-sale sticker applied to the blank side. There were some interesting ragtime numbers on this label, recorded as banjo solos by Vess L. Ossman, and a few mildly interesting operatic titles and Hebrew vocal music.

IMPROVED GRAM-O-PHONE RECORD

See Victor.

IRAGEN

The International Records Agency, of which Al Franck was director, issued seven records (two ten-inch, prefixed 1G-, and five twelve-inch, prefixed 2R-) during the mid-1930s. They are extremely rare today, almost unheard-of. The two ten-inch are by Ezra Buzzington's Rustic Revelers, a direct forerunner of the Original Hoosier Hot Shots, and piano solos by Lillian Crawford (one being Bix Beiderbecke's *In a Mist*), both from Electrobeam Gennett masters. The twelve-inch are piano solos of Medtner played by Harry L. Anderson; Sibelius and Grieg interpreted by Andre Skalski; Haydn's *Eloquence* and a collection of short Polish songs sung by the Music Makers, conducted by Skalski; songs by Alfven and Schubert; and a trombone solo by Jaroslav Cimera backed by a cornet solo by Ernest Pechin, both members of the Chicago NBC Orchestra.

The latter two sides were recorded in Chicago in the Homer Rodeheaver Studios, according to Mr. Franck when interviewed in 1966 by Ray Wile for *Record Research*. They bear matrix numbers in an 85000 series, as do certain Autograph records recorded in 1924. It may mean that Homer Rodeheaver and Orlando R. Marsh, who produced Autograph records, had some business links.

JEWEL

There are two distinct kinds of Jewel records. One obviously stems from the first Grey Gulls of 1920–1923, since a record with a maroon label and design with lettering in gold has been found numbered L-855, exactly 200 numbers behind the same coupling on Grey Gull, and with the same prefix. The matrix number proves it to have been recorded in the opening weeks of 1921. By 1923 the allocating of catalog numbers seems to have been abandoned, and the label was changed to orange-yellow with red design and lettering. The earlier type is pressed into the wax in the usual way. The later is pasted onto a Grey Gull pressing.

The second Jewel label is from the Plaza Music Company's group of makes, dating from about April 1927 and continuing until 1932. The numbers start at 1000 and reach well into the 6000s before being discontinued by the American Record Corporation. For much of their life, the later Jewels ran in step with Oriole, 400 numbers behind. The labels were originally green with black lettering, and later became dull red with gold printing. Early on, the true Plaza matrix number was suppressed, and a control number used instead. This procedure was eventually abandoned.

It is not known for whom Jewel records were manufactured. They are pressed in cheap material, and the labels have an undeniably cheap appearance. Whereas their namesakes from Grey Gull are so rare as to be almost unheard-of, the Plaza kind are common, and usually in poor condition. They may have sold at 15¢ each. Little of any musical importance can be found on Jewel apart from some mild jazz items by the Original Indiana Five, various Irving Mills-Ben Pollack groups known loosely as the Whoopee Makers, and a handful of others. These can, of course, be found also on associated labels, occasionally with different takes.

KEEN-O-PHONE

This black and gold label graces a vertical-cut disc issued by the Keen-O-Phone Company of Philadelphia during World War I or just after it. The trademark shows the conductor of an orchestra in front of an external-horn machine. Ray Wile reports that some issues on this label appear also on Rex (q.v.).

KEITH PROWSE

The London music publishers, Keith Prowse & Co., Ltd. of 21 Denmark Street, London, W.C.2, in 1927 sponsored the issue on Parlophone of eight outstanding jazz records from OKeh. That was in February and March. The following autumn, probably November, a further selection appeared, this time on the Keith Prowse label, specially designed for the purpose. There seems to have been only one issue on Keith Prowse, comprising three records: two sides from Gennett splitting the record between Andy Preer and his Cotton Club Orchestra and Ross Gorman and his Fire-Eaters; two more Gennetts, these by Jelly James and his Fewsicians; and two Brunswick-Vocalion recordings by Johnny Dodds and his Black Bottom Stompers, featuring Louis Armstrong on cornet and Earl Hines on piano. These cost 3s. each at the time, or about 60 cents. The label is large, printed in black and gold on white, and the design eye-catching. The pressing was apparently done by the English Vocalion Gramophone Co. Ltd., and is inclined to be rather rough and noisy.

KEY

Key records were sold exclusively by Selfridge's, the London department store, in 1933 and perhaps during the early weeks of 1934. They were chosen by pioneer British disc-jockey Christopher Stone from the Panachord catalog, and pressed by Decca. Only about thirty seem to have been made available, and all those under pseudonym. Most of these are dance or popular vocal records, a considerable proportion coming from the American Melotone catalog. Adrian Rollini and his Orchestra appears as "The Rhythm Aces." Annette Hanshaw, to her horror, was renamed "Ethel Bingham."

London recordings have four-digit matrix numbers prefixed GB- or TB-. The catalog series runs from S-600. The labels are off-white, printed entirely in green. The upper half showed an ornate key lying on its back, surrounded by the words "KEY" RECORD and "Chosen for Selfridge's by Christopher Stone," all in the same off-white as the lower half.

KILDARE

It is a matter of opinion as to whether Kildare as a label merits a place in a book of this kind. By no means commonly met with, the copies known to exist are all English Vocalion B- series pressings (mostly from Gennett masters), with the brand name pasted over with a small oblong sticker bearing the word "Kildare" in ornamental white lettering on a black ground. Though not certain, it is believed that these were sold in one of the large department stores in London. The date would probably be late in 1927 and/or during the first part of 1928. The Vocalion label itself was withdrawn during that time, and it could be that the Kildare sticker was used to disguise and thus dispose of out-of-date stock.

So much for the theory. But Mr. John R. T. Davies clearly recalls seeing a Kildare record which had a Vocalion-style label (square panel, segments ornamented in gold on cream, cream or yellow title rectangle below the spindle hole), but with the word "Kildare" printed in its usual position *on the label itself*, not pasted on to it. This was in a junkshop in Brighton, Sussex. As he was looking exclusively for jazz records, or at least those obviously jazz-oriented, and as this was by some non-jazz artist, he did not buy it. Its existence suggests that the brand may have been a continuation of the yellow-label Vocalion B- series, marketed briefly after Vocalion itself was abandoned. But in the absence of further examples and of any catalogs, supplements or press announcements, the scope and extent of this mysterious relic of fifty years ago must remain a matter for speculation—and diligent research.

LA BELLE

The LaBelle label is just that. As far as is known, there is no such thing as a LaBelle record. Copies that have been examined show that the blue, sometimes black LaBelle label, with its ornate gold decoration and the complete anonymity that cloaks the artists, was pasted onto existing Columbia stock pressings. As these all seem to date from 1919–1920, it is assumed that a similar arrangement existed at that time between Columbia and the promotors of LaBelle as had previously been the case with Standard and Harmony and others (q.v.), where Columbia also insisted that no artists' names be disclosed. Those other labels used Columbia's catalog number, whereas LaBelle has its own numbering system in a 5000 series prefixed AL-. Records by Wilbur C. Sweatman and his Original Jazz Band are known to have been issued this way, and probably other Columbia artists as well.

LEEDS

Some of the labels in this book will be seen to be akin to works of art. Others have the merit of sobriety and good taste, but are simply functional. Yet others are cheap and garish, and there are those that lack any kind of design and thus lack character. But the most outlandish of them all is surely Leeds, the pre-1910 product of the Talkophone Company. It was a single-sided record offering nothing more, apparently, than the standard light pieces, instrumental solos and popular songs of the day, anonymously. But it did so under an all-gold label on which the entire decoration and lettering is embossed—in gold. The decoration consists of a wide band of assorted leaves, flowers and berries round the rim. The title credit and other (very sparse) details appear on a lozenge-shaped panel below the spindle hole. The origin of the masters is uncertain; it could be Columbia.

LENOX

This is another extremely rare label, bright red with gold lettering and a tasteful, almost graceful design of five arcs segmenting the upper part of the label. The lowest number known is 104 and the highest 106. Nothing is at present known about who produced it, although the labels show the same control numbers as do their opposite numbers on Oriole, one of the Plaza group; and in the wax round the rim of the label can be seen the Plaza Music Company's matrix number. The A side of Lenox 104—*Charley, My Boy*, by the Liberty Syncopators (as indeed most of the issues are termed)—turns out to be by Fletcher Henderson and his Orchestra. It is likely that others by this and other name bands recording on Banner and its better-known affiliates may also be on Lenox, pseudonymously.

LEVAPHONE

Levy's of 139 Whitechapel High Street, London, E.1 was famous among jazz record collectors during the late 1920s and the 1930s as the principal importers of first-class rarities on Victor, Columbia, OKeh, Brunswick and other labels. Prior to this, in 1926, the firm issued its own records on Levaphone. Some of these were by Cliff Edwards, better known as Ukulele Ike. Pressed from Pathe Actuelle masters, they were issued on a pale lilac label with violet lettering and design.

There was also a very brief issue of exactly three jazz items on a black label with a dull red panel inset containing title and pseudonymous artist credits. The inset was surmounted by the word LEVAPHONE in almost copperplate script. The motto, "Pure Tone" on the base of the L, extended to meet the last "e" of the name. There was also a Tudor rose and other red decorations. All six titles are ascribed to the Dixie Plantation Orchestra, but in fact the first two (A-101) are by Sonny Clay's Plantation Orchestra, and the second (A-102) by Vic Meyer's Orchestra. The third disc (A-103) splits between McKenzie's Candy Kids (*The Morning After*) and the Tennessee Tooters (*I Had a Sweet Mama*). These very rare jazz discs are all from the American Vocalion catalog. One might well wonder why no further items of similar calibre were forthcoming; but see Oriole.

LIBERTY MUSIC SHOP

The Liberty Music Shops of 450 and 795 Madison Avenue, and 10 East 59th Street, New York City, during the mid- and late 1930s not only sold all kinds of records to a fashionable clientele but launched its own label. It featured "society" dance bands like Emile Petti, selected jazz groups, sophisticated cabaret artists, and stars of Broadway musicals. Thus the catalog contained the famous point numbers by Beatrice Lillie from *At Home Abroad, Set to Music* and *Flying Colors;* Ethel Waters singing *Hottentot Potentate* and *Thief in the Night;* several of the sort of record that could not then be played in mixed company without causing embarrassment, sung by Bruz Fletcher or Nan Blakstone; and dance items by Ted Straeter and his Orchestra. Most famous were the four sessions in 1939 and 1940 by Lee Wiley with various jazz groups accompanying her, and three in 1936 and 1937 by harpist Casper Reardon playing sweet, soft, rhythmic jazz of a most attractive and unusual kind, with a small group.

Columbia (or the American Record Corporation) provided most of the studio facilities. Decca made some of the Beatrice Lillie sides, and Victor the Ethel Waters. The results, despite the sophisticated material and Liberty's Park Avenue customers and the fancy $1 price tag, often came in shabby pressings. The records were well recorded and deserved better. About two hundred were issued before 1942, on a white label with dark blue lettering and smart typography. Later there were a few more 78s, and a number of LPs reissuing past glories.

LINCOLN

Lincoln records were announced in January 1924 as a subsidiary of the flourishing Cameo label. They cost 50 cents each, and their slate black labels, printed mostly in gold, featured a cameo effect with the likeness of Abraham Lincoln on it. The numbering began at 2000, and reached about 3400 before the formation of the American Record Corporation linked Banner, Cameo, Pathe and their subsidiaries and affiliates, and it was decided that Lincoln was expendable. In its six years of life, many Cameo titles had been issued on Lincoln, many under pseudonyms or at least under names other than those used by Cameo. The label aimed mainly at the market that was not interested in who was playing or singing as long as the all-important tune was there and it could be danced to, or listened to with inexpensive pleasure.

LITTLE WONDER

These 5½-inch records were produced by Henry Waterson between 1911 and 1919. Columbia did the recording and pressing. Many of the titles were interesting, as they were recorded by Columbia for their own label by artists of the calibre of Al Jolson. Little Wonder artists, however, are anonymous. The records have no paper labels, the title and number being etched on the tiny central area. Taking their size and cheapness (10 cents each) into account, Little Wonder reproduces the music remarkably well. Various examples of orchestral and band ragtime, however truncated, have also been reported. The catalog and matrix numbers are the same, beginning apparently at 1 and reaching 1300 before being discontinued.

LUDGATE

This British label was produced by an untraced customer of the Vocalion Gramophone Company, who pressed a few hundred different issues between 1921 and 1924. These are of the usual type of material found on cheap labels in Britain and the United States: popular dance records, vocals and light classics and novelties (so-called). The American component was drawn first from Gennett, but mostly from Vocalion. In both cases the American matrix numbers are heavily expunged, and a G- series number substituted. Nothing of great importance has yet been found on Ludgate, whose catalog series varied according to the category of the music. Most of them seem to have been in the 6000s. The labels are cream, with brown printing, employing a very crude block lettering for the title and artist credits, and little in the way of design. Ludgate records have one unusual characteristic in that each label gives the title and a vague description of the reverse side.

LYRAPHONE

The Lyraphone Company operated from 117 Mechanic Street, Newark, N.J. for the first four months of 1921, moving to 704 South 11th Street in May of that year. The label drew on Paramount for its material. The same titles by the same artists and the same coupling, as a firm rule at least until 1925, appeared in the 11000 series shared with Embassy, Mitchell, Triangle and others; which suggests that the Bridgeport Die and Machine Company pressed them. See also Lyric.

LYRIC

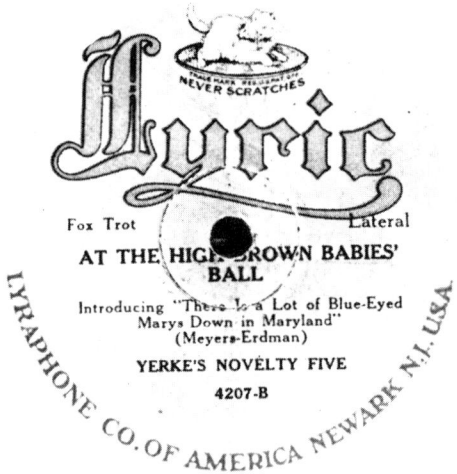

Lyric records were originally vertical-cut. They were manufactured by the Lyraphone Company of America, New York City, during World War I or immediately afterwards. This label is light blue, with gold lettering and the words LYRIC RECORD round the upper rim of the label, with a drawing of a lyre between the arc so formed. The lower half of the label shows a cat lying across a record and the slogan "Never scratches." The catalog serial is in a 6000 block, as are the matrix numbers.

In 1919 there was announced a Lyric lateral record with a grey label. The name LYRIC is printed in a kind of olde-Englyshe script, in orange, surmounted by the same cat, only a white one this time, and the same caption. The makers are shown round the lower rim, in orange, as Lyraphone Co. of America, Newark, N.J., U.S.A. The catalog serial is in a 4000 block, and matrix numbers seem to start at 12000. There do not appear to have been many Lyric lateral records issued, but in the autumn of 1920, a number of them appeared on Concert records (q.v.).

MADISON

This is the odd man out of the labels from the Grey Gull Company of Boston. It was produced from about 1926 until after the others in the group had been discontinued, including Grey Gull itself. Examples of 1931 tunes have been found in a matrix number range in the 4000s; yet Grey Gull and its affiliates or subsidiaries end at over 4000 in the summer of 1930 (see Grey Gull). This series, and one in a range from 5001 to 5041 (which by the titles covers 1926 to 1929), are the two series on Madison that are not part of the Grey Gull group.

Nor do the labels look obviously like those of the Boston parent. They are bright green with the word MADISON in gilt-edged white. There is a white and gold border, broken on either side behind two angel figures, the left holding a post horn and apparently playing it, the right holding a scroll. Both these are in gold, as are the words in minute upper-case lettering, "Madison Record Co." This firm had no corporate existence. The records were produced for sale in Woolworth's five-and-ten-cent stores, and cost a dime. They appear in red, black and dark brown wax. As might be expected in view of their price, the surfaces are noisy and do not wear well. The material offered is what was then regarded as ephemera.

Nevertheless, there are items on Madison that did not appear on Grey Gull or Radiex, as far as is known. One outstanding jazz issue that even merited reissue on the postwar Mouldy Fygge (sic) label is *St. Louis Blues* by a group named the Nashville Jazzers. Madison and Van Dyke are the only labels on which it was ever found, in each case bearing an obviously bogus matrix number which gives no clue as to when it was made, or by which musicians. It is obviously a coloured quintet. It was originally issued on Madison 50001 and subsequently changed, as all the 50000 series were, to a four-digit number, that omitted one of the zeros. A 6000 series is common to Madison and Radiex. One beginning at 8000 or 8001, can be found on Madison, Grey Gull and Globe. Another, starting at 8100 or 8101 is shared by Madison, Grey Gull, Radiex, Supreme and Supertone. The Madison 14000 series is paralleled by Grey Gull's 4000 block, except that Madison 14160 does not exist. It is numbered 4160, exactly as its Grey Gull mate. Madison's 18000, 22000 and 1600-1699 blocks can be found only on Madison. Exactly why these divers blocks of numbers were used—in some cases very briefly—is hard to figure out. There is the same variety of popular music on all of them: dance bands dominated by Mike Mosiello (trumpet) and Andy Sannella (clarinet, alto saxophone and steel guitar); vocals by Irving and/or Jack Kaufman and their prolific colleagues; Hawaiian and other instrumental "novelties"; and Wurlitzer organ solos. (It is worth noting another curiosity: Madison 1718 and Grey Gull 1718 are identical.)

Another strange feature about Madison records is that in some instances where Grey Gull or some other label of the family allocates a title to a number, Madison issues of the same number call it something different. Further, while the typography of Grey Gull and Radiex, at least, is identical, that of Madison is unlike the rest of the group, and indeed unlike all other labels. Madison's type is in *italics* throughout, even the catalog and matrix numbers. As with Grey Gull, large numbers of Madison records were obviously exported to England and sold in Woolworth's branches there—at half the American price and in competition with the British label specially provided for exclusive use in Woolworth's. How many Madisons were sold in England in this manner cannot now be hazarded, of course. While they are not as common as their eight-inch competitor, Eclipse, they still appear fairly frequently in British junk shops.

MAJESTIC

In the history of American record labels, there have been at least three named Majestic. The first was a seven-inch vertical-cut in the Edison style, operating from 247-253 West 19th Street, New York, where the Majestic Phonograph Company, Inc. had its head office (and studio?). The price was 25 cents, in keeping with the company slogan: "Gold in quality—silver in price." Despite this, very few copies can have been sold at the time, about 1917-1920, because the label is very rare. In fact, there is no physical label in the usual sense of a paper one pressed into or affixed to the shellac. The central area carries an etched design inverting the usual order of such things. The title and artist credits are above the spindle hole, with the manufacturer's name below it. An eagle with its wings spread out forms a kind of border to the lower rim of the design.

The second Majestic was also a short-lived issue, produced by the Olympic Disc Record Corporation for sale in Ross Stores, Inc. There are four known colours: black, blue, green and red, all printed in gold. The label name in openwork capitals across the widest part of the upper half of the label serves as a caption to a drawing of an ocean liner with four funnels, evidently the S.S. *Majestic*. The quality of Majestic records is quite good for the period, both as regards reproduction and surface noise. There are no matrix numbers visible in the wax, or shown on the labels. The catalog series is the same as Olympic's at the time (1923), in that the 1400s are dance records and the 1500s popular vocals and blues. This affinity between labels does not, however, mean that everything issued on Olympic automatically appeared on Majestic.

The following year, 1924, Ross Stores sold its own label (q.v.) briefly.

Toward the end of World War II, a third Majestic label made its debut, again with an eagle motif. These records are outside the scope of this book.

MANDEL

The Mandel Manufacturing Company of Chicago began operations on January 4, 1921 from company headquarters at 1455 West Congress Street. The masters used for pressing the records were made in New York mostly by Earl Jones. As head of Standard Records, a record brokering agency, he dealt in his own masters and various others. The time was 1919–1921, and possibly another year or two either way. The matrix serials are in a block of S-100 upwards, and were allocated indiscriminately to original Jones recordings and such as Lyric and Arto masters. The only known catalog series is in the 4000s. The label is quite attractive. A narrow gold edge surrounds a design in two shades of blue. The upper part is light blue-green, with the name Mandel in script in dark blue, outlined in gold. The lower part is dark blue, with all credits in gold and the manufacturer's name in pale blue-green around the lower rim. These records are extremely rare. The only announcement to the trade was in April 1921—probably the only foray the company made into the record market.

MARATHON

There was a Marathon record produced in England before World War I. It was a very unusual cut in that it was vertical but the groove was V-shaped and required a special type of soundbox. It was long-playing in that it outran the conventional 78 rpm record by several minutes. Nevertheless, it made no strong appeal to the public, and vanished quickly.

The American Marathon which concerns us in this book was an even shorter-lived venture. The Nutmeg Record Corporation announced to the trade in November 1928 that its new seven-inch record was ready for sale, to be known as Marathon. The jackets make some unusual remarks in their efforts to make the project a commercial success: "Marvelous Musical Miniatures—They Play the Latest Hits as Clear, as Loud, as *LONG* as the Usual 10-inch Records." The publicity department followed with the ambiguous (and, if taken the wrong way, ludicrous) piece of reasoning: "Why carry a clock when a watch will do? Done only by Nutmeg Record Corporation." The fine thread of the cutting in the grooves certainly ensured about two and a half minutes of playing per side. But the tendency to over-modulation made for a distorted effect rarely found on ten-inch discs playing slightly longer. After a few months, the label was discontinued. It is glossy black with gold printing. There is no design, simply the word MARATHON across the upper part, just above the spindle hole. The credits were below. The numbering began at 200 and the matrix series continued in the Emerson sequence in the 31000 block. It is believed the price was 15 cents a copy.

MARCONI VELVET TONE

This label is the only result of the heralded liaison between the Columbia Phonograph Company and Guglielmo Marconi, the eminent Italian scientist and radio pioneer. The label appeared on the American market in October 1907. It had a brief life, only a few months. Examples of the record are very rare today. The principle of the product is as modern as today: noiseless, unbreakable plastic records. It was half a century ahead of its time. The label insisted that though it was as "wonderful as wireless," the records must be played with gold-plated needles only, with each needle to be used twelve times. The advantages of having an unbreakable record—it did not make a scratching noise, and could be played twelve times without a needle change—were counteracted by the fact that ordinary needles, costing much less even though supposed to be used once only, could not be used. They ripped up the plastic grooves under the heavy metal arms of the time. Since the Marconi Velvet Tone record offered ordinary musical fare that could be obtained on (admittedly noisier) discs at the same price or less, records that could be played with cheap steel needles that did not wreak immediate havoc, the public soon passed a vote of no-confidence on Signor Marconi's invention, and continued to buy standard Columbia and Victor records featuring great artists that Marconi was never able to provide.

The label, printed in blue, white and gold, included Marconi's signature and details of the patents in white, with title and other credits in gold. It is quite impressive, like the advertising campaign that launched the records. The series began at 01 and carried its own catalog-and-matrix number. If a machine with a light tone arm and soundbox had been available at the time, the Marconi Velvet Tone-Columbia combine could have conquered the market. Forty-one years later, Columbia would pioneer long-playing records, noiseless and unbreakable. But then, Columbia had the machines to match, and thus sounded the death-knell of the 78 rpm disc.

MASTER

Impresario Irving Mills introduced the Master record in February 1937. It and its cheaper sister Variety (q.v.) offered a quality catalog that featured artists like Duke Ellington, Cab Calloway, Will Hudson, the new Raymond Scott Quintette, a number of jazz groups drawn from the Ellington band, and studio units whose records were aimed at jazz connoisseurs. But the venture foundered before the year was out. The few dozen records that were issued were transferred, along with the artists themselves, to Brunswick, the firm that had pressed the Master records.

The black label is printed in gold, the upper half showing an orchestra in session, decorated with triplets and semi-quavers. The brand name in ornate semi-Gothic is shown in an arc below the design, with the legend "Follow The Master." The catalog series beings at MA-101, and the matrix numbers have their own sequence beginning at M-100. This was continued, often with the prefix altered to WM-, on Brunswick and Vocalion, and even Columbia, until 1940. The pressings, like those on Brunswick at the time, are often rough.

MAYFAIR

Mayfair records were never sold through shops or stores, on newsstands or by mail-order. They were *exchanged* for coupons found in Ardath cigarettes, which were on sale in Britain at the time (1931-1933). The cigarette company issued regular leaflets showing what new records had been added to its catalog. Smokers could choose from among these. It is said that the London department store of Selfridge's bought up unused stock from Ardath in 1933 and sold them in its Oxford Street premises, at what price I have been unable to determine. The records are ten-inch and are numbered in a G-2000 series, at least to start with. After about G-2255, the first digit was dropped. The series continued to about G-330, at which point Ardath withdrew their offer and not long afterwards disappeared from the cigarette market.

The records present a "quality" appearance. They were pressed simultaneously by Edison Bell, Piccadilly and Warner-Brunswick. The glossy black label gives over most of the upper half to a block of gold with a small black insert bearing the brand name in flowing script. The surfaces are smooth and the recording excellent for the most part.

Mayfair offered a wide range of music drawn from the catalogs of the firms that did the pressing. Everything was issued under a pseudonym. The American Melotone catalog yielded gems by Joe Venuti & Eddie Lang and their All-Star Orchestra (as "The New York Stompers"), Benny Goodman and his Orchestra (re-named "Cliff Bryan and his Orchestra"), and Red Nichols' Captivators (as "Club Albany Orchestra"). The "Fifth Avenue Dance Band" is Howard Godfrey's Waldorfians, usually with Al Bowlly singing, these being London recordings from Piccadilly. Later on, Gene Kardos and his Orchestra playing *Business in F* and *Business in Q* (G-2193) are described, not altogether wrongly, as "The Rhythm Boys." "Marion Lee" is Annette Hanshaw, and "Milt Barson and his Orchestra" is Adrian Rollini and his Orchestra. And there are many others that offer interesting jazz solos. On the other hand, the titles supplied by Edison Bell seem to be of no interest as jazz or dance music. They are conventional light classics in simplified form. Some issues have the catalog number prefixed G-1.

Some Mayfair labels state that the titles on them were selected by Christopher Stone, Britain's first disc jockey and for many years London Editor of *The Gramophone*. His catholic taste, and his sympathy for hot jazz as well as the more conventional dance music and other popular forms, are quite remarkable in one who was not at that time a young man.

MEDALLION

This was a label of the post-World War I phonograph boom that seems to have died in the inevitable slump that followed in 1921. The trademark name was registered and use claimed by the Baldwin Piano Company of 124 West 4th Street, Cincinnati, Ohio, on June 25, 1919. The highest number in the series of ten-inch issues beginning at (presumably) 8101 is 8318, and that was made by Emerson on July 20, 1921; so it is unlikely that the life of the label extended beyond the early autumn of that year.

All Medallion issues were from the Emerson repertoire, and thus have matrix numbers in 4000 or 41000 blocks. Some of them are nine-inch pressings like Emerson, and are numbered 801 upwards. They do not seem to have reached higher than 866, however. These have matrix numbers in the 3000s.

The price was $1 for most of Medallion's life, but in April 1921 it was reduced to 85 cents. The label design does not change for the entire period of its existence. It is unusually attractive without being garish. The border is decorated broadly with cone-shaped figures. The title and artist credits are printed on a panel below the spindle hole, flanked on each end by an Olympic torch. The lower edge follows the curvature of the label. For about the first year, the colour scheme was in two shades of brown with white facing. Later it was dark green, printed entirely in gold.

The overwhelming majority of Medallion records are dance items. There are strangely few popular vocals. Indeed, there are about as many marches, sacred and Hawaiian issues as there are the usual Billy Murray-Irving Kaufman-Henry Burr type. Emerson seems not to have leased its personality records by George Jessel or Eddie Cantor to Baldwin for issue on Medallion. Those that were released on the Cincinnati label seem in the main to have retained their Emerson identity (although Walter Scanlan becomes "Walter Sullivan"; but Eubie Blake and Noble Sissle appear both as themselves and as "Willie Black and Ruby Blake").

MELODOGRAPH

An obscure Edison-cut vertical disc that probably lasted for a few months in the 1917–1920 era, Melodograph was the product of the Melodograph Corporation of New York. Apparently all issues were seven-inch. The label is black and white, embodying a representation of a lyre. The title and artist credits appear in black on a white panel below the spindle hole, and the manufacturer's name in white on black below this.

MELODY

This is another of the Olympic-originated labels. As far as can be ascertained, it bears the same catalog numbers in a 1000 series, no visible matrix numbers, and the same couplings as Olympic (q.v.). The records were issued during 1923.

MELOTO

Meloto piano rolls were on sale in England from sometime just after the end of World War I until the late 1930s, possibly later still. The lifespan of Meloto records, however, was very much shorter—from sometime in 1922 to about 1927, perhaps not as late. In this time some 600 records were apparently issued, beginning at S-1000. Though one of the cheaper British records, Melotos are very rarely met with. Meloto relied on the Aco repertoire, and may have had exactly the same lifespan (see Aco). The labels are violet, with a great deal of filigree ornamentation in gold in segments of the label formed by a hexagon, and more decoration above the word MELOTO in stylized olde-Englyshe script. The maker's name—the Meloto Co. Ltd., London—is shown at the bottom of the label. But this is almost certainly a subsidiary of Vocalion, even as Aco was, since Vocalion pressed all known copies.

Everything was issued under pseudonyms. The catalog consists of the usual pedestrian fare: dance music of little jazz interest, popular vocals and comic songs, light popular classics, instrumentals. The earliest issues probably include a few from the Gennett catalog, and there are believed to be other Gennetts among the last Meloto releases. Most of the American element occur between S-1100 and S-1600, and are from Vocalion. The matrix numbers are always tooled out, leaving no trace except occasionally. Under a row of X's showing through the labels, however, it is possible to determine the Vocalion matrix serial.

MELOTONE

Melotone was the subsidiary, less expensive label to Brunswick. It was introduced by the Warner-Brunswick Corporation on November 13, 1930. It survived the amalgamation with Banner, Cameo, Perfect and other labels to form the American Record Corporation in 1932, and continued to appear regularly until the spring of 1938.

The original label was a striking blue with silver printing. Today, when many 45 rpm records are printed in silver (are any still printed in gold?), this may not seem strange. But then it made an impact by its different appearance. The quality of recording was less impressive, unfortunately. Even after the Warner Brothers film company divested itself of the record side of its business, things were not noticeably improved for some time. A tendency to shrillness and a gritty surface belied the tradename. This is a pity, because for blues and hillbilly collectors, Melotone is a happy hunting ground. Jazz reissues and originals abound too. There are many interesting dance records by top bands of the time. The staple vocalist was Chick Bullock, who with studio groups invariably described as "his Levee Loungers," contributed a rich seam of music that was a neat compromise between the commercial output of Tin Pan Alley and small-band jazz by many of the top New York (and sometimes other) white musicians.

The important blues artists on Melotone include stellar names: Walter Roland, Bessie Jackson, Pinewood Tom (Josh White), Buddy Moss and Blind Boy Fuller. Country-and-western artists range from Goebel Reeves, the Texas Drifter, to Tex Ritter, via the Carter Family; not to mention Gene Autry, Bill Cox, Cliff Carlisle and Red Foley. There are personalities such as Jack Oakie, Bing Crosby (reissued from Brunswick), Frances Langford, Alice Faye, Eddie Cantor, Nick Lucas and Annette Hanshaw. And in the rawest folk music idiom, there was Leadbelly—Huddie Ledbetter.

The above all appear in a series issued as M-12000 to M-13457 (November 1930 to July 1935). Then the numbering system was changed for all ARC labels except Brunswick and Vocalion. Under the new system, the last two figures of the year, the month in that year, and the number of the record in either the popular or the race-and-hillbilly series formed the full catalog number. This meant that the sixth record in the popular issue for October 1935 would be numbered 35-10-06. If it was the sixth in the race series, the number would be 35-10-56. The numbering of race records began at 51, popular items at 01. From November 1935, the first part of this composite numbering system was altered to the last digit of the year. Thus, our sixth issue that month in the popular series would be 5-11-06. In race or country-and-western it became 5-11-56.

There were other Melotone series. In March 1931, the M-16000 block marked a group of Mexican issues that ended within the year at MS-16086. A series of fifty-three Cajun records, beginning at 18000, ended in August 1932, having also been launched in March 1931. A series of Hawaiian records, recorded mostly in Honolulu, appeared between June 23 and September 1, 1937 and were numbered 21001 to 21015.

For a time, between 1934 and 1936, the blue area of the label was changed to dark green, and the silver changed to gold. Later, the original blue and silver design was readopted, and with slight modifications of the "small-print" wording, continued to the end. The price of Melotone records was 50 cents, reduced to 35 cents in 1935. They were issued in England on Imperial, Panachord, Decca, Rex and Vocalion.

MELVA

Although this label claims that the trademark was registered at the United States Patent Office, no trace could be found by researcher Carl Kendziora. The company that produced the label was, appropriately, the Melva Record Company of Brooklyn, New York. All its twenty issues came from masters also used by Cardinal (C-700 series) and Lyric (14000 series) via Cardinal. The catalog series apparently began at 8001, and the highest known is 8020. The latest recording found on Melva is dated at the end of November 1921. Since there was probably only one issue, a batch of twenty, the November date suggests that the issues appeared early in 1922.

The known labels are in three colours: black, red, or green, with gold ornamentation which never changes. It shows the word MELVA on a broad gold bar across the top half of the label, almost tangential with the spindle-hole. The typography of this word is very unusual, and adds a strangely Oriental appearance to the design. Above the name is a motif that could have been lifted straight off the walls of a Pharaoh's tomb.

What happened to Melva; what, if anything, the word means, we do not know. It remains one of the more visually attractive of the myriads of labels on the American market in the years immediately following World War I. Nothing of aural interest, however, has turned up on the label!

MERRIT

The Kansas City music store of Winston Holmes produced the Merrit record during the late 1920s. As far as is known, the recordings are original, and obviously not the work of fully professional engineers. The rather bizarre design of the label includes a clown mask in cap and collar to the left and right of the spindle hole, facing inwards. Two quavers decorate the brand name, itself appearing in fancy lettering, and all this design is in gold on a mauve background. Details of the performance appear on a small off-white panel set below this design.

Despite the amateurish quality of the recording, and the rather garish appearance of the label, the Merrit repertoire contains some very interesting material by Negro artists. Outstanding among these are sides by George E. Lee and his Orchestra which are almost unheard of. There are also a few blues by local talent, and some sermons. The catalog series is in a block of numbers from 2000 upwards, but it is doubtful if more than a dozen or so different records were ever issued on Merrit.

METEOR

Described on the label as "The Star of the Talking Machine World," Meteor records made their debut in 1919 at the height of the post-World War I phonograph boom. The design of the label is unusual. It shows an elliptical figure around the spindle-hole bearing the above legend and the address, Piqua, Ohio, U.S.A. The brand name is in erratic ornate script, with a star and five gold rays to the right. The title and other credits are given below this design, with the title of the reverse side, described thus, in the segment above the central design.

Numbering seems to have begun at 1200 or 1201. The matrix series probably began at 31000 or 31001. The label is exceptionally rare. Apart from a collection of dance and near-jazz items of the period, the releases were of little musical interest.

METRO

Produced during the early 1920s by the Metropolitan Record Company of New York, this was apparently a label devoted to Irish music. It is black, with the entire design and lettering in green, not the usual gold. It includes the opening eight bars of *The Harp That Once Thro' Tara's Halls* on a stave fitted round the rim of the label, and an Irish harp with an angel figurehead surrounded by eighteen shamrocks! The only known issues are traditional Irish folk songs. Their origin is unknown. There are no catalog numbers, and the matrix numbers vary so much as not to fit into any known series. *Eileen Alannah* by Thomas Troxel, for example, has 135 on the label. In the wax are 14609 and 10725, the latter destroyed but legible. The other side has *The Meeting of the Waters* sung by Bobby MacWhaite: 139 on the label, 586-1 in the wax.

Another Metro label, also Irish but having no connection with the foregoing, also appeared during the 1920s, "made expressly for Tom Ennis, New York." Tom Ennis was an Irish pipes player who made a number of sides in New York for OKeh in 1921. The music on the record made specially for him is not his. It is a typical Irish patriotic song backed by a version of *The Foggy Dew*, both sung by one Thos. O'Kelly; but its origin is unknown. The label is red with gold lettering and design.

METRO-GOLDWYN-MAYER

The relatively recent label known as M-G-M, originally featuring artists under contract to the film company of that name, is well-known as a major popular label today. It began in 1947. As early as 1928, however, there was a black-labelled Columbia product whose issues were numbered in a 1001-P series. It relied on songs from M-G-M films that were recorded and issued on Harmony. If the Harmony issue was backed by a song not from a Metro-Goldwyn-Mayer film, the record issued under the famous lion trademark and the motto *Ars Gratia Artis* was re-coupled with one that was. Consequently, there is no "marrying" the Harmony-Diva-Velvet Tone combine with these records. As the labels tell us, they were designed for use in Loew's theatres everywhere. The -P series was used for special records of all kinds produced by Columbia in the earliest days of the talking picture industry (see also Publix). Metro-Goldwyn-Mayer's issues consisted of agreeable but rarely outstanding dance records, occasionally varied with sides by such artists as Annette Hanshaw and Irving Kaufman.

METROPOLE

The first Metropole records appeared on the British market in April 1928. They cost 3s. (about 60 cents) and seemed well made, smooth-surfaced products, electrically recorded and of a high standard—until it became obvious that the same titles by the same artists were being issued on Piccadilly a few months later at half the price.

About 300 Metropole records were issued between that first list and the last, just over two years later. Numbers ranged from 1001 to something slightly over 1300. For the last fifty or so, American recordings from the Grey Gull complex were used, as on Piccadilly. Early on, there had been some strange couplings on Metropole. Irish ballads backed by Gounod's *Ave Maria* as a violin solo; a dance band playing a fox trot on one side with a male voice chorus singing *Polly Wolly Doodle* on the other—these are examples. This curious policy was soon abandoned, however, in favor of some interesting music: Sir Edward German conducting a studio symphony orchestra playing his *Henry VIII* Suite; Fred Elizalde and his Rhythmicians playing two dance numbers with Al Bowlly singing; and from Grey Gull, a jazz quartet of unusual quality playing *In Harlem's Araby* under the name of The Bohemian Dance Band. Hot solos can be found on records credited to Al George's Red Pepper Band, George Fisher and his Kit-Cat Band, and the Montmartre Mad Hatters.

The Grey Gull masters are in their usual 3000-4000 series. Metropoles bearing matrix serials other than these are in a 1000-4000 range, usually prefixed XX, which are from Piccadilly. Very early, there was a series beginning at M-1, which seems to be original. The labels are glossy black with gold printing. The upper half of the label depicts in line drawing the Big Ben clock face and tower, with the motto, "A Striking Record."

Some records from the first Metropole listing were part of a fund-raising campaign, the proceeds of which were donated to private hospitals. Selected records were sold for 2s. 6d. (about 50 cents). Along with the records went a Metropole Ballot. Competitors had to estimate the popularity of the records on the list. The first winner, Major J. Reynolds of Kelvedon in Essex, marched off with one thousand pounds (then about $4,000).

MITCHELL

A news item in *The Phonograph and Talking Machine Weekly* for September 10, 1924 reported that the president of the Bridgeport Die and Machine Company was "on the road." Among other cities in a wide-sweeping itinerary, he was bound for Detroit, Mich. It would seem that one short-lived result of this odyssey was an arrangement with the Mitchell Phonograph Corporation of 3000 Gratiot Avenue to launch its own label. Mitchell would use BD&M for its supply base and the Emerson-Radiex-Oriole complex as its source for masters. The BD&M Mitchells—no one ever calls them "the Mitchell," but that is how they are labelled—are a rare breed, distinguished-looking in chocolate brown with lettering in gold. The brand name sweeps at an angle of about 30 degrees to the horizon across the upper half of the label. It is in copperplate script with the word RECORD in italic block capitals on an underlining "tail" from the last letter of the name. Bridgeport Die and Machine went bankrupt in July 1925, so the arrangement with Mitchell cannot have been much longer than a year, if that long. The fact that known specimens all bear the same catalog numbers as the same items on such labels as Broadway, Puretone, Triangle and Lyratone suggests that perhaps they were sold only in the Gratiot Avenue store. Indeed, Carl Kendziora suggests that they may never have been *sold* at all in the normal way, but rather may have been given away with one of the company's machines. Whatever the facts, the BD&M Mitchell disappeared early in 1925.

But that is not the end of the story. Early in 1926, judging by the material on known examples, the corporation took another flier at marketing records, by some method or other. This time the source was the Grey Gull catalog. These Mitchell records bore green labels with gold lettering in the Grey Gull typography of the time, and Grey Gull catalog numbers. This proved to be a brief appearance, possibly for one issue only.

MONTGOMERY WARD

This, one of the most famous of all mail-order houses, featured records in its catalog back in the 1930s. At first they were pressed by Victor from items in its own or its subsidiary Bluebird's repertoire. Some excellent jazz and blues items were used, together with country-and-western recordings of great interest and rarity. The series was numbered in four figures, prefixed M-. The labels are black or dark blue with gold lettering. A design of semi-circles covered the entire upper half of the label concentrically, with the name of the label appearing in block capitals round the lower rim. Being a Victor product, they are of course of excellent recording and pressing quality. A further series from Eli Oberstein's Varsity label was issued in 1939-1940, again with similar material. This series did not last long—nor did its parent label (q.v.).

MOXIE

This was a label for one record only, designed to advertise the soft drink of the same name. Both sides feature the same advertising jingle. One side is sung by Arthur Fields, the other played as a fox trot by Harry Raderman and his Orchestra. Both were made by Gennett in its New York studio at the turn of 1921-1922. The label shows a man holding a bottle of the beverage with obvious pleasure. Not surprisingly, there is no catalog number.

MOZART

A vertical-cut of the Edison type from the 1917-1920 era, apparently associated with Lyric (q.v.). The dull blue label is printed in gold. The words "Mozart Record" and "Mozart Talking Machine Co." circumscribe the label between two circles. A portrait of the composer is shown in a white circle above the brand name in gold script. The catalog numbers are in a 9000 series. Matrix numbers seem to be in two parallel blocks: a 6000 block followed by a take digit, followed by another number in a 1000 block synchronized with the first.

MUSE

This label, produced by the American Record Manufacturing Company of Framingham, Mass., had a short but checkered career. Muse began when Cameo did in February 1922. It used Cameo masters, catalog numbers and artist credits until just before the end of the first hundred issues (starting at 200 or 201). Production under the Muse name was later resumed with numbers starting at 300 or 301, as far as can be traced. But on these, for the first forty or so, Plaza-Banner, Emerson and Grey Gull masters were used, and under pseudonyms. After this brief flirtation with non-Cameo material, Muse took up with Cameo again, but with different catalog numbers and couplings, and still more pseudonyms. The highest Muse number, as reported by Carl Kendziora, is 429. Mr. Kendziora points out that Cameo's sidekick label, Tremont (q.v.), seems to start at about that number. He suggests that Muse was originally pressed for Kress Stores; *vide* the Muse sleeves. But Kress dropped the line, leaving the Framingham factory with Muse records to sell. Unable to find a replacement customer, they probably changed the name to Tremont and marketed the discs themselves for about another hundred issues.

The Muse label is black, with all printing in gold, and the word MUSE in heavy block letters on a treble stave of music—of a sort—in the form of a scroll. There is no maker's name or store outlet on the labels until after the brief use of non-Cameo masters—which lends credibility to Carl Kendziora's ingenious theory.

NADSCO

One of the earlier affiliated labels in the Grey Gull complex, Nadsco probably made its first appearance in 1922. The records were still being issued in 1925. The usual label is maroon, with gold lettering and a design utilizing a hexagon in a gold ring. The segments were filled with a curlicue pattern, and the hexagon itself contained the brand name in bold lower-case type, with the usual credits in Grey Gull typography. There is no maker's or any other name shown. Although an inexpensive type of label, Nadsco records are not common compared with others in the same group. One of the most interesting issues is Nadsco 1283, on which Negro bandleader and arranger Leroy Smith and his Orchestra play *Harlem's Araby*, which also appears on Everybody's, Globe and Radiex. The band made very few records, and most of those are on uncommon labels like Blu-Disc, Everybody's, and Up-To-Date—from which session came the Nadsco issue.

NASSAU

Nassau records were pressed from the earliest Imperial (q.v.) masters during the first decade of the century. Many if not all of them are pseudonyms or even anonymous. The labels are dull black, with the brand name on a scroll across the top half in gold. All credits, such as are shown at all, appear on the lower part. As far as can be traced, there is nothing of great musical or historical importance here, although it is possible that some early ragtime music by banjoist Vess L. Ossman and various studio orchestras may have been issued.

NATIONAL

There have been four American record labels under this name. The first two were more or less contemporaneous. One was the product of the National Certificate Company of New York. It was pressed by the Bridgeport Die and Machine Company and had catalog numbers in the same 11000 series as Puritan and others. The other National was the product of the National Record Exchange Company of Iowa City. It had a 12000 catalog series. Unlike its namesake—which was also derived from Paramount—this National is linked with Paramount's popular series. Thus, National 12190 is the same coupling as Paramount 20190. The New York-based National number for these is 11198.

The date of these two series is 1922-1924. In 1925 came a third National, derived from the Emerson catalog of that date, in a 1000 catalog series. The fourth National made its debut toward the end of World War II and is outside the scope of this book.

The original National issues from Paramount contain much of interest to jazz collectors but little else other than conventional dance music and popular vocals. Pseudonyms for such names as Fletcher Henderson and Jelly Roll Morton (or "Marton" as National 12251 prints it) are not used as a rule, but a great many bands of no great consequence were dubbed "Frisco Syncopators." The Original Memphis Five and the California Ramblers both have representative issues on National. The labels are blue with gold lettering and design.

203

NATIONAL MUSIC LOVERS, INC.

This somewhat unwieldy name, and the deluxe appearance of the variously coloured shields on the labels, suggest a connoisseurs' limited edition available by subscription basis at a handsome figure. But in fact all the issues on this presumably cheap make came from Paramount, both types of Emerson, Olympic, and latterly Plaza-Banner, etc. The first known issue was in October 1922, at which time the organization producing them was operating from 354 4th Avenue, New York City. By the time the label disappeared in 1928, the address had changed to 327 West 36th Street.

The principal catalog series started at 1000 and reached at least 1208. Within this were a number of series, all with shields on a background including a stripe to the left of the spindle hole. The shields were usually graced with gold bands, and each shield had its own distinctive colour scheme:

Series	Shield colour	Band colour	Stripe colour	Lettering colour
Band and Concert	Blue	Gold	Blue and white	Gold
Dance Series No. 1	Red	Gold	Red and white	Gold
Dance Series	Red	Gold	Red and white	Gold
Hymns and Sacred Song	Dark green	Gold	Green and white	Gold
Irish Song	Gold	Light green	Gold and white	Black
Latest Song and Dance Series	Red	Gold	Red and white	Gold
Novelty	Orange	Gold	Orange and white	Gold
Old Time Song (originally)	Gold	Black	Gold and white	Black
Old Time Song (later)	Black	Gold	Black and white	Gold
Operatic Song	Purple	Gold	Purple and white	Gold

The original Old Time Song series and the Irish series have the name of the make in black across the top of the shield, along with the category name. All the others are white.

The dance series—all of them—provide the only records likely to be of interest to collectors. Here the jazz collector can have a field day with Fletcher Henderson, the Six Hottentots, Jack Pettis, and the California Ramblers from Plaza (some via Pathe), not to forget Fred Hall titles, credited correctly, from the Emerson group. These were all derivatives from other labels. But there were two series comprising records evidently made either by or for National Music Lovers. These are numbered 101 to 116 and are Old Time Songs (the first of two such series above) and 201 to 212, the Operatic Songs. Another curious occurrence early in the career of this label is the duplication of catalog numbers, 1032 to 1039. One issue has a bright red shield and is from Plaza. The other has a dark red shield and is from Paramount. The A side of each pair is credited to the Master Melody Makers, the B to the Music Lovers Dance Orchestra. The first fourteen supplements are each allocated a letter of the alphabet, A to N, but after this the designation was dropped. The last fifty issues or so are described, correctly, as electrically recorded.

It is probable that some at any rate of these series were sold through the mail. A 1924 advertisement offers eight Old Time Favorites for $2.98 plus postage. The records could be returned without charge if found unsatisfactory. This may explain why NML records are not rare compared with some of their contemporaries. The recording quality is as good as comparable records of the period, as are the surfaces.

NATION'S FORUM

These records, recorded and produced by Columbia, are among the most valuable, historically, of any ever produced during the 78 rpm era. They consist entirely of the voices of prominent political personalities of 1918 to 1920, and in addition those of General Pershing, Commander-in-Chief of the Allied Armies, and of Eamon de Valera, American-born Irish-Spaniard who fought to establish first the Irish Free State, then the Republic of Ireland, as a political entity apart from the United Kingdom.

The idea of recording these voices, most of whom never made any other records, was that of a famous attorney from St. Louis named Guy Golterman. He is himself on record (in print, not sound) as saying that on a visit to the Library of Congress in 1917, he was musing on the fact that although Washington's Farewell and Lincoln's Gettysburg Address are there for the reading, their voices are lost to us. But why, now, should their political descendants not be recorded?

Soon after the entry of the United States into World War I, the State Department set up the Committee on Public Information for issuing war news to the press and for conducting speech campaigns by 40,000 public speakers called the Four Minute Men. The Committee was urged by Golterman to record the famous of the time in speeches designed to encourage the war effort. It lost no time in arranging with Columbia to record such as Secretary of the Navy Josephus Daniels; labor leader Samuel Gompers (he was the first in line); Secretary of the Treasury William Gibbs McAdoo; and many others. These records, and those that followed throughout 1920 in preparation for the Presidential election that year, appeared in a variety of labels—some green, some gold, mostly black. In many cases the label featured a photograph of the speaker. (One exception is the 1920 record devoted to a talk on "Law and Order" given by the Governor of Massachusetts, one Calvin Coolidge. Eighteen recordings were made in 1918, all ten-inch. The twenty-six numbered and three unnumbered 1920 recordings are all twelve-inch.

The speakers for the war effort recorded in New York between January and June, 1918. General Pershing appears to have recorded in France. His record has an English matrix number. The 1920 campaigners recorded, as often as not, in their homes. At $2 for a few minutes' speech, blank-backed or coupled with some standard and unrelated orchestral title from the Columbia domestic catalog, Nation's Forum records were not the kind to attract vast sales. Once their purpose had been served (the War won, the President elected), the public viewed them as obsolete. It was fine to go to a political meeting and hear the voice of an important member of the Washington hierarchy, but few customers cared to pay heavily for a recording of the event. Hence, some of these records have never been found. And when the election results were actually broadcast from Station KDKA in Pittsburgh on the night of November 2, 1920, the public realised that by buying a radio they could get all the political speeches they wanted free, without even having to wind a motor or change a needle. It was the *coup de grâce* for Nation's Forum.

NEW COMFORT

A rare member of the Grey Gull complex. Numbered in a 5000 series, it contains no outstanding collectors' items as far as is known.

NEW FLEXO

These black flexible records made their debut on the American market in 1925, probably about February. By the autumn they had vanished. (See also Flexo, a much later vintage.) New Flexo records have no paper labels. The brand name, title and artist credits are printed rather crudely in brown on the smooth central area. It requires little effort to remove them. Hence some have turned up that are completely unidentifiable. The source shown on surviving legible copies is the Warner Record Company of Kansas City, Mo. Since the items in the slender catalog are all originals recorded in Kansas City rather than leased from New York jobbers, they offer no well known names and little of interest except to jazz collectors, who have been known to find intriguing items by, say, Johnnie Campbell's Orchestra. Much research remains to be done on this strange brand. In view of its home base, it could be rewarding to those interested in recordings of territory bands and artists.

NEW PHONIC

Carl Henry, Inc., of New York City produced this label in 1927-1928. It drew from the Plaza-Banner catalog, suppressing the original matrix numbers in favour of the 1000 series of control numbers used on such Plaza affiliates as Banner, Jewel and Oriole. Pseudonyms for the various dance bands and popular singers that seem to have constituted the catalog—if that is the correct term— were in general use. The label is very rare, and thus it is difficult to assess what Plaza material may have been used. Technically the product is no better and no worse than its associates in the group: electrically recorded, but nasal and lacking in bass clarity, and with rather gritty surfaces. The design of the label is attractive. It is crimson with gold printing, the upper rim being decorated with a stave of music, with the words NEW PHONIC in two lines of type. The catalog numbers are apparently in the 1000 range. But the only known copies are centred round 1200, and may be limited to only a handful of issues.

NORDSKOG

"First on the Pacific Coast," claim the labels of Nordskog records. They were introduced in 1921 by Andrae Nordskog of Santa Monica, Cal., where one of the offices of the Nordskog Phonograph Recording Company was situated. There was also a studio and factory in Los Angeles. This factory had the capacity to produce a million records annually, according to a document produced many years later by Nordskog himself. Whether this claim was ever put to the test is doubtful. Nordskog records of any kind are exceptionally rare.

They are also outstandingly interesting. They have a known catalog number range of only 3001 to 3027. But in that collection of little over two dozen issues are to be found the only known recording by "Cyclonic" Eva Tanguay (*I Don't Care*, of course); some songs by folk-song arranger Thurlow Lieurance, accompanying his wife; piano solos by Charles Wakefield Cadman, composer of such standard ballads as *At Dawning;* the initial recordings of Abe Lyman's Orchestra from the Cocoanut Grove in the Ambassador Hotel, Los Angeles, and of Herb Wiedoeft's Cinderella Roof Orchestra. The most interesting to a jazz and/or blues collector are six sides by Kid Ory's Jazz Band, under the name of "Spikes' Seven Pods of Pepper." Two of them are instrumental, two accompany Ruth Lee, and two back Roberta Dudley. These were all issued with the picturesque Sunshine (q.v.) label pasted over the black and gold Nordskog.

These historic records, the first ever made by a Negro New Orleans jazz band, were recorded, it seems, in Spikes Brothers' Music Store at 12th and Central Avenue, Los Angeles. They certainly do not sound like they were made in the professionally equipped studio that we are told was used by Nordskog early in the 1920s. The balance of the instruments is very poor, and the whole band is under-recorded. In addition, there is little to suggest that here was a pioneer jazz band from the very birthplace of the idiom. Musically and technically, the Ory Nordskog records are perhaps the strongest contenders for the title of the most disappointing records in jazz. Stories vary as to whether Spikes ordered the Ory records from Nordskog and pasted the Sunshine label on them, or whether Kid Ory himself "broke with the Spikes Brothers and pasted his own [Sunshine] label over the Nordskog," as Andrae Nordskog maintained thirty or forty years later. My own view is that Spikes decided to sell the Ory records in its store, since it had recorded them; and Spikes did so, under its Sunshine label. For according to Nordskog, Spikes failed to pay him for the records, and he won a judgment in Los Angeles County Superior Court following a suit by Nordskog to obtain the full amount due from Spikes for selling "hundreds" of the records. (We might be excused for pondering the fate of these "hundreds"—although nearly sixty years is of course a long time.)

Before the installation of the plating and pressing plant in Nordskog's own factory, this work was done by Arto in its factory in New Jersey. Evidently Arto also printed the labels, which bear the type-face identical to that of Arto and its affiliated labels. Arto also supplied certain masters. Sides by the California Ramblers, the Original Memphis Five, and others under pseudonyms, and by Arthur Fields as himself, can be found on Nordskog as well as on Arto and the other Eastern labels. A Nordskog document reports that after Arto went bankrupt in 1923, it was found to possess about eighty sets of masters, mothers and stampers of Nordskog couplings. Nordskog filed a $20,000 claim for the loss of these in the Bankruptcy Court in New Jersey, but received nothing. Around the time of Arto's demise, Nordskog seems to have bowed out of the record business under its own name, although it probably pressed discs for other firms.

Nordskog labels come in three colours: red or black, with gold lettering and design, and gold with black lettering and design. The maker's name is printed in large block capitals round the lower rim of the label, with the legend, "The Golden-Voiced Records," in quotes in smaller, lower-case print just above. The top half shows the brand name in elegant semi-copperplate script. The other claim, about being first on the Pacific Coast, appears against a vague background of cloud formation, and is also in semi-copperplate, as is the title. The composer and artist credits are given below the spindle hole.

ODEON

The original Odeon record is not American, but Franco-German. When the International Zonophone Company was bought by the Gramophone Company in London and the Victor Talking Machine Company in the United States, its managing director, F. M. Prescott, promptly formed the International Talking Machine Company. He was backed by the former Paris agents for his Zonophone products, Ullmann Frères, which had a factory in Weissensee, near Berlin. There he produced the world's first double-sided records, which he named Odeon after one of the most famous theatres in Paris. A simple representation of the building appeared on the labels, the internationally registered trademark for the company.

The European Odeon catalog contained superb examples of the operatic talent of those times. Foremost were Lilli Lehmann, the soprano, whose career extended back to Bayreuth and the first performances of Wagner during the composer's lifetime thirty years earlier; tenor Wilhelm Gruning, singing the little-heard title rôle of Leoncavallo's *Roland von Berlin,* which he had created; bass Oreste Luppi; and Czech soprano Emmy Destinn, also singing the rôle she had created in *Roland.* There were dozens of titles from composers as widely different as Wagner, Mozart, Schubert and Smetana. In London a number of sides were cut by a young Irish tenor of twenty-four named John McCormack. The Odeon McCormacks were not only superb art; they were deluxe examples of the recording engineer's art. For years they were followed by others like them by other singers, many of which have since joined the exalted ranks of artists whose work is treasured by collectors.

The earliest American Odeons were single-sided. Their appearance was standard in neither size nor colour. They were 10¾ inches in diameter and pressed in a rich blue wax, with labels depicting a Red Indian chief in full natural colour on a pale fawn or off-white background. Examples of the European opera gems were issued in the United States, but there was nothing recorded there comparable to the products of the Odeon studios in London, Paris or Berlin.

In 1910 Odeon became part of a combine known as the Carl Lindstrom Company, which had acquired control of Beka and Favorite as well. The huge new company presented formidable competition to the Gramophone and Columbia companies, until the outbreak of World War I in 1914 caused the suspension of all trade relations with the Allied nations.

Before the United States entered the conflict on the side of the Allies, Carl Lindstrom had placed his affairs in America in the hands of Otto Heinemann, who was evidently a German-American and thus able to continue in the phonograph business during hostilities. (See OKeh.) One of his lines after the war ended was a new American Odeon. These were quality records made in the OKeh studios in New York and elsewhere, including the reopened Odeon studios in Europe. Gradually the popular items on Odeon were phased out and left to OKeh to market which it did with enormous success. Serious works from abroad, and sometimes from the New York studios, continued to appear on Odeon. The records had dark blue, almost black labels, gold lettering and design, and an unmistakably aristocratic air. Starting in March 1921, the ten-inch popular Odeons were issued in a 20000 series and the twelve-inch in one beginning at 3000.

The Otto Heinemann Phonograph Corporation had become the General Phonograph Corporation of New York in 1919. It flourished as such for some seven years. Then, on October 15, 1926, *Talking Machine World* carried the news that Columbia had purchased the OKeh and Odeon Record Division of General Phonograph. Nevertheless, everything continued as before until 1929. Then the Odeon label, defunct since 1922, was revived for the West Coast trade. It used certain items from the OKeh catalog, numbered as on OKeh, with the prefix letters ONY-. After a few of these had appeared, the numbering was altered to ONY-36000. Just over two hundred records, many of them not issued on OKeh but emanating from that company's studios, appeared during the next two years, before prevailing economic conditions forced the abandonment of the project.

These later Odeons have the most dignified design of them all. The label is black, with only the Odeon trademark and the words ODEON ELECTRIC above the spindle hole. A broad-bordered semi-circle below embraced the title, artist and other credits in gold, like all other printing. The general design thus maintains the appearance of Odeons the world over. An Argentine or German Odeon bears much the same likeness to an American Odeon as does a French, Italian or Scandinavian. (In England, they have rich brown labels and are usually called the Parlophone Odeon Series.)

For quality of sound and surface smoothness, American Odeon, being a product of the Columbia Phonograph Company, are unsurpassed. At a time when many other popular records had noisy surfaces and were produced with indifferent recording techniques, Odeon presented for 75 cents a magnificent product that today seems incredible for its natural beauty. Of particular interest to jazz collectors are the sides by Miff Mole's Little Molers that have no vocals, unlike the regular OKeh issue of the same titles. Almost all the top jazz names on OKeh are represented on Odeon: Louis Armstrong, Clarence Williams, Frankie Trumbauer, Duke Ellington. On the acoustic Odeons of a decade earlier, however, there is nothing comparable in jazz, just some excellent recordings of dance music that rival the best that Victor and Columbia were issuing at that time.

OKEH

When Otto Heinemann set up the American branch of the Carl Lindstrom empire in 1916, he began to think in terms of a wholly American label to complement the Odeons that had become his legacy. He decided on a make of hill-and-dale record cut in such a way that by adjusting the soundbox on the phonograph, any kind of machine would play it with either a sapphire or a steel needle. He took his own initials, then selected an Indian word meaning "It is so" or "So be it." As pronounced by members of the Indian tribe, the word sounded like "Okeh." The first labels showed the word in block capitals, gold on a dark blue ground. The type emphasized the OkeH. A brave's head was encircled by the O. The first of these was announced in September 1918. The catalog numbers began at 1000 and the matrix numbers at 100, with a letter after 100 to denote the first, second or whatever take.

The catalog of the period shows the usual popular songs, standard ballads and sacred numbers, military bands and dance music, and some unusual records for those days by the Berkshire String Orchestra and Quartette offering Grieg's *Romanze in G minor*, Haydn's *Minuetto in G minor*, and Verdi's *Prestissimo in G major*—not at all the kind of music that might be expected on a label specializing in Irving Kaufman, Collins and Harlan, the Van Eps Quartette, the Green Brothers' Novelty Band, Henry Burr, and such. The back cover of the catalog dated February 1919, however, lists two sides under the heading "Instrumental." These are *Ja Da* (1155) and *Ole Miss* (1156) by the New Orleans Jazz Band, whose pianist and leader was Jimmy "Schnozzola" Durante, but whose other members were all New Orleanans. It was the only genuine New Orleans jazz on records at that time other than the music of the Original Dixieland Jazz Band on Victor, Aeolian Vocalion and Columbia. "Guaranteed to tickle the toes of... every man and woman in whose veins flows no buttermilk but—blood," effused the copywriter, "once it gets into your blood you'll dance on until the fire department stops you." It seems a pity that records like these did not sell well enough to make them easier to find today.

Exactly a year later the vertical-cut OKeh record was abandoned in favour of the more universally accepted lateral-cut. The labels, unchanged in design, were accordingly emblazoned with the word LATERAL in capitals larger than those used for the titles shown immediately below it. This format did not last long. By the end of 1919, the colour scheme was maroon with all printing in gold. The Indian remained a little while longer, and the brand name was still spelt OkeH. These lateral records were numbered 4000 upwards. After the first issues, the matrix series was restarted at 7000, having reached about 800 in the vertical-cut sides. The earliest laterals were also numbered in this block. In the spring of 1920, the entire label design was changed, apart from the colour scheme. The name OKeh was spelt in flowing script across the upper half, with the first *two* letters in capitals instead of the first and last. Otto Heinemann had renamed the firm the General Phonograph Corporation in 1919. Now he stressed the "OK" in the brand name rather than his own initials.

To the New York studio of the General Phonograph Corporation on February 14, 1920 came a pretty coloured girl with her manager, Perry Bradford, to record two "character" songs, as they were termed. She was Mamie Smith, who had been trying without success to catch on with other companies. Milo Rega and Fred Hager, the musical directors of OKeh Records, liked what they heard. That spring they issued Mamie Smith's first record on OKeh 4113, *You Can't*

Keep a Good Man Down and *This Thing Called Love*. It sold well enough, though not sensationally. But Fred Hager was sufficiently impressed to have Mamie Smith back in the studio in August, this time with a Negro jazz band to provide a more spirited accompaniment than the rather tame backdrop at the first session. The titles were *Crazy Blues* and *It's Right Here for You*. No sooner had it been announced in November 1920 than demands for it among coloured communities shot the sales figures up to 75,000 copies.

Obviously there was a vast untapped market for genuine Negro blues and blues-inflected jazz. There had been coloured artists on records before, but every one of them played music aimed at white audiences. Mamie Smith was recalled again and again to make records with her Jazz Hounds, as the accompanying group was called. Other girls with blues to sing were engaged to record for OKeh, and in the summer of 1921 the famous OKeh "Race" series was introduced, starting at 8001.

This became one of the richest sources of supply for jazz enthusiasts. Few indeed were the great jazz, blues and gospel artists who never made an OKeh Race record before the series was discontinued in the summer of 1935, after 966 issues. Nor was the standard of music the only consideration. OKeh recording quality was at the time, and has been ever since, a byword among collectors, a criterion by which all others were judged. In Charles Hibbard, the recording wizard, and Ralph Peer, of the artists' department, and Clarence Williams, the musical director, OKeh had an unbeatable team. The recordings, even those made by the acoustic process, stand comparison with the acknowledged best of their kind. This is the series that gave the world the first records under Louis Armstrong's name; that provided the best examples of how King Oliver's Jazz Band sounded in 1923; that preserved the varied music of Clarence Williams himself; and by issuing the results of numerous tours to such cities as Atlanta, New Orleans, San Antonio, Detroit, St. Louis and Kansas City, gave us examples of the talent that played or sang there. Blues singers Eva Taylor, Margaret Johnson, Virginia Liston, Sara Martin, Esther Bigeou, Sippie Wallace, the mysterious Cleo Gibson (whom many consider was the real Empress of the Blues, Bessie Smith herself); and their male counterparts Texas Alexander, Lonnie Johnson, Mississippi John Hurt, Sylvester Weaver—all were OKeh artists for long periods in their recording careers. Preachers such as the Revs. J. M. Gates and Johnnie Blakey, and the Elder Richard Bryant, made gospel records with their congregations that captured authentic, vivid pictures of living faith at work.

There was also a series beginning at 45001 that covered the country artists. Frank and James McCravy sang hillbilly hymns to their own guitar accompaniments; Earl Johnson and his Clodhoppers, recording in Georgia, left no doubt that they were absolutely genuine. Fiddlin' John Carson, Henry Whitter and his harmonica, and ragtime-tinged dance music by the Aiken County String Band, the Carolina Mandolin Orchestra and the Salem Highballers recorded healthy, invigorating performances whose aesthetic value today is beyond assessment. There were even records on OKeh (the 65000 series) devoted to West Indian calypso music by real calypsonians. The 14000 series covered Jewish and Yiddish music and humour of all kinds. A 9000 series brought memories of Europe at its happiest to immigrants from all over that war-torn continent. There was a 16000 series for Mexicans.

The domestic OKeh series beginning at 4000 reached 4999 in December 1923. It was immediately followed by a 40000 series that continued to 41588 in August 1935. These too, though designed principally for customers looking for dance bands playing current hits, included items of enormous value to jazz collectors—again the products of Ralph Peer's numerous field tours. Not all the bands in this series were white. A high percentage is from the Race series, among them King Oliver, Clarence Williams, Louis Armstrong and Duke Ellington. Almost as important, the number of fine bands that only made one session—and that for OKeh—is legion.

On the vocal side, the old regulars continued to record laterally as they had vertically. But OKeh also developed new top singers such as Annette Hanshaw, Johnny Marvin, Aileen Stanley, Seger Ellis, Smith Ballew and Vernon Dalhart. They cut instrumental novelties by the so-called Jazzologist Supreme, Boyd Senter, who wrenched outlandish cackles, squawks and gurgles from his clarinet (but also proved, every so often, that he could play as well as the best of the rest). There were solos by Senter's accompanist on guitar, Eddie Lang; organ solos by Emil Velaszco, under the name "Richard Jordon"; and violin solos by Dr. Eugene Ormandy, later to become one of the world's greatest symphony conductors. Last but not least, there was the extraordinary OKeh Laughing Record. Pressed from a master made in Berlin by one of Lindstrom's labels, Beka, it was issued there as "Original Lauf-Aufnahme." It consisted of the keeper of a *bierkeller* and his *frau*, both gifted with most infectious laughs that they could turn on at will; which they did all through the record, laughing uproariously at a clumsy effort at cornet playing. Listeners invariably find themselves laughing along with the record. It sold into the millions.

In 1926, for a few brief issues, the maroon OKeh label became bright scarlet. This soon changed not its colour but its design. A lozenge-shaped gold plaque was introduced, bearing the word TRUETONE, the new process by which OKeh records were made from that point. Photographs in contemporary trade journals show Charles Hibbard at the control panel of what must be some form of electronic technique for recording. The records themselves lack the tonal range and crispness of the later OKeh electrics made after Columbia took over Heinemann's business in October 1926. Yet these early electrics are still excellent examples of mid-twenties recording. There is a clean bass response that acoustic recording never gave, and a fullness and breadth of tone in other registers that was rare in the old system (unless Hibbard happened to have been in charge of recording those too). After Columbia absorbed OKeh, the Truetone label disappeared. The Viva-Tone Columbia (Western Electric) became the standard recording system for both labels.

Through 1927 and most of 1928, OKehs were red and gold, slightly more decorative than in Heinemann's days of independence. (He remained as President and General Manager of what was now the OKeh Phonograph Corporation of 25 West 45th Street, New York, with its own studios in Union Square.) In the late summer of 1928, without the slightest altering in the design, the labels were changed to glossy black for all categories, and remained black for the next four years or so. During the Depression, various label changes took place. The large label was reduced to the new standard size, 2.9 inches in diameter. OKehs began to appear in a bewildering variety of colours: maroon, red, black, even bright blue. It is interesting to note that up to the end many jazz and folk items recorded nearly a decade earlier were still available under their original numbers. For most of its colourful and fascinating career, the OKeh record was 75 cents for ten-inch issues, $1.25 for twelve-inch. (One of the latter was a blues coupling by Eva Taylor, surely the only twelve-inch blues record issued prior to the mid-1940s.)

From 1935 to 1940 there were no OKeh records. In 1939 the Columbia Broadcasting System reactivated the Columbia label, discontinuing Brunswick. The following year Columbia transformed the thriving Vocalion label into the revived OKeh. It didn't look much like the OKeh collectors knew and almost worshipped. It had a mauve label printed in gold, with the OKeh name somewhat as before but in a different script, less elegant. It continued with numbering from where Vocalion had reached in June 1940, in the 5800s. This continued after the war, right into modern 45 rpm singles in the 1950s.

OKeh recordings can be found on Odeon labels the world over. Their British outlet was and still is Parlophone, despite the fact that in England, Parlophone is one of the EMI group of labels, while in the United States, OKeh remains in the CBS group. This, it appears, is due to a special agreement between Lindstrom, Heinemann and the Parlophone Company which made Parlophone's right to OKeh material exclusive and permanent. (See also Parlophone.)

The following chart shows the first matrix number, actual or estimated, to have been made at the beginning of each year:

	New York	"Location" recording
1918 (c. June) (vertical)	100	
1919	c. 500	
1919 (c. July) (lateral)	7000	
1920	7200	
1921	7670	0-8000 (Odeon only, New York)
1921 (June) (new series)	70000	
1922	70385	0-8200 (Odeon only, New York)
1923	71140	c. 8350
1924	72230	8500
1925	73071	8828
1926	73890-74444 (Dec. 10)	9501-9982 (Nov. 27)
1926 (April 16) (new series)	80001	
1927	80275	80517-80626; 80741-80932; 81300-81399; 81600-81767; 82000-82099
1928	40000	400200-400599; 402000-402226
1929	401489	402227-402412; 402598-202857; 403100-403193; 403300-403453;
1930	403579	403800-403813; 404050-404199; 404300-404375; 404400-404419; 404600-404801
1931	404802	405000-405095
1932	405121	

OKeh records made between the summers of 1932 and 1935 have either ARC or Columbia matrix numbers. There were also 480000, 490000 and 495000 series, mostly used on Odeon and Parlophone. Some of these are re-numberings of regular OKeh masters. Others indicate non-vocal takes of regular dance records issued on OKeh with vocals. The revived OKehs of 1940 onwards have normal CBS series masters (q.v.).

OLYMPIC

The coming of Olympic records was announced in the *Talking Machine Journal* of March 1921. The Olympic Record Corporation, incorporated in Maryland with capital of $260,000, notified the trade that the first release would be on April 15. The office of the Corporation was at 1666 Broadway in New York City, with a recording studio and factory in Brooklyn. The parent firm was the Remington Phonograph Corporation, of which Philo E. Remington was president.

A month later, there appeared an announcement of seven different series of Olympic records, the numbers given below being the first issue in each:

14101	Popular vocal
15101	Dance
16101	Hawaiian
17101	Standard vocal
18101	Instrumental
19101	Operatic
20101	Sacred

After November 1921 there were no further issues, and indeed no further press references until the *Talking Machine Journal* of June 1922 noted that the firm had been reorganized as the Remington Radio Company. But nothing more was ever heard of records from either Remington firm. On July 15, 1922, the *Talking Machine World* said that the Brooklyn plant had been purchased by Pace & Fletcher, makers of Black Swan records, and reorganized as the Fletcher Record Company, Inc., to operate exclusively for Black Swan.

Black Swan itself sold out to Paramount in April 1924, and the *Phonograph and Talking Machine Weekly* of April 9 recounted the grim story of the failure of the original Remington Phonograph Corporation in December 1921. The officials were put on trial for fraud in the sale of the stock. The *Talking Machine Journal* carried a further note on Olympic records, which were revived by the Columbia Music Roll Company of 721 North Kendzie Avenue, Chicago, Ill. A few records were issued as a result of this, but the second resuscitation proved as profitless as the original issue three years earlier.

The Fletcher era of 1922-1923 produced Olympic records with numbers around 1400-1600 in exact step with the same titles on Majestic and other labels. None of the various kinds of Olympic records has a visible matrix number. The catalog number, suffixed -A or -B, has to suffice. This gives the source of recording when it shows up on Black Swan (even white artists from Olympic were issued on Black Swan's 2000 and 10000 series), Banner and Phantasie Concert Records. The label design is black with gold lettering and design, the latter including a naked male athlete standing on a small dais marked "Olympic Records," in the act of hurling something that could be a discus—or a record. The setting for this gymnastic feat is a clearing between two rambler rose bushes, each with three blooms and vicious-looking thorns. In view of the fate of the original corporation that produced the records, this design seems almost sinister.

The repertoire of the first Olympic records is not unduly exciting, and that of subsequent revivals is exactly akin to Majestic (q.v.). There are two issues on the 1921 Olympic, however, that should interest popular and jazz archivists. Both are by Lindsay McPhail, pianist-composer of the long-established jazz standard, *San*. One of them is a piano solo of this very tune, although as played by its creator, it lacks most of the colour and zest that dozens of bands managed to infuse into their subsequent recordings of it. The other is a typical Dixieland quintet known as McPhail's Jazz Orchestra of Chicago, playing another McPhail composition, *Zowie*. If the band was Chicago-based, and it probably was, it provides an interesting example of what basic white Chicago jazz was like in 1921.

OPERAPHONE

This was another firm specializing in vertical-cut records. Its full title was the Operaphone Manufacturing Corporation, New York. It appears that both the Edison and Pathe systems were used in the years between 1916 and 1919. In 1919 and 1920 some lateral-cut records were also produced. The latter-day vertical Pathe issues were actually pressed from Pathe masters, but little of any great consequence is known to have appeared. A few pseudo-Dixieland performances by the Joseph Samuels bands, notably the Synco Jazz Band, account for the jazz items. The rest were mostly standard ballads, light instrumentals and popular vocals. At least this fare almost justifies the company motto on the labels: "Music for Everybody." There were eight-inch issues to begin with, but most of the output was in ten-inch form, numbered 31000 upwards. The head office was in Long Island City, N.Y.

ORIOLE

Oriole was a 25¢ label sold in McCrory's stores, beginning in 1921. Many of the initial issues were from Emerson, and some were from Grey Gull. But for most of Oriole's life of nearly seventeen years, the Plaza-Banner complex, and from 1932, the American Record Corporation, supplied the masters.

The series began at 100 as a popular music label featuring mostly dance music, popular vocals (including vaudevillian blues artists), and an occasional light classic. The label is deep orange with black lettering and design. It shows an oriole singing amid some indeterminable foliage. In 1927, this was changed to a much less attractive dull black. The design was unaltered, except that the oriole became black and white with one gold wing visible. The leaves are gold throughout, and the brand name is white, edged in gold and slightly larger. Until 1926, the Plaza or the Emerson matrix number appeared in the wax and on the label, the Plaza being preceded by the figure 3 on the label only. After this, the Plaza control number was used until ARC took over Oriole. Then the Plaza matrix numbering system was resumed, without extra digits or suppression.

The orange labels and the pre-ARC black-and-golds do not wear well. They are inclined to be gritty, and the acoustic Plaza recordings have of course the nasal, bass-less character found on Banner, Domino, Regal, and similar labels. The pre-ARC electrics sound muddy. The ARC issues are constricted and not very interesting in the bass. They improve considerably from about 1935.

At that date, the old Oriole series, by then some distance into the 3000s, was changed to fall in line with Melotone, Banner, Perfect and Romeo, all of whose domestic dance records began to be numbered according to the year (usually the last digit), the month and the number on the monthly supplement, starting at 1 for dance and vocal popular records, 51 for "race" and "hillbilly" issues.

There had been in the earlier 1930s an 8000 Oriole race series catering to the Negro market. It featured an interesting array of blues talent and an occasional gospel or instrumental item. There were also hillbilly items, and these remained in the elaborate, all-embracing ARC style of numbering from September 1935 to the end in April 1938.

The most interesting issues from a jazz collector's viewpoint are the orange labels. Here can be found a wide variety of talent from Clarence Williams' Dixie Washboard Band to Joe Candullo and his Everglades Orchestra. Most of the truly interesting ones are described as being played by the Dixie Jazz Band. The two bands mentioned above, as well as the New Orleans Jazz Band, Luis Russell and his Orchestra, and the California Ramblers, are all included under this widely used pseudonym (which was by no means restricted to bands of jazz interest). Several "Dixie Jazz Band" items seem to have been issued only on Oriole, so we cannot be completely sure which band was involved in some cases.

The catalog numbering of the late twenties is in step with that on Jewel (q.v.). Thus we can find identical recordings on both Oriole and Jewel, four thousand numbers apart. E.g., Oriole 2087 is the same coupling as Jewel 6087.

The London firm of Levy's made several attempts to launch their own Oriole label, but theirs was at all times an expensive product. In May and June 1927, fifteen large buff-cream labels with brown lettering appeared under the Oriole imprint. They offered highlights of the Vocalion race catalog by Lil's Hot Shots (Louis Armstrong's Hot Five), Clarence Williams' Washboard Band, Jelly Roll Morton, Sonny Clay, Dewey Jackson and his Peacock Orchestra, Fess Williams' Royal Flush Orchestra, Jimmy Bertrand's Washboard Wizards, and Duke Ellington and his Kentucky Club Orchestra. There were also some fine blues records by Rosa Henderson, Edmonia Henderson and Viola McCoy. The race items were numbered 1000-1012, and there were two by white cabaret artists numbered 2000 and 2001. In 1931 and through to 1935, Levy's launched a new Oriole label. Much smaller, black and silver in colour with a microphone motif, they were numbered P-100 to about P-120. They included only recordings made in London, but by talent such as Adelaide Hall, Harry Roy and his Bat Club Boys (their *Pussy* became a kind of classic of recorded *double entendre*), and Stanley Black and his Modernists with Nat Gonella. In 1935 came records made in France by Freddie Taylor and his Swing Men from Harlem, and by a new string group known as the Quintette of the Hot Club of France whose guitar soloist, Django Reinhardt, was considered very promising. Some of these had gold where there had been silver, and the numbers ran from LV-100 upwards. This enterprise shrivelled and died like its 1927 predecessor. In 1950 Levy's tried again, and with some success. It issued pressings from various postwar American labels as well as some made in London; but these are beyond our scope in this book. One collectors' piece appeared on a single-sided Oriole made by Levy's at the end of Duke Ellington's visit to England in June and July 1933. He was interviewed by the late Percy Mathison Brooks, Editor of *The Melody Maker*, after playing a few bars of slow, wistful music on the piano. If you bought six Ellington records from Levy's, all at once, for a total of £1 10s.—say about $7.50— you received the record of Duke's speech free. It is not clear why Levy's chose to use the name Oriole for its records. The labels have no trademark, and the oriole is not a bird known in Britain.

OXFORD

No origins are given on any Oxford records I have examined or heard of. I therefore assume that they are the product of a phonograph manufacturer of the first decade of the century who quite legally drew on Victor and Columbia alike for his repertoire. As far as is known, there is no physical catalog of Oxford records. They have large, dull purplish-blue labels decorated with the brand name in florid script in gold across the upper half. The title and the artist's name (sometimes, but not always) and record number are shown below.

Examples from Columbia date from 1905 or 1906 to 1911. The original matrix number in a 3000, 4000 or 19000 series is used as the catalog number. Both these and the sides made apparently by Victor—though they have matrix numbers in a different series from the regular Victor issues—carry stickers on the blank side that give the usual patent details and/or warnings about copying and other misuses of Oxford records.

The Victor-type pressings look and sound as if they were pressed in Camden, N.J. For example, Oxford 585 is an anonymous banjo solo that sounds markedly like Vess L. Ossman. The song is *Bay State Quick-Step*. There is orchestral accompaniment. The catalog number and the other lettering on the label are in the same typeface as all Victors of the 1904-1914 decade, and it is *embossed* in the wax in the twelve o'clock position in the same curlicued style as Victor used from 1904 to 1942. Yet in the wax there appears in minutely *engraved* type the number 6865, which on a Victor is a twelve-inch recording by the great baritone Emilio de Gogorza of an aria from *Faust!*

The answer probably lies in the Zon-O-Phone subsidiary of Victor, which also used Victor typography, of course, but which had its own matrix serials and repertoire. Oxford records from Zon-O-Phone are unlikely to produce much of collectors' interest other than the occasional ragtime numbers; but the Columbia pressings have already produced rare sides by important personalities like Bert Williams, Josie Sadler and Blossom Seeley, all of whom get label credit.

PAN

Throughout the course of phonograph record history, there have been mavericks: the flexible, the rigid but unbreakable, the labelless, the strange groove cuts. The Pan record is none of these, but it is unique as far as is known. Its label (green with border, maker's name and brand name in white, artist and title credits in gold) is triangular in shape. The only known specimens bear catalog numbers in a range between 2001 and 2009, which betokens a limited distribution and an even more limited catalog. All are standard music: one military band item of well worn Sousa marches, one coupling of violin solos, and one of well known operatic arias sung by a Mme. Genie Fonariova. The military band and violin items are aurally identical to the same titles, in the case of the violin solos the same artist credit, as on Lyric. Vera Barstow is the violinist, and her Lyric bears the matrix number 14017. Her identical Pan is numbered 41013. The military band, anonymous on Pan, bears Lyric matrix numbers 12068-2 and 12071-2. Both of Mme. Fonariova's titles appear on Arto under her name. The company producing these strange-looking discs was the Pan Phonograph Company, nothing more. It was probably another of the machine manufacturers that in the boom-or-bust year 1920 (the date is suggested by the fact that popular songs and tunes with nearby matrix numbers on Lyric are 1920 numbers) decided to try issuing records and cashing in on the boom—and went bust.

The original source of the masters was Earl W. Jones of New York, who supplied Arto and Lyric (q.v.). Each label allocated its own matrix numbers, but the 41000 series was Jones's own.

PANACHORD

The British branch of the newly formed Warner-Brunswick Company launched its Panachord label, in step with its American opposite number Melotone, in May 1931. The records cost 2s. (about 40 cents). At a casual glance they were indistinguishable from Melotones. The numbering started at 25001, and by the time the subsequent owners, the Decca Record Company, had decided to discontinue them in November 1939, the numbers had reached 26046. There was also a twelve-inch series numbered upwards from 9001, but this was desultory in its appearance and short-lived.

Panachord at the outset had a rich blue label printed entirely in silver, exactly as had Melotone (q.v.). Even the flowing script, in which the brand names were printed in blue on silver just above the spindle hole, was made to look as if written by the same hand—and perhaps it was. After about a year, Panachord dispensed with the silver and printed everything in the then more conventional gold. It claimed manufacturing links with Warner-Brunswick even after Decca had assumed production in 1933 and were so advising customers with the legend "Made by Decca" above the spindle hole where the words "Electrically Recorded" (apparently considered necessary even in 1931-1932) had run.

The new make had been in existence exactly three months when the price was reduced to 1s. 6d. There it remained until February 1935 when it was reduced still further by Decca to 1s., all this without loss of quality. Indeed, if anything the cheaper issues were smoother-surfaced than their pioneer predecessors. In September 1937 the price was back to 1s. 6d. There were no further price changes.

Panachord was a name originally intended, apparently, to suggest that the repertoire was all-embracing. Yet the monthly supplements always depicted a satyr playing Pan-pipes, perhaps to suggest that the music was enticing, beguiling, alluring. If you happened to be a devotee of hillbilly-cum-country-and-western music, this was no less than the truth, for Panachord is today one of the most sought-after labels among such devotees. Tex Ritter, Goebel Reeves ("The Texas Drifter"), Marc Williams, W. Lee O'Daniels, Glen Rice and the

McCravy Brothers were featured on Panachord throughout its eight and a half years. The Colt Brothers' record of *Eleven More Months and Ten More Days* (25029), issued on the second Panachord list, was a nationwide hit and outsold all the other versions. If you were a jazz connoisseur, you would regard the titles labelled as Jack Wynn (or Winn) and his Dallas Dandies as worth examination, for they could be by the Original Memphis Five (*Lovey Lee* and *How Come You Do Me Like You Do?* on 25008), or by King Oliver's Dixie Syncopators (*Someday Sweetheart* on 25035). On 25047 there was Chick Webb's *House Hop*, ascribed to Earl Jackson's Musical Champions. From 1936 onwards it became common knowledge that anything credited to Dick Robertson and his Orchestra was, with the exception of Robertson's own vocals, well worth a place in any jazz collection, potboilers from Tin Pan Alley though the numbers were. Four of the finest jazz sides of all time, by Joe Venuti-Eddie Lang and their All Star Orchestra, were issued on Panachord 25151 and 25168.

The rest of the catalog covered literally all kinds of music other than the most elevated serious works. Cornet solos, piano-accordions (singly and in droves), street pianos, Wurlitzer organs, and even Alpine horns recorded in the Bernese Oberland could be found on Panachord; for by the mid-1930s, European recordings as well as American and British began to appear. The Rhythm Maniacs, long a staple of the Decca catalogs, were issued on Panachord with vocal refrains in German. Among the British regulars were Arthur Lally and his Orchestra, Sam Browne the crooner, and top dance bands such as Joe Loss's and Lou Preager's. There were many American studio dance bands too. Those credited to Len Herman and his Orchestra usually turn out to be exceptionally fine small-band jazz. The Personality Girl, Annette Hanshaw, also had ten sides issued on Panachord. Two American bandleaders were sparingly represented; Woody Herman and Ted Weems, the latter featuring vocal refrains by his young Italian-American vocalist, Perry Como.

The outbreak of war in September 1939 may have been what decided Decca to withdraw the withering Panachord label from the market. It had dwindled to one or two issues a month, where once there had been ten, fifteen or more. With a similar repertoire being issued on Decca's other cheap label, Rex (q.v.), Panachord became superfluous. Boasting few big sellers, it was, as I have said, a connoisseur's label at a poor man's price. Wartime conditions left no room for such luxuries.

Melotone issues on Panachord originally appeared with the Melotone catalog number (M-12000 series) indented in the wax. No matrix number was visible either there or on the label. But after early 1932 and the takeover by the American Record Corporation, the original catalog number disappeared and the five-figure matrix number, usually in the 11000-23000 block, appeared instead in the wax and on the label. (The C- prefix indicates a Chicago recording.) English Panachords of the first year or so have no matrix numbers easily discernible, but they can sometimes be seen scratched by hand *very faintly* and usually in mirror form inside the concentric ring to which the run-off spiral leads. In Decca times, the matrix numbers have GB-, TB- or DR- prefixes. American Deccas are of course distinguishable by their 38000-39999 serials, or 60000 series of numbers, or DLA- prefix if recorded in Los Angeles. Records with lower-case letters suffixing the matrix number, usually three (e.g., bkp, hpp) are of European origin.

PARAMOUNT

Of the American labels most likely to cause excitement among jazz and blues collectors, Paramount stands out. It was the product of the New York Recording Laboratories, Inc., whose executive office was in Port Washington, Wisc., where it had been established in 1916. The pressing plant was in Grafton, in the same state, but the studios were located at 1140 Broadway in New York City, although many sides were recorded in Chicago, and from the end of 1929, in Grafton itself.

The first Paramount issues were vertical cuts in a 2000 series, then a 3000 series of catalog numbers. These were supplanted towards the end of 1919 by a lateral-cut disc (33000 series) that remained the Paramount record with which collectors are familiar, until its withdrawal from the record world in the summer of 1932. There were several catalog series. The 3000s were country-and-western. The 12000s were "race" records (between August 1922 and August 1932, when the last of the series, 13156, was issued). The 20000s, issued between 1919 and 1929, were the dance and popular vocal items. And there were other ethnic series devoted severally to German, Spanish, and other languages.

For the first seven years or so, until August 1926, the labels of all Paramount records were blue, with all printing in gold. The trademark for most of that time was an eagle standing on the world, wings outspread to form an inner ring to the upper contours of the label. (Until sometime in 1920, probably about October, the eagle is seen standing on something much less cosmic—to be exact, the lid of a table-model phonograph.) In 1926 the colour changed to black. Shortly afterwards the legend "Electrically Recorded" appeared, first in lower-case type to the right of the spindle hole, then in upper-case on either side of it and almost above. The lower-case type disappeared in November 1928 and no major changes took place in the remaining four years.

At the beginning of 1921, the managing director of Paramount was a man named Spitz, who had worked in sales promotion with Victor and Columbia. The recording manager was A. E. Satherley, who seems to have remained in this position at least until the company began using masters cut by Orlando R. Marsh in Chicago. The first date for these was 1924, and in 1926 they became regular items in the Paramount catalog. The Starr Piano Company of Richmond, Ind. has files that reveal that in the months between March and October 1929, certain masters were made to Paramount's order. The chart at the end of this chapter shows the approximate dates of the different types of recording to be found on Paramount.

In April 1924, Paramount absorbed the Black Swan catalog (q.v.), and its "race" series from 12100 to 12189 was set aside for reissuing whatever Black Swan issues were considered marketable. By this time the company was already marketing Broadway, Famous and Puritan records, using Paramount masters. In the popular dance music and vocal lines, many of the best-selling Paramount issues were also issued on these labels, especially on Broadway. Although Paramount continued to make original records in Chicago from the summer of 1927, and began making them in Grafton two years later, many issues on the 20000 series in the late 1920s were leased from Plaza. Thus, a best-seller like *Big City Blues* or *Do Something* could and did appear on Banner, Domino and Regal, the Plaza group; on Jewel and Oriole, the chainstore subsidiaries; on Pathe Actuelle

and Perfect, on Cameo, Lincoln and Romeo, and on Paramount and Broadway as well!

Paramount advertising was mostly aimed at the Negro population. It is surely significant that in the decade of the "race" series, some 1,147 issues were announced, while in the decade between the first 20000 popular series and the last, there were less than 900. The biggest star of the race series was Ma Rainey, the almost legendary blues moaner who exerted such an influence over Bessie Smith. There were others, too. Classic blues records by Elzadie Robinson, Ida Cox, Alberta Hunter, Irene Scruggs, Edmonia Henderson, and male singers Charlie Patton, Blind Blake, Blind Lemon Jefferson and Charlie Spand filled the catalogs over the years. There were blues piano records of incalculable importance by Henry Brown, Will Ezell, Cow Cow Davenport, Jimmy Blythe and Blind Leroy Garnett, amongst others. Relatively few instrumentals by jazz bands appeared on Paramount, apart from Lovie Austin's Blues Serenaders, Jimmie O'Bryant's Famous Original Washboard Band, various equally small groups under Jimmy Blythe's name, and one-shot items by Freddie Keppard's Jazz Cardinals and John Williams' Synco Jazzers. There was a fair proportion of gospel material, much of it conventional spirituals sung by unaccompanied quartets and quite probably issued with the white market in mind as much as the coloured.

Readers interested in the Paramount advertising methods and the exact contents of the famous race series are strongly advised to write to the publishers of *The Paramount 12000/13000 Series*, compiled by Max Vreede, the distinguished Dutch collector. The address is Storyville Publications & Co. Ltd., 66 Fairview Drive, Chigwell, Essex IG7 6HS, England. In these minutely documented pages will be found reproductions of advertisements in *The Chicago Defender* between August 1922 and April 1930, and of various leaflets and record sleeves.

At the beginning, Paramounts cost 85 cents. They were reduced to 75 cents in 1921, and that price does not seem to have changed. The various series all cost the same. The surfaces of Paramount records vary from smooth and almost noiseless to gritty and harsh—the latter particularly true of the electric black-label issues. The recording of the acoustic blue labels is quite adequate without being sensational. The electric black labels are inclined to be shrill and nasal, or "pudding-y," lacking adequate balance between top and bottom frequencies. Thus, King Oliver's Jazz Band, recorded acoustically in 1923, is clean and quite natural-sounding, whereas Junie Cobb's Windy Rhythm Kings allow the bass too much prominence when recorded electrically in 1929. The vast majority of Paramounts are regular black wax pressings, though for a short time during the latter part of 1923 and the first months of 1924, a reddish-brown wax was used.

Most labels can claim at least one or two *curiosa* issued under their imprints. Paramount's must go on record, if that is the correct term. One involves some—not all—copies of Paramount 20026, issued in November 1920. It consists of (Ben) Selvin's Novelty Orchestra playing the big hit of the time, *Avalon*. The reverse is the Newport Society Orchestra, another Ben Selvin band, playing *Whispering*, an equally huge success. This coupling, one would think, was a sure-fire all-time million-dollar hit. It did sell quite well, in fact, but not *that* well. *Avalon*, rather under-recorded, is given the usual tasteful Ben Selvin treatment, with Nathan Glantz's saxophone and Frank Clegg's xylophone featured. But in the tenth bar of the second chorus, there begins a strange sound like a carpenter at work on some hollow object like floorboards, or some kind of closet. The noise continues intermittently until the end of the performance, out of time and therefore obtrusive. Whoever passed it for issue must have been half asleep while listening to the test record—if indeed such was ever made. It may be significant that a few weeks later Selvin's Novelty Orchestra was called upon to make *Avalon* again, this time without the contributions of an over-zealous do-it-yourself pioneer in some adjoining room.

The other known oddity on Paramount appeared in the race series on ten sides, 12534 through 12538. Each side contains a broadcast account of one round of the famous heavyweight championship fight between Jack Dempsey and Gene Tunney at Soldiers Field, Chicago, on September 22, 1927. One matrix number was allocated to this singularly unmusical performance, the round number serving as the "take"! The appearance of the set in the race series seems especially odd, since neither fighter was a Negro. As an historical document, it is certainly of great value, almost certainly the first live recording of a sports event, and certainly the first issued to the public. But evidently that public did not feel inclined to invest a total of $3.75 even for Gene Tunney's famous "long count" victory over the Manassa Mauler, who never fought a major bout again.

The following chart shows the approximate first matrix number in each block used by Paramount during its fifteen years. There were other blocks of numbers as well, all recorded in Chicago in 1924. They began at 6000, 8000, 9000, and 10000. Each seems to have consisted of only a hundred sides. One side of Paramount 12250 is numbered 9099, the other 10000, but they are obviously from the same session by blues singer Thelma LaVizzo. It is possible that all these blocks were made in the same studio, on a contract arrangement: that is, not in a studio devoted exclusively to Paramount, but one occupied in providing masters for private and semi-private use as well as for occasional major-league concerns. If so, the numbering system of this studio must have been irregular, changing with the completion of every hundred masters. There was also an 11000 block that went beyond 11100. This seems to have begun towards the end of 1925 and continued into 1926 at least as far as the early summer.

1917 (date unknown)	1				
1918	c.200				
1919	c.350				
1920	c.500				
1921	c.730				
1922	c.960				
1923	c.1270				
1924	1637				
1925	c.1980				
1926	c.2400				
1927	c.2790	3070	4090	20000 (September)	
1928				c.20230	
1929				c.21100	L-1 (November;
1930					c.L-100 Grafton only)
1931					c.L-700
1932					c.L-1250

The 7000-9000 series seen on Paramount dance and popular vocals of 1928-1929 are from Plaza-Banner, and the 14000-15000 series are from Gennett (both q.v.).

PARLOPHONE

Parlophone as an American label deriving entirely from OKeh (q.v.) was one of short duration, between 1929 and 1931. Some of its issues, devised principally for the West Coast, bore the same catalog numbers as OKeh for the same couplings, prefixed by the letters PNY-. The same prefix was used from the end of 1929 for a 34000 series that also produced identical issues to OKeh, on a selective basis. Additionally, there were some non-vocal recordings by dance and jazz bands that were never released on OKeh at all. Everything came out under some of the most ingeniously allusive pseudonyms in the history of recording. Annette Hanshaw, for example, was renamed "Janet Shaw." Frank Trumbauer became "Tom Barker." The Casa Loma Orchestra was "Hal Laska and his Orchestra," and on one issue simply "The Castle Orchestra." Smith Ballew was convoluted into "Kyrle Bell." Yet two of the most prominent jazzmen recording for OKeh were given names quite unlike their own: Louis Armstrong appeared as "Ted Shawne" and Miff Mole as "Gilbert Marsh."

The American Parlophone PNY-34000 series could boast of some two hundred issues. Then it was discontinued. Its products were splendid, examples of the finest that science has ever produced on any 78 rpm label. They were in essence OKeh records, resembling these even to the glossy black labels printed in gold and the manufacturing credit given to the OKeh Phonograph Company, with title and artist credits in the same typeface as Columbia and OKeh had used for their West Coast issues. The trademark, however, was a gold circle enclosing a morning-glory-horn disc phonograph with a £ sign superimposed, all in black, exactly like the English Parlophone labels since they first appeared in November 1923.

Parlophone in England was the first major label from Germany to appear after World War I. The parent firm, Carl Lindstrom, set up a factory in the county of Hertfordshire, some distance from London. From there it became a force to reckon with in the British record industry. Other labels came, flourished briefly, and were gone. Parlophone remains to this day, one of the original triumvirate forming the vast Electric and Musical Industries Ltd. (EMI) combine. To be sure, it merged with Columbia in 1927 and promptly appeared as superb laminated pressings with virtually noiseless surfaces. But even before this, the OKeh recording technique and the smooth material for pressing proclaimed them a superior product indeed.

The artist's manager and recording chief was Oscar Preuss. In charge of the OKeh selections and dance and popular music generally was Ted Sommerfield. To him must go the eternal thanks of all jazz collectors in Europe for having issued so many superb performances by so many of the top jazz and blues artists then recording for OKeh. Thanks to him, enthusiasts outside the United States could keep abreast of the latest developments in the history of jazz as they were happening. Thus England was favoured with the little-known but important bands as well as the top names. Of course there were records by Bix Beiderbecke, Frank Trumbauer, Joe Venuti, Eddie Lang, Miff Mole and Louis Armstrong. But there were also examples of the Arcadia Peacock Orchestra, the Arcadian Serenaders, Merritt Brunies and his Orchestra, Sol Wagner, Jack Linx, Frank Quartell and Clarence Williams. Blues singers Margaret Johnson, Eva Taylor, Sara Martin and Ada Brown were represented, Miss Johnson's superb record of *E flat Blues* and *If I Let You Get Away with It* (E-5187) becoming a

best-seller that survived in the catalog from its issue in June 1924 until September 1931, long after acoustic records (it was one) were considered obsolete. The publicity attending the issue of this remarkable record is interesting: "Sung by Margaret Johnson, a coloured Artiste, with true meaning of the Blues. Somewhat quaint when first heard—played again, you get them—played once more, they have got you."

Popular though this first Parlophone blues record was, it was the Parlophone Laughing Record (see OKeh) that tickled the British public when it was issued on E-5500 in December 1925. The E-5000 series was issued on a bright red label with gold lettering and design, including the same horn phonograph and £ sign as later appeared on American Parlophone, but in gold on red. (The antique machine, already obsolete for playing records when adopted as a trademark by Parlophone in 1923, finally disappeared from the labels early in 1936, leaving the £ sign in proud if lonely possession of the commanding position at the top of each label.) The E- series continued until July 1931 when E-6428, the last of the line, was issued. The price was still 2s. 6d. (50 cents or so). In November 1926, a "royal blue"—actually a rich purple—label prefixed R- was introduced at 3s. The numbers were interlinked with those of another E- series devoted to Irish, Scottish, Welsh and (inexplicably) Hawaiian records that still cost only 2s. 6d. Thus, if a Parlophone with a 3000 catalog number had a red label and was recorded by, say, the Pipers of H. M. Royal Scots Guards, or the Irish fiddler Patrick J. Gaffey (from OKeh), or Ferera's Hawaiian Quartette (also from Okeh), it would not be possible to find a purple R- series record with the same 3000 catalog number. Eventually these red-label regional recordings were continued in an E-3800 series that also included Hebrew and Yiddish performances. The purple Rs continued uninterrupted until May 1928 and R-3543. The series was recommenced the next month at R-100 with a brand new recording by Sophie Tucker, then appearing in London. She had recorded just before leaving New York. On hearing the sides, she was quoted as saying, "For the first time my records sound like Tucker." Along with stars of Miss Tucker's calibre were more hot jazz by the same front-rank musicians as had graced the R-3000 series; first-class dance records; and sides by the Goofus Five, elevated to the more expensive label from the red E- series that had introduced them to England in 1925. On the R-3000 series, for some unaccountable reason, they had been renamed "The Goofus Washboards," although at no time was a washboard ever used on any of the Five's records.

In 1928 some curious mislabelling was perceptible on the royal blue Parlophone label. Clarence Williams' Washboard Four, which really did use one of these "novelty" instruments, was issued as "Louis Armstrong and his Original Washboard Beaters," although Armstrong himself did not take part in either title. Williams himself was the vocalist, and his near-Armstrong guttural style brought forth the opinion from one British reviewer that he sounded like someone trying to talk in a dentist's chair with a mouth full of wadding. Armstrong was even then beginning to mean something at least to a select circle of Parlophone's clientele, so when Duke Ellington's beautiful record of *Black and Tan Fantasy* was issued on R-3492, it too was credited to Louis Armstrong and his Original Washboard Beaters. Again, no washboard was used, of course. Frank Trumbauer's Orchestra playing *Borneo* appeared as by the Goofus Five and their Orchestra. Miff Mole's fine *Crazy Rhythm* (no vocal) was issued as "Sam Lanin's Famous Players and Singers." A genuine Louis Armstrong title, *That's When I'll Come Back to You,* was entered in the catalog and on the label as by

Butterbeans and Susie, accompanied by Louis Armstrong's Washboard Beaters, as was its coupling, *Mama, Why Do You Treat Me So?* Another reviewer, faced with this record, authoritatively informed his readers that "Butterbeans is what Louis Armstrong's wife, Susie, calls him."

The latter title was Parlophone's attempt to bowdlerise the original OKeh title, *Gully Low Blues*. This was not the only example of a jazz title being altered. There had been two versions of *Take Your Black Bottom Outside* made by OKeh, both issued on Parlophone, each with a different title. Clarence Williams' Washboard Five, renamed "Original Washboard Beaters"—strangely without involving Louis Armstrong—could be heard on R-3381 playing this number under the title *Yale Rhythm*. Sara Martin, rechristened Margaret Johnson and accompanied by Clarence Williams' Blue Five (renamed Clarence Williams' Dixieland Orchestra) sang it on Parlophone R-3506 as *Stop That Black Bottom Dance*. A very neat compromise between a desire to cash in to the full on the Black Bottom dance craze, and a wish not to offend the apparently hypersensitive customers—or more probably, the Lord Chamberlain's office, which then had the power to ban anything offered for entertainment that seemed salacious or even mildly suggestive. (In November 1938, Parlophone issued Eddy Duchin's *Ol' Man Mose*. It was instantly withdrawn on the grounds that the vocalist, Patricia Norman, used a four-letter Anglo-Saxon expletive repeatedly throughout.)

The R- series consolidated its popularity with jazz connoisseurs in November 1929 when the New Rhythm Style Series was launched. Drawing for the next two and a half years on jazz classics from the OKeh catalog, this series of sixty records was mixed in the numerical sequence with straight dance records, American and British alike, and with a raft of imports from Germany and Austria by the orchestras of Barnabas von Geczy, Edith Lorand, Dajos Bela, Jack Bund, the Orchestre Mascotte, and the Pavilion Lescaut Orchestra. In May 1932 the Second New Rhythm Style Series began. Over the next ten years came other series devoted to the jazz connoisseur, and latterly to those whose penchant was for big-band swing.

By the time the Second New Rhythm Style Series appeared, the only British dance band on Parlophone was Harry Roy's. He continued in that position until he began recording for Regal Zonophone in 1940. The follower of Continental dance music continued to be as well catered to as the jazz aficionado, but the collector of country-and-western music received such scant attention from Parlophone—despite the rich OKeh catalog of well over 500 issues—as to drive him straight into the arms of Panachord (q.v.). Parlophone, like many British labels, frequently issued the offbeat record. An example is the Laughing Record already referred to. It was subtitled *That Kruschen Feeling* in England, as a little free advertising for a make of health salts. Another is a record (R-1164) issued in April 1932 to commemorate the bicentenary of the birth of Josef Haydn. It plays seven examples of the music Haydn wrote for mechanical *floetenuhr* or flute-clock, the machinery of which can be heard working before, during and after each piece. On Parlophone R-1614 is an extraordinary record that sold extremely well, unlike the Haydn memorial issue. It was by Kanui and Lula, evidently two Hawaiian singers and guitarists recording in Paris. They sing *Oua, Oua,* which is evidently a song about a dog of some kind. The vigorous beat and the persistent repetition of the title make it one of the most entertaining of its genre.

In common with its EMI partners, HMV and Columbia, Parlophone in February 1935 dropped the price of its dance and popular vocal records, and many light instrumental items also. They were all gathered in a new magenta-labelled series starting at F-100. Relatively little of any American material appeared on this label. The mainstays became Harry Roy and his band; a small group backed by the pipe organ in the London studios and issued as The Organ, The Dance Band and Me; Nat Gonella and his Georgians; Joe Daniels and his Hot Shots in "Drumnasticks"; and a million-dollar hit in the form of utility dance music played straight and in severely accurate tempo. The word used on the label and in the publicity was "strict," and no more suitable description could have been chosen. The leader of this brassless sextet was dancing champion Victor Silvester. American bands rather shyly issued on Parlophone in the late 1930s included Bert Block, Kay Kyser, Eddy Duchin, Jan Garber and Emery Deutsch.

The twelve-inch Parlophone series was purple, latterly black-labelled, and always in a series beginning at E-10000. Some 1,500 issues appeared before the last 78 rpm was pressed. Few were of American origin, although many derived from Odeon appeared in America on that label. There was also the Parlophone-Odeon label, brown and gold, featuring mostly the voices of tenor Richard Tauber and sopranos Gitta Alpar and Conchita Supervia.

The following chart will give an approximate idea of the date of recording by Parlophone in its London Studios, usually situated in Maida Vale or St. John's Wood. Strict chronology does not seem to have been necessarily observed, so the details are thus rather less exact than I would like:

Year	Number
1923 (c. July-August)	E-100
1924	E-270
1925	E-620
1926	E-770
1927	E-1120
1928	CE-1750
1929	CE-2270
1930	CE-3000
1931	CE-3700
1932	CE-4400
1933	CE-4900
1934	CE-6350
1935	CE-6770
1936	CE-7380
1937	CE-8000
1938	CE-8850
1939	CE-9500
1940	CE-10240
1941	CE-10660
1942	CE-10880

PAR-O-KET

Manufactured by the Paroquette Manufacturing Company of New York, the seven-inch Edison-type cut hill-and-dale Par-O-Ket record sold at 25 cents a copy between the autumn of 1916 and the end of 1917. The label was not the normal paper type. It was either etched into the material or stamped on it. Researcher Bob Colton recalls seeing one many years ago and received that impression from casual inspection.

The strange character of the recording and its labelling is matched by the methods of production. According to the late Fred Van Eps, the pioneer banjo master, Par-O-Ket records were owned and operated by the artists themselves, notably singer Harry McClaskey, better known to record historians of all kinds as Henry Burr or Irving Gillette. If this is so, it must be remarked that their knowledge of music and its performance surely exceeded their business acumen, or how to manoeuver through the cut-throat jungle of the record business as it was constituted even then. The venture limped along through the opening months of America's entry into World War I. Then Henry Burr seems to have dispensed with the services of a pressing plant and a studio equipped with Edison recording gear, in favor of having the major companies distribute his records.

PATHE, PATHE ACTUELLE and PERFECT

The story of Pathe reaches back into the 1890s. Charles Pathé, proprietor in partnership with his brother Emile of a bistro near the Place Pigalle in Paris, saw and heard an Edison phonograph at the annual fair in Vincennes. He persuaded Emile that the installation of a similar machine in their bar would be a most useful asset to their business, as it turned out to be. In 1894, the brothers began manufacturing a facsimile of the Edison machine in a factory in Belleville. In another suburb, Chatou, they built another factory that same year for making cyliner *blanks*. By 1896 this side of the business had expanded to include making records of all kinds, from the usual military bands and comedy artists to stars of the Paris Opéra-Comique. The recording studio was situated at 98 rue du Richelieu, Paris, along with the head office of Pathé Frères Pathéphone. It was the nerve centre of an expanding business that also produced various models of Le Coq, the name given to the phonograph, of which the trademark was and is to this day a cockerel in full cry.

By the turn of the century, Pathe had reached an agreement with the Anglo-Italian Commerce Company of Milan. The agreement authorized Pathe to issue outside Italy cylinders of front-rank Italian opera singers, including a young Neapolitan tenor named Enrico Caruso. Although today these Caruso cylinders, the first recordings ever made for public use by the great singer, sound light in texture and without the warmth and richness that characterize his subsequent Victors, they are obviously by him. They carry a rather garbled announcement by the singer himself, the accompanist beginning to play before the speech was complete.

In October 1906, having established recording studios in London, Milan and Moscow, Pathe announced a vertical-cut disc with grooves, recorded on exactly the same principle of indentation as its extremely popular cylinders. (Popular, that is, in France; everywhere else they ran second to lateral-cut discs.) These discs appeared in most unusual sizes. The conventional 7-, 8-, 10- and 12-inch diameters were rarely used by Pathe, which sold its wares on 8½-inch, 11-inch, 14-inch and even 20-inch discs, with a wide selection of machines on which to play them. The playing speed was 90 rpm, and the grooves were wide. They had to accommodate a jewel in the shape of a ball about .005 inches radius. Further, the pitch of the groove was much less than that of the average 78 rpm disc, and it fed outwards from the centre. It almost seemed as if Pathe, in its attempts to capture a large slice of the first phonograph boom, was determined to be different even if it killed the company. (As far as the United States and Britain were concerned, it nearly did.) Moreover, there were no labels. The details of title and artist were moulded into the smooth surface where a label is normally found, and inked in with a cream-coloured substance.

In 1914 an American branch of Pathe under the management of the pioneer actor-comedian-recording artist Russell Hunting was set up in New York. By now Pathe's home office in France had decided that no further cylinders were to be issued. Discs were to be of less outlandish dimensions, with the grooves feeding *towards* the label. And a label there must be. For American issues, the

label was black or violet, with the rooster crowing on a gold *disc*, the bird himself being red. The matrix series began at 65000, and the records were to be played at 80 rpm. Almost the only characteristic remaining from the former Pathe discs was the vertical-cut recording.

From the start, it was obvious that Pathe in the United States was a major label. The company succeeded in capturing such operatic celebrities as the young lyric tenor, Tito Schipa, French soprano Fanny Heldy, basso Adamo Didur, baritone Mario Sammarco, and many others of comparable stature. Shortly before his victory in the Presidential election of 1920, Warren G. Harding recorded some addresses for Pathe. They were even issued in England, but only as a memorial to the President after his death in 1923.

Then came the first admission that the much glorified sapphire ball might not be the best method of playing a record. The groove, indented to receive the ball, had lost favour with the American as well as the British public. In September 1920 Pathe announced a "needle-cut" record for the American market. It was named Actuelle. Its popular issues were to cost the same 75 cents as its vertical-cut predecessor, which had been reduced from 85 cents in 1920. The

vertical-cuts would of course continue to be issued, as indeed they were until November 1925. The Actuelle catalog numbers would be the same as Pathe, with a prefix O. This was dropped in December 1925. The popular catalog series began at 20000. There was also a 22000 series.

Actuelle records were made by the same method as the Pathes, by dubbing from a huge master cylinder pantographically; except of course that the cutter used for them moved laterally, removing shavings of wax from the master block as it did. Pathe masters continued to be indented as before. The studios were located at 18 West 42nd Street, New York City. Surviving artists who recorded for Pathe during the 1920s remember vividly seeing the cylinder and the recording machinery actually in the studio. One musician, of an enquiring and mechanical turn of mind, took a long, close, fascinated look at it, and was abruptly told to mind his own business, in so many words. In 1923 the studios were moved to 150 East 53rd Street. It may be that the matrix series, which by November of that year had reached more than halfway through the 70400s, was changed to 105000 upwards because of the changed location.

Before the move, another extension of the Pathe empire took place. The *Talking Machine World* of June 15, 1922 advised the trade that the first issue of Perfect records was to take place in July. The first of these, numbered 14000 upwards, had a black label with simple gold lettering and an octagonal figure in gold, encompassing the word PERFECT in a gentle arc above the spindle hole. The Actuelle label also had an octagonal frame for the entire gold printing, but *its* frame was as ornate with filigree leaves and fronds as Perfect was plain. Pathe also had Le Coq, whereas Perfect at no time in its life, which extended to April 1938 as one of the American Record Corporation's labels, used him as its trademark. Instead, Perfect adopted something much more decorative. Behind the arc of the brand name and above it rose the sun, flooding the upper part of the label. Kneeling over the word PERFECT in an attitude of worship were two shapely girls, completely naked. Belatedly but noticeably, they followed the dictates of fashion. In the early 1930s their long, flowing locks were cut to a neat bob. The label itself was black at the start, and soon changed to maroon.

The 14000 series was allocated exclusively to dance records on Perfect. There was also a 100 series for "race" records (numbered 7500 up on Pathé Actuelle). The 11000 series was a miscellany of comedy songs and patter, Hawaiian and sacred and standard instrumental and vocal items, corresponding to Pathe Actuelle (0)20000-(0)22000s. Perfect 11167 is the same as Pathe Actuelle (0)21094, and the two series are synchronized from this point on. Numbers 11500-11546 covered operatic and other more serious music, the equivalent of assorted Pathe Actuelle (0)25000s and some (0)20000s and (0)27000s. From 11547 upwards is the Star series, corresponding to Pathe Actuelle 25115 upwards. The 12000s are Perfect's popular vocal records, the equivalent on Pathe Actuelle of the first 79 of these in the miscellaneous (0)20000-(0)21000 series. Perfect 12080 is the same as Pathe Actuelle's 32001, and from this point they coincide. The dance series was roughly the same as the contemporary Pathe Actuelle (0)20000 catalog until 14181. From 14182, the equivalent of the newly introduced Pathe Actuelle (0)36001 series, these too coincide (except for Actuelle 036091, which should match Perfect 14272; but this became Actuelle 036092. Eight records later the error was discovered, and Actuelle 036091 was paired with Perfect 14282, after which everything tallies). The last Pathe Actuelle issue was 37089 in March 1930, after which Perfect survived alone for eight years.

Perfect never acknowledged the Pathe parenthood. The labels, when they gave information on the subject at all, credited manufacture to the Perfect Record Company of Brooklyn, New York, sometimes divulging in press notices that the exact location was 20 or 34 Grand Avenue. Pathe had its factory at 10-34 Grand Avenue. Its 75-cent record would not deign to link publicly with the 50-cent Perfect, still less when Perfect was reduced to 39 cents, or three for $1, in 1924 or early 1925. Actuelle was pressed in black shellac. Perfect for most of the Pathe years was reddish-brown. Both labels showed their matrix numbers in minute, neat handwriting indented into the wax and showing through the label with varying degrees of clarity. The absence of a suffix indicates a first take, -A a second, -B a third, and so on. This holds good until the spring of 1927. Then, gradually, both began to appear with sunken labels: that is, the central area carrying the matrix number (which never appeared on the labels) was removed in the processing, and labels were pressed in their place, with rims overlapping the gap thus created by about three-sixteenths of an inch. This discographically frustrating state of affairs lasted until the late summer of 1928, when labels flush with the surface of the record once more became the rule.

The two catalogs did not confine themselves to masters cut in the Brooklyn studios. In 1924, 1925 and 1926 they drew on Ajax masters in the 31500 series, masters recorded in Chicago by Orlando R. Marsh (three-digit matrix numbers by Boyd Senter, "The Jazzologist Supreme"), and a considerable number from the Plaza-Banner repertoire. These were numbered in the late 5000s-early 6000s according to the originals on Banner, Domino and Regal, without necessarily giving the take digit.

In January 1927, Pathe began to go over gradually to electric recording. Some months earlier, the Compo Company in Lachine, Quebec, Canada began supplying masters recorded electrically in New York for Pathe. These were in their E-2000 series, while the electrically recorded Pathe-made masters continued in the established series, then standing at 107269. The supply of Compo masters seems to have dried up about the time of the introduction of the sunken-label pressings.

In January 1928 came the merger between the Pathe Phonograph and Radio Corporation, as it had become, and Cameo Records. The result was that most of the biggest hits were issued on both labels simultaneously, each with a matrix number in the respective series (four figures for Cameo, q.v., six for Pathe). Not everything was recorded for both labels. When either label used a master unilaterally, it allocated only its own serial number. If Pathe subsequently decided to issue an existing Cameo title, say, the Pathe Actuelle and Perfect pressings were marked with a Cameo matrix number, and sometimes with both this *and* a Pathe number allocated at the time of selection for issue on Actuelle. The converse also happened often.

Late in the summer of 1929, the American Record Corporation took over the entire Plaza and Pathe-Cameo complexes. Thenceforth all records issued on these labels bore matrix numbers in Plaza's existing series, then just crossing over from the 8000s into the 9000s. By the late summer of 1935, Perfect was assigned the same numbers as the other surviving labels. Thus the catalog number of each Perfect indicated the month and year of issue, and the individual number in that month's supplement. Perfect 7-11-08 was therefore the eighth "popular-dance" series Perfect issued in November 1937. The eighth "race" or "old familiar tunes" series that month would be numbered 7-11-58.

The mid-thirties Perfect label, apart from the shorn-haired sun-worshippers, was little different from its independent 1920s predecessor, except that the colour was no longer maroon but black. It changed to violet. Then, with the renumbering system of 1935, it changed again to bright blue with silver lettering, and a much plainer design. No strutting cockerels to link with its Pathe origins long ago. No naked, sun-worshipping maidens. Simply the word PERFECT in slightly italicized block serif capitals straight across the upper half of the label. It was in line with "modern" design of the decade. There is no doubting that the involved filigree border on Actuelle labels, and the cosmic effect of the sun and its attendant votives, were rather Old World—but so very much more distinguished-looking! The Perfect trademark in its original form was never registered. The final plain one was granted on June 20, 1939, following an application by the President of the American Record Corporation, R. W. Altschuler, two years before. But by then Perfect had been discontinued for fourteen months. The application claimed use of the trademark since December 31, 1925: a strangely inaccurate date, since Perfect had by that time been on the market and selling extremely well for three and a half years.

As we have seen, the French home office had been quick to establish a

London branch. The earliest English Pathes looked exactly like their French counterparts. When the American branch began supplying masters, the English pressings looked very much like their American opposite numbers. When the "needle-cut" Actuelle was introduced into England in September 1921, however, its label presented a very different picture. The octagonal frame complete with filigree work in gold was there, and the general pattern was much the same as in America. But the backdrop to the frame was a dull green, and the contents of the frame were what the catalogs and monthly announcements termed "ivory" (a kind of off-white) or "pink" (of the most delicate pale rose tint). On this, all printing was in black. The brand name was faced in gold. The scripted *Pathe* did not appear at all until some seven or eight hundred issues were issued. When it did appear it was in red, like Le Coq; and there was Le Coq proudly standing on a shiny black disc with a circular gold background. The first Actuelle ten-inch was 10100, costing 3s. or about 60 cents. The first twelve-inch was 15100 and cost 4s. 6d. These records, pressed in curiously brittle material but with remarkably good surfaces, appeared monthly until December 1928, when the British branch was sold to Columbia. Soon afterwards, the factory in the northwest London suburb of Stonebridge Park was vacated.

The Actuelle catalog in its seven years presented the connoisseurs of opera and jazz alike with some treasures. The great singers have already been referred to. But where other major companies in England, with the exception of Parlophone and perhaps Brunswick (on a much smaller scale), seemed to be blissfully unaware of the existence of jazz classics and the potential market for them, Pathe with its Actuelle label gave that section of its customers such gems as almost all the records made in New York by a Red Nichols group called The Red Heads (and for good measure included some Nichols sides by a trio that never appeared in the USA at all); a generous helping of Original Memphis Five sides; some early Duke Ellingtons; a parade of titles, many with exciting jazz accompaniments, by Annette Hanshaw, who had made her recording debut for Pathe at the age of fifteen in 1926. Most remarkable of all, Actuelle issued all four Pathe sides by a Negro band called the Dixie Jassers Washboard Band. There were also clarinet solos by Boyd Senter for those whose sense of the ridiculous could tolerate them, and others by Jimmy Lytell for those who preferred clarinets that sang rather than squawked and giggled. Besides all this, there were many interesting dance bands, including the ubiquitous California Ramblers, usually under the name of the Golden Gate Orchestra.

Popular vocalists of the calibre of Lee Morse ("The Unique," as she was subtitled) and "Ukulele Ike" (Cliff Edwards) flooded out of Stonebridge Park on Actuelle. From masters cut in Paris came pressings by Maurice Chevalier, the boxer Georges Carpentier (singing, not telling of his exploits in the ring), and an American Negro dance band directed by drummer Louis Mitchell. The London recordings have matrix numbers in a 78000-79000 and a 90000 series, the French in a 5000-6000 block.

Exactly a year before Pathe sold out to Columbia, the British branch launched the English Perfect label, starting the numbering at P-301. The last one was P-432, as far as can be traced. The price was 1s. 6d., the quality every bit as good as the expensive Actuelle. Nothing outstanding appeared on English Perfect with the exception of a strangely non-commercial recording by a quintet of jazz musicians, an instrumental version of *Everybody Loves My Girl* (P-378). Ascribed, as many bands on English Perfect were, to Meyer's Dance Orchestra, it was never issued on any other label anywhere as far as is known.

The English Perfect looked very much like its American counterpart, except that it was pressed on a superior black shellac and had a bright red label. Both labels produced by Pathé Frères Pathéphone in London bear a date, finely etched by hand in mirror writing and visible inside the rim of the smooth area round the labels. This is *not* the recording date, but the date of processing that particular master.

This chart shows the approximate first matrix number recorded in each year from 1916 to 1929, in New York:

    1916 65000
    1917 65900
    1918 66530
    1919 67380
    1920 68300
    1921 68980
    1922 69570
    1923 69984 (last known in this series 70454, November)
    1924 105045
    1925 105755
    1926 106520
    1927 107315
    1928 108000
    1929 108570

For ARC matrix numbers following the above, see Banner.

PEACOCK

Peacock's Stores produced this very rare label for sale exclusively in its own shops, mainly in the Midlands of England, during the mid-1930s. Two companies were contracted in turn to supply the masters: British Homophone, which used its own London-recorded Sterno masters, and Decca, which produced Peacock records from issues in their low-priced Panachord catalog (q.v.). The Sterno-derived issues are in a series apparently beginning at BP-600 or 601. These, of course, have matrix numbers in a S-3000 series. British Homophone also produced an eight-inch Peacock label in a PS- series akin to its more usual Plaza label. It is not known exactly where this began or ended, but several hundred may have been issued. The Decca-based Peacock issues are in a P-100 series. As might be expected, the surfaces of these are usually faultless.

Everything so far discovered on Peacock was issued under pseudonyms. Most of the repertoire from both sources was of the popular and light music variety. The attractive royal blue label is printed in gold, the design embodying a spread-tailed peacock across the entire upper half, with the brand name in italic script superimposed.

PEERLESS

Whether this label qualifies as American is a matter of some doubt. The name was issued as a trademark in Mexico City in November 1944 to one Ed Baptista, who had claimed its use since April 1921. Why it should have taken him nearly a quarter of a century to file application for the use of a trademark appearing on so few records—the label is very rare—is something that may never be known.

In this book, we are not generally concerned with labels used since 1942, as one variant of the Peerless design seems to have been (and that apparently recorded in Mexico.) The earliest known Peerless records were pressed by the Starr Piano Company from masters it recorded and had used for pressing its own Gennett records (q.v.). Evidently Peerless began issuing early in 1922. Number 1001 is *The Sheik* by Sam Lanin's Orchestra and *Stars* by Nathan Glantz's Orchestra, issued at that time on Gennett under their correct names. Peerless credits both to the National Dance Orchestra. How long the arrangement with Starr lasted, and what else was issued in 1922 on Peerless, is not known.

The label is red with lettering and design in gold. The brand name appears in red on an ornate gold scroll arching over a gold P on an oval red background set in a quadrilateral gold frame. There is no indication as to origin or manufacturer, but the typeface used for the title and artist credits is the same as Gennett used at that time. There is nothing on the label to suggest that a Mexican customer was the distributor, or that the records were designed for the Mexican market. All the printing is in English.

PENNINGTON

A news item in the *Phonograph and Talking Machine Weekly* for June 4, 1924, tells us that the Bridgeport Die and Machine Company of 174 Elm Street, Bridgeport, Conn. had just launched the Pennington label for the Newark, N.J. store of L. Bamberger & Co.

These, like other BD&M labels (Broadway, Puritan, Triangle, Carnival, Mitchell and others), were drawn mostly from Paramount, with some from Emerson, Olympic and Blu-Disc. The latter provided the extremely rare Duke Ellington recording of *Rainy Nights* and *Choo Choo* issued on Pennington 1437 as by Chic Winter's Orchestra. Olympic supplied a rough but interesting *Copenhagen* by Al Turk's Princess Orchestra on Pennington 1436. This is credited to the Golden Gate Orchestra. Its backing, *Eliza,* from the Paramount label, is likewise credited to the Golden Gate Orchestra, and really is by them. (The Golden Gate Orchestra, to confound matters further, is *really* the California Ramblers.) Emerson was represented by some Original Memphis Five sides, unusually interesting for their titles.

All these are recordings of high quality, pressed on acceptable wax. The label is dark brown. The lettering, the inner concentric ring, the horizontal frame for the brand name in block capitals, are all in gold on white. A reference to L. Bamberger & Co. is in white in an arc round the lower rim. A gold olde-Englyshe P in an oval white frame, surrounded on either side by white symmetrical fronds, completes the pleasing appearance.

The catalog numbers seem to follow Paramount/Broadway sometimes, but are mostly in the four-figure 1000 series mentioned above. The venture into records by Bamberger's was short-lived. A little over a year from the date of the announcement, BD&M went bankrupt. Nothing more is known of Pennington records.

PERFECT

See Pathe.

PHANTASIE CONCERT RECORD

Little is known about this very rare and ephemeral label. It came and went at the end of 1921, lasting perhaps into the early months of 1922. Some issues were evidently connected with Lyric. The material was identical, and the only difference in the catalog numbers was a figure 1 in front of Lyric's. Others are known to have been recorded by Criterion in New York, for Cardinal-Clarion. Among them were some by the coloured cabaret artist Dorothy Dodd, whose records were issued on Phantasie as "Josephine Baker." Miss Dodd, however, was in no way related to the great comedienne from St. Louis who settled in France in 1925 and lived most of her life there. The Dodd records have three-digit C- prefix matrix numbers and are numbered in the 17000s for whatever catalog may have contained them.

PHILHARMONIC

Philharmonic was a label produced by Varsity records for Firestone Tires. The deep red labels with gold lettering and design have as a rim decoration an impression of the treadmark of a tire. The gold is a very pale tint. The records appeared during the winter of 1939-1940, and presaged the coming of major labels whose gold was also anemic.

Varsity material, Varsity typography, but slightly less than even the mediocre Varsity surfaces are apparent on the few Philharmonics I have seen. The catalog series is FR-1 upwards. Included are records by such world jazz notables as the "Father of the Blues," W. C. Handy himself, with a small band, and Jack Teagarden and his Orchestra. A globe shows the North and South American continents and a suggestion of Europe, and is surmounted by a humanoid figure with outstretched arms above the brand name. The latter is printed in rather small serif capital letters. The records are not easy to come by.

PHONOCUT

This was another short-lived Pathe-type vertical-cut record of the 1917-1920 era. It was made by the Phono-Cut Record Company of Boston, Mass. The label is black, with gold lettering and a design which embodies a scroll carrying the manufacturer's name superimposed on a globe map. It is believed that nothing of great musical or historical importance was issued on this make.

PHONOGRAPH RECORDING CO. OF SAN FRANCISCO

This was a small recording company that never issued records publicly. It recorded, processed and pressed to order whatever its customers desired during its period of activity in the late 1920s. Its chief claim to fame, if that is the word, lies in the fact that one of its products has survived, a coupling by Jack Danford and his Ben Franklin Hotel Orchestra that included cornetist Lu Watters. Later Watters became the spearhead, with his Yerba Buena Jazz Band, of the revivalist movement of the 1940s.

PHONOLAMP

A Phonolamp is a contraption apparently put on the market in 1920 or 1921 by the Electric Phonograph Corporation of New York. It consists of an electric lamp with a built-in phonograph. It was not, however, driven electrically, nor does it reproduce records by this means. It would seem that Phonolamp records, of which probably less than a dozen were issued, were given away with the machine. They were products of the Grey Gull complex, numbered from 1000 at least to 1007. Popular dance tunes and songs of 1921 have been found on Phonolamp records. It is unlikely that there is anything of greater significance there.

The label itself is white, printed in dark blue. The song title appears in an arc round the rim of the upper half, enclosing composer credit, catalog number and artist credit. The entire lower half is occupied by the word PHONOLAMP (subtitled, in upper and lower case, "Speaks for itself") in bizarre lettering starting and ending in small capitals that grow to their largest with the central O, which encloses a drawing of the Phonolamp itself. However rare Phonolamp records are, the same music is to be found on Grey Gull. The machine of the same name must be a unique collector's item.

PICCADILLY

Costing half the price of its parent label Metropole, Piccadilly records at 1s. 6d.—say 30 cents—were quite a bargain. They always maintained a high standard of recording and manufacture during their life of nearly four years between October 1928 and April 1932. Piccadilly produced two series of records. The popular had white labels with gold overlay round the rim and all printing in black. They started at 100 and reached 924. The classical series had vivid red labels exactly like the others in every other respect. It started at 5000 in February 1930 and reached 5127 in January 1931. These red-labelled records were 2s. They were probably introduced to match the Broadcast Twelve series that had been established at the same price for eighteen months. As far as is known, all the issues in this series were recorded in London in the studio in Metropole House, Finsbury Square, London, E.C. 2.

Recorded in the same studio were the English popular series. Issued on 825 white-labelled Piccadilly records, their labels first showed a broad gold rim strewn with various instruments of the orchestra. They soon dispensed with this rather frivolous design but retained a drawing of Eros, the statue of the god of love resting on his pedestal in Piccadilly Circus, London. Many of the dance records and a sprinkling of popular vocals were of American origin. Those with matrix numbers in a 31000 series were from Emerson. They were issued, like many of the Piccadilly dance catalog, under imaginative pseudonyms. The Kentucky Freebooters was one. Then followed the White Star Syncopators and the Astoria Dance Players, the Cunard Dance Band and the Fifth Avenue Dance Band. Emerson soon disappeared as a source for Piccadilly. For most of the rest of its career, the label drew on Grey Gull until the latter vanished from the American market in the summer of 1930. Piccadilly records from Grey Gull have two sets of matrix numbers. The original Grey Gull 3000-4000 numbers are usually indented heavily in the smooth wax round the label, close to the concentric groove linked to the playing track. So too are the Piccadilly numbers, also in the 3000s, and often preceded by the letters XX.

The chapter on Grey Gull gives all the information that can be gleaned about these records. The pressings on Piccadilly are usually smoother and cleaner than those on anything in the Grey Gull complex. Other than a somewhat corny version of *St. Louis Blues* and a superb quartet version of *In Harlem's Araby* (credited to the White Star Syncopators), there is not much of jazz interest on Piccadilly, though the Grey Gull house band sometimes provides a worthwhile hot soloist. The Piccadilly records most likely to interest a specialist collector are the many by such bands as Percy Chandler's, Howard Godfrey's, Earl Melville's (Hawaiian instrumental), and Jack Leon's, all of which feature Al Bowlly as vocalist. They are rare, and well worth searching for. Bowlly can also be heard on two sides by Percival Mackey and his Concert Orchestra (*When the Lilac Blooms Again* on 288, and *Up in the Clouds* on 264, the latter issued as by the Ever-Bright Boys and not without its jazz interest). Records by Billy Cotton's Band, renamed the Bohemian Band, or Jack Harris's Orchestra, described as Tunney's Floridorians, are also of some interest. Several British bands made all or almost all their records on Piccadilly, among them Allan Selby, Jack Leon, Jock McDermott and Jerry Hoey.

When the supply of Grey Gull masters ceased, Piccadilly evidently made some agreement with the American Record Corporation for selected masters. Two sides by Whispering Jack Smith and two by Ruth Etting, as well as several dance records and two by the famous singer of cowboy songs, Gene Autry, appeared on Piccadilly. Most of these also appeared simultaneously on Edison Bell Winner and/or Imperial.

The following chart shows approximately the first Piccadilly matrix number recorded each year in London:

```
1928 (c. June)  1001
1929            1515
1930            3340  (matrices between 2199 or 2200
                       and 2999 or 3000 were not used)
1931            4160
1932            4600
```

The series was continued by the Octocros label, heir to the Piccadilly catalog until it too went out of business in 1937. There were no American masters on this label, as far as is known.

PLAYERPHONE

The Playerphone Talking Machine Company of Chicago produced this ver-Jewel Ball Point (around the upper rim). The brand name in flowing script, set at an angle of about 30 degrees to the horizontal, occupies the rest of the upper half. The price, 75 cents, is shown to the right of the spindle hole. The label is extremely rare. Its repertoire is not likely to include anything of outstanding interest—unless Roy Spangler's superb ragtime piano solos (see Rex) are to be found on Playerphone.

tical-cut record from the same master source as Rex, Empire, Imperial and Rishell during the years around the first World War, using the same 5000-series catalog numbers. Proclaiming itself "The Quality Record," the reddish-brown label with gold lettering instructs that the record be played with Playerphone

PLAYTIME

As might be expected, this seven-inch 78 rpm record is designed for children. Its repertoire included all kinds of songs and music likely to appeal to the young. The selections were recorded by such varied artists as Irving Kaufman, who made a seasonally cheerful record of *Jingle Bells* for the 1932 Christmas trade, and soprano Margaret Daum, who sang *Sweet and Low* and *The Doll Song* in 1941. The records were made by ARC, then CBS. The earlier issues had suitably illustrated labels. Latterly they were yellow with all lettering in black.

PORTLAND

The enterprising British firm of Curry's, dealer in electrical appliances of all kinds as well as bicycles and accessories, produced three labels during the 1920s. These were its own, Portland (both q.v.) and Westport. Portland, like Westport, was pressed by Edison Bell Winner and used its masters. These occasionally included material from the Gennett catalog, mostly by Bailey's Lucky Seven. There was also a version of *Somebody's Wrong* (9078) by a Chicago-based band called Porter's Blue Devils. As with other Edison Bell products, Portland bears that company's matrix numbers, in the 7000-8000 block. Where a Gennett master was used, the original handwritten Starr Piano Company's matrix number is left untouched. There do not seem to have been many Portland records issued during the year or eighteen months of their life (1923-1924). Fewer than a hundred would seem to be a fair estimate.

The label is purple, lighter in tint than usually found on purple-labelled records. All the printing and design are in black. An odd feature of the design is that, above the brand name across the upper half, there is the word CURRYS in upper case, arc-shaped, with a panel underlining it and bearing the legend "1927 Ltd." Yet all the known dance records and popular songs issued on this label are firmly from the period three of four years earlier. They would have had no sort of appeal in 1927, especially since by that date electric recording was featured and widely publicized on even the least expensive labels. Portland is also unusual in that its label bears *three* advertising slogans: "As good as a Curry cycle" in an arc over the top, "Always Gives Satisfaction" on a panel below the brand name, and "A Record That Provides Endless Pleasure" around the lower half. The 9000 series is the only one known to have been used on Portland, which issued everything under the same pseudonyms as the Edison Bell Winner equivalent.

PRINCESS

Manufactured probably between 1917 and 1920 by the Sapphire Record and Talking Machine Company, Metropolitan Tower, New York City, Princess records were vertical-cut discs of the Pathe type (as suggested by the name of the makers). Little is known about them. They are very rare. The label is pale yellow with all lettering in blue. The maker's name runs around the upper rim of the label and the address around the lower, with the initials of the company and the full name, Princess Sapphire Record, across the label below the maker's name.

PUBLIX

A custom-pressed Columbia product designed to plug the "theme songs" from Paramount films in the early years of movie musicals, Publix records were pressed from existing masters recorded for the Harmony label (q.v.). By the time they came into being, Harmony's "boxy" acoustic method of recording had thankfully been abandoned. Publix records thus have the advantage of the superb recording system then used by the Columbia Phonograph Company for all its products. Publix records were designed mainly for use—and presumably for sale—in theatres showing Paramount musicals. Their distribution was therefore limited, and the label is rare. It is glossy black, printed throughout in gold. The design suggests a steering wheel, quartering the label so that the upper part frames the familiar Paramount Pictures trademark, a mountain with an arc of stars above it. The word PUBLIX in sans-serif block letters is shown below the Paramount logo. The description of the music is given in the right-hand quarter. The lower quarter shows the usual title, composer and artist credits, but in minute type because of the space limitations caused by the steering-wheel design. Reading almost requires a magnifying glass, particularly for the matrix number. Publix catalog numbers come in a 2000-P series. Fewer than a hundred were issued.

PURETONE

The name Puretone is unfortunate in the context of the history of American records. It is easily confused with another, more common label from the same factory: Puritan (q.v.), made by the Bridgeport Die and Machine Company of Bridgeport, Conn. The two makes enjoyed, if that is the word, a contemporaneous existence for about a year, maybe a little longer. Their numbers are similar, if not identical. Puretone's seem to be restricted to a block in the mid-11000s. The label is unusually attractive, a deep maroon slightly darker in tone than the brown wax of the pressing itself. A gold rim inside the edge, a pair of parallel gold bars nearly half an inch apart across the upper half just above the spindle hole to form a white panel with the brand name in simulated olde-Englyshe characters in gold surmounted by two white lilies amid strands of curlicue foliage also in gold—it all adds up to a striking design quite unlike any other. No clue is given as to which of B.D.&M.'s customers ordered the Puretones. The lower rim of the label merely credits the Bridgeport factory as manufacturer, in white capitals. The usual credits are in gold, but in a typeface not usually found on other B.D.&M. products. The price is shown as 75 cents.

The masters derive from Paramount. The recording quality is adequate, the surfaces reasonable. But one could buy a pair of dance tunes or popular songs or well worked light classics on Victor, Columbia, OKeh, Brunswick, Vocalion or Gennett for the same price, and by nationally known artists. This may be the reason why Puretones are so rare. They probably disappeared early in 1925, as the manufacturers went bankrupt that summer.

PURITAN

Puritan records bowed in the *Talking Machine World* in the January 15, 1920 issue. They were manufactured by the United Phonographs Corporation of Sheboygan, Wis. The soberly attractive black and brown labels with gold lettering and printing featured a girl playing a virginal. The numbering was in a 9000 series. Before fifty records had been issued, a similar design added the words "America's Best Record." This modest claim was maintained throughout the remaining seven years of Puritan's existence. The numbers later included an 11000 series.

The black changed to blue in 1921, and the brown was omitted. From March 1, 1922, Puritan records were put on sale as manufactured by the Bridgeport Die and Machine Company of Bridgeport, Conn. They cost 50 cents, and reverted to black and gold. Some specimens now showed a cameo effect of a Puritan's head in profile, black on white. These, according to contemporary literature, were distributed in the area east of the Ohio and north of the Potomac.

The *Talking Machine World Trade Directory* for 1923 shows the New York Recording Laboratories, Inc. as manufacturers of Paramount, Broadway, Famous and Puritan. Yet Bridgeport Die and Machine is listed as manufacturer of Triangle, Broadway—and Puritan. And copies of titles issued by Paramount, in late 1922 as all Puritans of this date were, show the New York Recording Laboratories of Port Washington, Wis., as the makers. These use a bright blue label with gold lettering and design, with no place for either the stern Puritan or the damsel at the virginal. This label is instead festooned with grapevines. This design remains to all intents and purposes unaltered until Puritan was discontinued in 1927. The background colour became more purple than blue, finally reverting to black. For the last two or three years there was no indication on the label as to who the manufacturer and/or distributor was. Early in 1924 the 75-cent price was included on the label, as it was on the quality labels of Victor and the rest. By the summer of 1925, with B.D.&M. out of business, Puritan was *all* Paramount.

From the latter part of 1925 into the first few months of 1927, Puritan drew as much from Plaza's repertoire, via Paramount, as from Paramount originals.

Those with matrix numbers in a block between 500 and 3000 are from the latter source. Those having a 6000-7000 series number, without a take digit, in addition to a three or low-four-figure control number, are from Plaza. Unlike some others that drew from Paramount, Puritan offered some fine jazz and blues items, from the Original Memphis Five to King Oliver's Jazz Band, from Jimmy Wade's Moulin Rouge Orchestra to the Six Hottentots (a kind of Red Nichols Five Pennies group). For the most part a B.D.&M. production, the quality of the surfaces is quite good, and Paramount's recording in the acoustic era was frequently of comparable standard. Due no doubt to being distributed on a wider scale than the Paramount-originated labels that were sold only in one store or chain, Puritan lasted longer than the others. Finding a specimen is still a source of joy to a jazz, blues or dance band enthusiast. The allocation of a different catalog number to each side in some cases (Fletcher Henderson's *Prince of Wails* backed by Sammy Stewart's *Copenhagen*, for example) only adds to the joys of speculation as to what else will be found on this enigmatic label.

PURITONE

This label was the property of Strauss and Schram, Inc., the Chicago mail-order house. Pressed from Columbia's Harmony masters but with no numerical relationship to the Harmony catalog, they appeared in 1928 and existed for perhaps a year, possibly slightly longer. At 75 cents each—the red label tells us that much—they were as expensive as the fine quality Columbia, OKeh, Victor and other major labels. The catalog series seems to have begun at 1001-S and continued for about a hundred issues. The label is very rare. Such items as are known are all straightforward dance and popular records. This is not to say, however, that other, more interesting fare may be awaiting discovery under the Puritone label.

QRS

The QRS Piano Roll is the longest-established merchandise of its kind in the United States. Beginning before World War I and continuing today, it offers a wide spectrum of music for the player-piano. There were three kinds of QRS records in the 1920s, all of them actually or potentially of interest, mainly to jazz collectors—and all of them as rare as the piano rolls are common.

The earliest known QRS record not only drew from the Gennett catalog but even used the Gennett catalog *number* and label colour-scheme. This is a dark navy blue with gold lettering. There is no design. The label is inner-ringed doubly, the outer being just twice as wide as the inner. Around the upper rim are the letters Q·R·S, the middle R being smaller than the large Q and S. Under the letters are the words TRADE MARK in small upper-case lettering. Under this is the word "Record" in lower case. Around the lower rim run QRS COMPANY CHICAGO, U.S.A. and the numbers and title, composer and artist credits in the usual position. One QRS record is identical to Gennett 5271. Since one of the most sought-after jazz records of all is King Oliver's Creole Jazz Band on Gennett 5276, one can be forgiven for speculating on the possibility that this, evidently considered at the eleventh hour as unsuitable for issue on Gennett, might—*might*—have been taken up by QRS. . . .

When these Gennett-type QRS records were issued is uncertain. It could be any time from as far back as Gennett itself (q.v.) right through into the second and more familiar QRS era of 1928-1929. At that time the Gennett studio in Woodhaven, Queens, New York City was used to produce two distinct series, R-7000s ("race" issues, many by Clarence Williams and his Orchestra, some by his Barrel House Five, and various by extremely rare and interesting blues artists, urban and country alike) and R-9000s, a country-and-western series. These QRS issues have glossy black labels printed entirely in gold. The enigmatic initials—no one seems to have established exactly what they signify—run across the central area and again above, enclosed in a wreath with a lyre sending out thirty-four zigzags denoting lightning and affirming that "Q.R.S. PRODUCTS are Better." An arc of twenty stars surrounds the upper rim of the label. Six more stars go round the lower, broken by the announcement QRS CO. MANU-

FACTURERS OF MUSIC ROLLS AND RECORDS. The firm and brand name thus appear three times, each time with the R in noticeably smaller type than the Q and the S.

The third type of QRS has a somewhat smaller label than the three-and-a-half inch label on the second. It is red with gold lettering. The design is similar, except that the lower rim states "Recorded by Cova Recording Corp., New York City." The catalog series is Q-1000 to at least Q-1055. All seem to date from late 1929 to the summer of 1930. All that is known or that can be surmised about this Cova QRS is that in April 1929, according to the *Talking Machine World* for that month, the QRS Company in Chicago merged with the DeVry Corporation, which produced movies, including sound films. It seems likely that the red QRS issues are a product of this union. Their matrix numbers range from about 1700 to about 2400. Those of the black labels that preceded them are from about 100 to about 500 and came out between the summer of 1928 and the spring of 1929. Thus, a gap of some 1,200 numbers. Can we infer that at least some were recordings for the soundtracks of DeVry films?

One of the most interesting points about the Cova QRS catalog is that many were issued in England on Goodson (q.v.) during the summer and early autumn of 1930, when Grey Gull was in decline and thus unable to supply further American recordings of the latest hits. The Goodson supplements and catalogs of the time contain listings of several sides by a band called the Cova Cavaliers. Such examples as have been found show that these are indeed from Cova QRS. The matrix numbers are etched by hand in the central area rather than heavily indented in the inner side of the concentric ring forming the limit of the run-off, as in the Grey Gull style.

The repertoire of the Cova QRS record, as best can be determined, follows much the same pattern as that of dozens of small labels of the previous decade: dance records (nothing of much importance to a jazz collector, although some are of interest, notably those by Stew Pletcher's Eli Prom Trotters), popular vocals, comedy numbers and instrumental novelties. Their great rarity is undoubtedly due to their having made their debut at a time when the Wall Street debacle had shocked the national economy into semi-paralysis. As to quality, both of these and their black-label forerunners are remarkably good. The Gennett-type issues of 1923-1924 are of course exactly as good or as bad as the Gennetts themselves.

RADIEX

Radiex, throughout the 1920s, was one of the Grey Gull complex of labels. Its repertoire, appearance and quality had all the characteristics of Grey Gull (q.v.). It underwent a number of designs in its nine years of life. One of its earliest was a bright vermillion label with a gold ring two-fifths of an inch inside the rim of the label itself. The brand name in lower-case lettering appears across the upper half, underlined and surmounted by a gold bar, each end decorated. The title, composer and artist credits, and the catalog and matrix numbers, are all printed in black. The general appearance is rather tawdry. Many of the masters used for this 1000 series are from Emerson, Paramount and Plaza, as were Grey Gull's. No origin is named on these early issues.

The later 1920s saw a much more attractive design, a new catalog series, and credit on the labels to Grey Gull. The exact wording is "Recorded by Grey Gull, Boston, U.S.A." It is printed in small lower-case type on either side of the spindle hole, on a label entirely cross-hatched in rich blue. The brand name is printed in a gentle arc in gold, with a white background to each letter, the whole on a deep blue background. The details of the recorded performance are in black. The border of the label is dark blue, gold and white in a rather complicated design.

In October 1928, the trade was notified of no fewer than thirty-eight new issues on Radiex, each disc to sell at 14½ cents each. Despite the sales promotion, their rough surfaces and coarse recording held scant appeal to the public. Within some eighteen months or so, Radiex had vanished. The records were pressed on a dark chocolate brown material, and wore out easily. Like Grey Gull, large numbers seem to have been shipped to England during the 1930s and sold in Woolworth's and similar stores, at what was then the sterling equivalent of dime-store prices.

RAINBOW

This semi-private record bears the obvious label design: a rainbow in full natural colour on a greyish-blue background. All printing was in black or dark blue. The recording was apparently done by Gennett, or independently. The power behind the label was gospel-singer and trombonist Homer Rodeheaver, who also recorded for Victor and indeed for most labels extant in New York during the 1920s. Rainbow records are apparently all acoustically recorded. As far as is known, they consist entirely of gospel songs, hymns and popular sacred music.

REGAL and REGAL ZONOPHONE

There were two Regal labels during the 1920s. The American one was a fifty-cent chain-store label drawing from Emerson masters. It made its first appearance in the spring of 1921 at 901. On reaching 999, the numbers leapt to 9100 and continued in this series until 9999 in April 1926. The next allocation was 8000. This series also continued to the millennium at 8999. Next in line was 10000.

By the early months of 1923, Regal had turned to Plaza for its masters. This remained the source of supply until the summer of 1931, when the arrangement was discontinued at about 10400. A short-lived new series was introduced at that time, starting at 100 or 101. Only a few issues appeared before the American Record Corporation absorbed all the Brunswick and Plaza labels and phased out several, Regal among them.

Of all the Emerson-Plaza labels, Regal was the plainest. Printed in gold on glossy black, the design consisted of a wide gold ring round the rim, about two-fifths of an inch inside it; the word "Regal" in lower-case type across the top half; the title, composer and artist credits below; and the notation "© 1921" at the bottom of the lower half. This never changed, except that the introduction of electric recording brought in an E on a gold disc to the left of the spindle hole in 1926. The last issues were pressed with smaller labels.

The material issued on Regal was remarkably varied. It followed the course of its label-mate Banner, of course. Regal sometimes even used the same pseudonym as Banner occasionally varying the coupling. The quality of recording, especially the early Emerson and Plaza acoustics, is clean and well balanced. As with Banner, the electrics are inclined to shrillness and later to muddiness. A mint copy of a Regal record reproduces with little surface noise, something which cannot always be said of certain more expensive makes of the time. The collector of jazz and blues can find many enjoyable items on Regal by such as Bessie Brown, Nettie Potter, the Dixie Washboard Band, Joe Jordan's Sharps and Flats, Lanin's Southern Serenaders, the Original Memphis Five, Clementine Smith, the Six Black Diamonds, and Noble Sissle and Eubie Blake. Later on came Fred Hall's Jazz Band, Jack Pettis and his Band, Cab Calloway, Duke Ellington and Clarence Williams. Dance music from Sam Lanin, Fred Rich, Ben Selvin and Vincent Lopez; interesting vocals by Chick Bullock, Irving Kaufman and Billy Jones; folk music by Irish, Hawaiian and other groups—all can be found on Regal. Distribution was nationwide. Few labels are met with more frequently.

The British Regal was introduced in April 1914 as a cheap Columbia subsidiary. The label was then as it remained for the whole of its independent life up to December 1932: magenta in colour, with all the printing and lettering in gold. At the outset the design included a representation of the ceremonial orb, sceptre and mace used in the coronations of British kings and queens, complete with velvet cushion for the orb. These were surmounted by the brand name in an arc around the upper rim of the label, flanked by a warning about copyright. Soon after the end of World War I, in 1919, the orb, sceptre and mace were dispensed with. The copyright warning took their place, between the brand name and the spindle hole. For the next three years Regal labels presented a rather empty appearance. Then the copyright notice was set straight across the top of the label, above the brand name. This too was printed straight up, between two parallel gold bars. This plain but less vacant design remained, with slight modifications, until the merger with Zonophone.

The label was introduced with tremendous double-page spreads in the trade press accompanying sections of its ready-made catalog, inherited from Columbia. This was done with a panache rare in the history of British records. The price was 1s. 6d. By the end of the war in 1918 it had doubled, to 3s. In September 1921 the price was reduced to 2s. 6d., or about 50 cents—by coincidence the same figure as the American namesake, with which there was no connection. Exactly ten years later, the price came down again—to 1s. 6d., where it had started. This was maintained until February 1935, when it dropped to 1s., only to be raised to 1s. 3d. in March 1937 and back to 1s. 6d. in September 1937. The war and its purchase tax jacked the price up again. In November 1949 the Regal Zonophone label was abandoned.

The original Regal catalog series began at G-6000. It reached G-9473 by February 1930. In March, all Columbia products were re-numbered, Regal starting at MR-1. Hitherto, Columbia and Regal had shared the British allocation of matrix numbers, the curious jigsaw detailed in the chapter on Columbia, through the A- prefix series almost to A-10000. Now this was to be Columbia's alone. Regal made a new start with WAR-1. Later the prefix became CAR-, and stayed so. The amalgamation with Zonophone made no difference to either the MR- catalog series or the CAR- matrix series.

With the amalgamation came an attempt to combine the original colours of the two labels. The REGAL remains in its position between the parallel gold bars, surmounting ZONOPHONE. Both names are in white. REGAL was outlined in red and backed with gold, ZONOPHONE backed with red. Above the bars is a vermillion segment with italic gold print warning about copyright. Below, the lower half of the label is green, with all details in gold. The outer rim of the whole label is red. The general appearance is tasteful and colourful, distinguished and attractive, with no floral tributes or curlicues of any kind. Beginning at MR-745 in January 1933, this design remained in use until two months after the February 1935 supplement. This brought in the shilling Regal Zonophones with bright scarlet labels of exactly the same design, but with all printing in gold. It never changed materially again in the remaining fourteen years of its life. The last of the line was MR-3814, a contemporary recording by Gene Autry.

Regal as an independent product was of the finest quality, as good as Columbia in its brilliant recording and velvety surfaces. It offered everything: opera in English and ballads of all kinds by singers of the calibre of John McCormack, Lenghi-Cellini and Violet Essex; country-and-western numbers from the American Columbia catalog by Riley Puckett, Harry C. Browne, Dan Hornsby, the Three Georgia Crackers and the Alabama Barnstormers; quality dance records by American and British bands, the very cream of the international elite in this field; popular vocals, sacred records, instrumentals and brass bands aplenty; and always the novelties, which might include bird imitations, speeches on conditions in the trenches in Flanders by a Left-wing politician (and a soldier who won the Victoria Cross), jokes by the editor of *Tit-Bits*, then as now a rather garish humorous tabloid, and music-hall sketches that sold to capacity. After the formation of the Regal Zonophone partnership, the novelties grew even more varied, with records by Master Denis Gonet, the thirteen-year-old with a tenor voice like a grown man's; a "sensational discovery" in the person of a singing millworker; a singing dirt-track racer; a heavyweight boxer (he sang, too); the members of the Grandfathers Club, whose ages totalled nearly a thousand years; a duet on two cinema organs in theatres five miles apart; slivers of soundtrack from outstanding movies; and even one disc, two sides, by the Memphis Jug Band, recorded seven and a half years before on Victor, issued without any publicity, and fast deleted. It remains one of the most sought-after of all Regal Zonophone records (MR-2331).

That was in February 1937. The big sellers then were the dance bands, of which Joe Loss flew the flag for Britain. There were dozens from Victor's Bluebird catalog. British customers could sample the bubbling of Shep Fields and his Rippling Rhythm and the jazz of Wingy Manone and his Orchestra. There were Hot Lips Page and Vincent Lopez, Tempo King and his Kings of Tempo, Gray Gordon and his Tic-Toc Rhythm—and, in 1939, a few tentative sides by two new bands that were just exploding on the American scene. They were led by Artie Shaw and Glenn Miller.

A month after Miller's *Moonlight Serenade* was issued on MR-3090, World War II broke out. American releases shrivelled up almost to nothing. Where once the output of new issues every month had frequently been thirty, it was now down to a dozen . . . six . . . then perhaps one a month. One of the most lively

British labels became another war casualty. It outlasted hostilities by four years, and its catalog remains a model of quality and quantity at an incredibly reasonable price.

The following chart shows the first Regal/Regal Zonophone matrix numbers made in each year up to 1942:

1930 (February)	WAR-1	1937	CAR-4370
1931	WAR-476	1938	CAR-4820
1932	CAR-970	1939	CAR-5228
1933	CAR-1660	1940	CAR-5648
1934	CAR-2446	1941	CAR-5940
1935	CAR-3150	1942	CAR-6240
1936	CAR-3800		

For details of American Regal matrix dates, see Emerson for the 41000-42000 series and Banner for the 5000-10000 series.

RESONA

This was another store label produced in the first half of the 1920s. Early issues bear numbers in the 11000s and are from Paramount masters pressed by the Bridgeport Die and Machine Company of Bridgeport, Conn. These are very rare. Their successors, which first appeared in the autumn of 1923, were pressed from Federal masters (q.v.). These are numbered as Federals are, but with a 7 in front of the 5000 catalog series. The matrix numbers have a take digit *preceding* the actual number, which in any case is different from take to take.

Resona records from Federal have black labels with no design but with a gold ring as a border. The brand name runs in large script at an angle of about 30° to the horizontal across the upper half of the label. The words "The Charles William Stores Inc., New York City" follow the inner side of the gold ring around the lower part of it.

The stores had used the name "Resona" since January 1916, according to their claim for rights. But the name applied to phonographs. There were no Resona records on the market as early as that. The records continued to be issued even after Federal had disappeared in the spring of 1924. Some were from Emerson, and a good selection from Plaza, the latter continuing into the autumn of 1925 and bearing Plaza matrix numbers in the 5000-6000 block. The repertoire was the usual selection of light classics, ballads, comedy, instrumentals, popular vocals, and above all dance records. The latter do not appear until more than 300 items in the other categories had been issued. Then, in a 75000 catalog series, they run to about 75500 and the demise of the label.

REX

There are two very different makes of 78 rpm records labelled Rex. The earlier is American, produced by the Rex Talking Machine Corporation of Wilmington, Del. between 1912 and 1916. The numbers run in a 5000 series. The recording method is vertical, in the Pathe manner. The label is black, printed in a strange fawn colour throughout. The words REX RECORD are faced in white around the upper rim of the label, with the maker's name and the advice "Use only sapphire point on this record" in two lines of upper-case lettering around the lower. The logo is an Edison type of disc phonograph with its lid open, playing a record. Behind it is a bearded face with a crown. A right hand holds a record and the whole design is swathed by an elaborate scroll bearing the words "A Royal Entertainer." The price is shown as 75 cents.

Many labels from this era were content simply to feature popular songs, dance music and light classics. Rex was no exception, as far as the great rarity of the label allows research to discern. But it also put out two sides (each backed by some trivial popular number of the time, 1913) by an obscure pianist named on the label as Roy Spangler. He plays *Cannon Ball Rag* on Rex 5024 and *Red Onion Rag* on Rex 5026, reissued later on 5342. Two sessions are involved here. Whether any similar music was also recorded *and issued* remains to be seen. Meanwhile, the beauty of both titles and the splendid performance make each record a classic. There was also a twelve-inch Rex 1000 series, apparently much shorter-lived than the ten-inch. In May 1917 the Imperial Talking Machine Company purchased all the assets of Rex.

The later Rex is British. It was launched by the Crystalate Gramophone Record Manufacturing Company Ltd. of 60 City Road, London, E.C.1 in September 1933 at 1s. (about 20 cents). The makers of Imperial records (q.v.) were plunging into the cheap record market with a quality product costing a dime less than their existing label, which in any case was allowed to die seven months later.

Rex, "The King of Records" as the label proclaims it, began at 8001. Before the last was issued in February 1948, over 2,200 had appeared. First there was a black-label series. It became bright red with black lettering and the brand name in white during World War II. There was also a U- series of Irish music with an appropriate green label carrying exactly the same design as the regular issues: a shield bearing the word REX in gold, supported by two heraldic lions. At the outset they were black on gold, and looked fierce. After about thirty issues the colour scheme was reversed. The gold lions on a black background grew larger, more lifelike, more dignified. The gold rim to the label was printed in black with the words BRITISH MADE around the upper half and HEAR WHAT YOU LIKE—WHEN YOU LIKE around the lower.

The promise in the slogan was of course not kept. There was dance music, but no jazz other than the occasional hot performance of some popular song of the day. Popular vocals abounded. Here the jazz enthusiast could find interesting accompaniments to Chick Bullock, who was well represented throughout the first thousand issues. There were light classics played by string orchestras, cinema organs, piano-accordions, even chirping canaries. The sometimes noisy surfaces also carried comic sketches, Gracie Fields, Larry Adler and his harmonica, piano medleys of six songs per record by Charlie Kunz, and exactly similar records by Primo Scala's Accordion Band. But, unlike Broadcast in 1928, Rex made no attempt to provide the less affluent public with concert music or opera. The Silver Jubilee issues of May 1935 (with expensive-looking labels featuring full-colour portraits of Their Majesties King George V and Queen Mary) and the Coronation issues of exactly two years later (with similar portraits of Their Majesties King George VI and Queen Elizabeth) featured patriotic music. One lone issue, Rex 8957, offered Bing Crosby (*Home on the Range* and *Blue Prelude*) at a shilling when his latest recordings on Brunswick were selling at two to three times as much. About the same time, late 1936, several American stars turned up on Rex: the Boswell Sisters, the Mills Brothers, Cab Calloway, Vincent Lopez, Joe Haymes, Johnny Johnson and Smith Ballew. In 1934 there was even one Rex—8335—of Benny Goodman's Orchestra under the pseudonym "Hollywood Dance Orchestra" playing *Stars Fell on Alabama*. Rex 8051 offered "Bob Causer and his Cornellians" as a disguise for a New Orleans band of Negro musicians, under the leadership of Joseph Robechaux, playing *Swingy Little Thingy*.

This superior dance music was issued from the ARC catalog. Crystalate shared access to it with Decca. In March 1937 Decca took over the record division of Crystalate and proceeded to issue occasional items from American Decca along with much the same British fare as before.

The original Crystalate matrix series began at F-500 or F-501. Often nothing of this, nor of an ARC matrix number where one applied, was visible in the wax around or under the label. Sometimes all that could be seen of either was a faint hand-etching that showed through the paper. By the end of the Crystalate era, the numbers had reached about 2260. Under Decca they continued, with a prefix R-. The Crystalate studios in Broadhurst Gardens, Hampstead, London N.W.3 were also taken over by Decca, and are used by Decca to this day. While redecorating and modernizing the building in the spring of 1962, some workmen found a hollow wall holding a number of Crystalate ledgers for sessions on every company label except Rex. Though there was a huge scrapbook of every Rex label from the beginning, nothing has ever been found to show exactly when any London-recorded Rex title was made. The following will show approximately the first matrix number in each year up to 1942:

1933 (c. July)	F-500	1938	R-2560
1934	F-650	1939	R-3201
1935	F-1130	1940	R-4200
1936	F-1660	1941	R-5210
1937	F-2130	1942	R-6590

RIALTO

Two distinctly different Rialto labels were introduced into the American record market during the 1920s, with absolutely no connection between them. Both were short-lived. The later one was apparently sold by the Rialto Music Store of Chicago in 1924. Recorded by Orlando R. Marsh, it had like his Autograph label no catalog numbers. The only known example is *London Blues*, a piano solo played by its composer, Ferd (Jelly Roll) Morton, as the label has it. The label is bright blue, with an ornate design in the form of leaves and curlicues. The reverse is another Marsh recording, one Frank Collins accompanying himself on ukulele while singing *I Never Miss the Sunshine (While There's Moonshine Around)*. Piano solos are seldom big sellers. This one, sold only in one music store in the whole country, is certainly no exception, even with some rugged country humour on the other side. The recording is reasonably good. The surface, at least of a copy in excellent condition, is tolerable.

The earlier Rialto also has a bright blue label, with much ornamentation and printing in gold. It was produced by the U.S. Record Manufacturing Corporation, Long Island City, New York in 1921. Apparently there were at least seven issues in a 6000 catalog series. The label has a gold upper half with RIALTO in studded block letters in gold on a blue panel describing a slight arc above the spindle hole. Behind it is what appears to be a kind of firecracker display. Six sparkling semi-circles are seen overlapping above the panel, with six sparkling columns emanating from the same spot to the right of the spindle hole below it. The title, composer and artist credits are all printed in italic capitals. The tiny repertoire seems to consist of dance music and popular songs. The matrix numbers apparently begin at 100 or 101 and have numerical prefixes (usually 5, but also 8 and 12), the meaning of which is unknown.

Several other eccentricities should be noted about this Rialto label. The same material appears on another U.S. Record label known as Hits. Hits has the same catalog numbers, except that they are exactly 4000 numbers behind those on Rialto. There is also an Apollo label in an exactly similar 5000 series, and an Emerald numbered 3000. Perhaps stranger still is the fact that the Dandy label of the mid-1920s duplicates the design of Rialto, except that Rialto's blue is

Dandy's black, and the gold design and decoration on Rialto is white on Dandy. An anonymous electrically recorded Rialto in black and gold is reported by Carl Kendziora of a pair of Italian songs of unknown recording date. Here again the label is exactly the same design, without the maker's name.

RICH-TONE

This short-lived label derived from Gennett masters made between the summers of 1921 and 1922. It retailed at 85 cents, although the major firms, Gennett included, had reduced their popular lines to 75 cents early in 1922. Perhaps this competition proved too stiff.

The Chicago-based Phonograph Record Exchange of America was the parent of Rich-Tone. Little of musical interest appeared on its fifty or so issues. The occasional Ladd's Black Aces (alias the Original Memphis Five) was listed as "White Brothers' Orchestra." Bailey's Lucky Seven, a small Sam Lanin band, were re-named the Jazz Harmonizers. The label is little more than a curiosity, without even visual attraction. It is black, with gold lettering and modest design. The catalog series begins at 7000 or 7001.

RISHELL

The Rishell Phonograph Company of Williamsport, Pa. produced Rishell records during and probably just after World War I. The 5000 series fit exactly the Imperial-Rex-Empire-Playerphone issues with the same numbers for the same couplings. The 1000 series is identical to the early vertical-cut OKehs. The brand name just above the spindle hole supports a violinist playing in front of a Rishell machine. The credits are all printed in blue on a grey ground. A wordy slogan celebrates "The old master's violin and the RISHELL, both with wood sounding-chambers for the sweetest tone produced." Instructions about playing the disc with a Rishell sapphire ball complete the design. At least one Rishell record in the 5000 series is printed in Hebrew script, so at least part of the catalog was designed for Jewish listeners. The OKeh element may include the New Orleans Jazz Band titles on that label. The interesting ragtime piano solos on Rex and associated labels could also have been issued by Rishell.

ROMEO

The third of Cameo's subsidiaries to appear, Romeo made its debut in July 1926. Its catalog series began at 201. The records sold in the S. H. Kress chain stores for a quarter. Romeo was absorbed into the American Record Corporation label complex in 1931 and continued to appear eight years and over 2,300 records later, long after its sister-labels, Cameo and Lincoln, had vanished. The label itself is a rich cherry red, with the lettering and design in gold. No maker's name is shown. Around the inner side of the gold ring around the rim appear the words "Copyright 1926. Made in U.S.A." The brand name is shown in compressed block capitals above the spindle hole, flanked and surmounted by lozenge-shaped panels decorated simply with short parallel lines. After Cameo had adopted electric recording for about three years, Romeo began to acknowledge the fact under the brand name. For dates of recording, see Cameo and Banner. Some early Romeo issues have a strange number that does not fit in with any Cameo serial, in a block of three digits. Most Romeo issues are under pseudonyms, the same name being used for more than one artist in many instances.

ROSS

This Bridgeport Die and Machine Company product sold in Ross Stores during the latter part of 1924 and the opening months of 1925. Drawn from Paramount, Emerson and probably Banner-Plaza, the label is turquoise blue, with lettering and simple decoration in gold. A white panel between parallel gold bars across the upper part of the label bears the name ROSS STORES in gold upper-case sans-serif letters. The numbers are in the basic 11000 series used in synchronized step with Broadway, Puritan, Triangle and the other B.D.&M. labels. The Ross label is very rare. In view of the material that may be available on it, it may repay close research.

ROYALE

Eli Oberstein, during the 1930s the leading A&R man in the RCA Victor studios, launched Royale as a companion label to his Varsity (q.v.) in the autumn of 1939. About a year later, the venture folded. In that time, however, some very interesting material was released. The ten-inch issues numbered 1700 upwards. A twelve-inch series numbered in the 500s. Reissues they were in many instances, but there were original records by such bands as Richard Himber's and Johnny Green's. The reissues included important sides by the Quintette of the Hot Club of France. There were vocal records by singers of the eminence of Jan Peerce, Louis Graveure, and the Don Cossack Choir. The blue labels present the brand name in gold, surmounted by a rather unusual-looking crown and transfixed with a gold arrow. Royale bears close scrutiny. It offers some fine music of the period. See also Varsity.

ROYCROFT

This was a label recorded by Cameo in 1927 and 1928 for distribution by William H. Wise & Co., 50 West 47th Street, New York City, on behalf of the Roycrofters, the arts and crafts society founded by author Elbert Hubbard, of East Aurora, New York. The brief catalog covers mostly choral works performed by the English Singers. Even the lettering on the labels matches the music. It is a kind of old-Englyshe style, although the brand name is in modern lower-case lettering. The words "Living Tone Record" (surely a generous exaggeration) are in broken script, also of modern design. The words are surmounted by a circle bisected horizontally, a double-barred cross emerging from the upper half and a capital R enclosed in the lower. Numbering seems to start at 151 and apparently does not go beyond 200.

SAVANA

This is one of the rarest British labels of the 1920s. Very little is known about its origins. Its use of Plaza masters (and Imperials made in London), the typeface on the labels, and the general appearance of the few known specimens show that they were pressed by Crystalate; but for what retailers is not known. There were ten- and seven-inch issues. Only the larger size appears to have used American masters. So far as is known, nothing of great importance appears on Savana. A side by the Buffalodians (*How Many Times?* on 1592) and one by Jack Pettis and his Band (*Ain't She Sweet?* on 1599) are of mild interest as hot dance music. Where the catalog series begins and ends and whether anything more exciting was ever issued, are questions that still await answers. The only name apparently used for dance bands was the Savana Serenaders. Other artists are probably given pseudonyms too.

The label is light blue, but not pale. All printing is in black. The upper half of the label is decorated with a treble clef to the left and the same, mirrored, to the right. A naked, apparently male figure holding a post-horn to his lips leans on each clef, forming an open-topped arch with the word SAVANA in heavy block letters reaching from the knee of one horn player to that of the other. The label assures us that the records are of British manufacture. Production of known examples can be dated as early to mid-1927. I can in fact remember buying one seven-inch Savana in December of that year. I rather think it was from unsold, obsolete stock. It is likely that the label vanished around that time.

SCALA

The Scala Record Company began issuing records in England in 1911. They were pressed in Germany from masters cut by other firms, mainly Beka. After World War I a new Scala label was introduced. It included pressings made in England from London-recorded masters and from stampers supplied by the Starr Piano Company of Richmond, Ind. and the Aeolian Company of New York. This postwar label is an attractive rich green. A drawing of the famous Milan opera house appears in pale green to the right of the upper half. The word SCALA flows in gold script at an angle to the left, with the words TRADE MARK in gold block below. The lower half is a pale green semi-circle bounded in gold and bearing the credits and numerical details in black. The design is as unusual as it is tasteful.

Would that the repertoire was in the same category! Aimed at record buyers of modest means, it mainly released the usual popular vocals, light classics and dance music. Among the latter it is possible to find occasional items of jazz interest like the Original Memphis Five's *Loose Feet* from Vocalion; their *alter ego*, the Southland Six, playing *Runnin' Wild*, also from Vocalion; and Pinkie's Birmingham Five playing *Headin' for Louisville*, from Gennett. The latter bears the improbable pseudonym of "D'Arcy's Cabaret Combination," as did several Scala dance band issues of 1925-1926. Earlier ones frequently appeared as the Broadway Band. The aforementioned Vocalions were both credited to Vorzanger's Band. Strangely, Victor Vorzanger was a real bandleader, a Hungarian violinist whose Broadway Band recorded for Scala in London. As such it received correct label credit. The band is rough and not readily acceptable to those with ears attuned to more sophisticated music. But Vorzanger's are almost certainly the first *jazz* records made by a band of mixed American Negro and British white musicians. They were made during the summer of 1922. The band then transferred to Aco, which re-routed the Vorzanger records back to Scala. They were sometimes issued thereon as the Broadway Band, and on at least one record as "Jaggers Elite Orchestra."

The pre-war Scala numbering began at 100, and this seems to have been resumed after the break caused by the war. Certain Scala issues were numbered in a 1000 series coincident with the main one and including the same kind of material on the same type of label. The British branch of Aeolian, the Vocalion Gramophone Company, pressed the latter-day Scalas. When Vocalion suspended all its ten-inch Vocalion and Aco catalog, Scala was also discontinued. The numbers had by then, autumn 1927, reached nearly 900. The majority of Scala issues are acoustic, on somewhat noisy surfaces. The recording quality of the titles made for the company itself, as distinct from those made by Starr, Vocalion and its British branch, is quite good. The Vorzanger sides reproduce at least as well as many by better-known bands on more expensive labels.

SCHUBERT

A vertical-cut disc on the Edison Diamond Disc pattern, Schubert was manufactured during the years around the first World War by the Bell Talking Machine Corporation of New York. They are ten-inch records and have labels divided into a green upper half and a yellow lower half. The lettering is the opposite colours from the background. Thus, the portrait of Franz Schubert surmounting the upper part of the label, the words "Reg. U.S. Pat. Off." and the name Schubert are in yellow. The instruction "Use steel needles" appears to the right of the spindle hole. The label was of brief duration. As far as is known, nothing of outstanding interest was issued.

SHAMROCK STORE

From its name and from the musical content of the only known examples, this is a label aimed principally at customers of Irish origin. The square label, with corners clipped to make it into an irregular octagon, is black, with printing in gold and no decoration of any kind. The typography matches that of Plaza, the origin of the masters used on the copies known to exist. These date from 1928 and 1929. The catalog numbers, however, are from 1934, 1935 and 1936. This suggests that they were reissued later. They were sold in the Shamrock Store at 1334 Third Avenue, between 76th and 77th Streets, in New York City. The address is given on the upper half of the label. Collectors of Irish music will undoubtedly regard Shamrock Store records as of unusual interest. It is unlikely that anything but Irish music ever appeared on the label.

SILVERTONE

There are five distinct kinds of Silvertone records. One is an eight-inch issue of limited distribution produced by British Homophone during the mid-1930s. It offered no American-recorded material. The few issues had blue and silver labels with a stroboscopic rim.

The other Silvertones are American, and derivative. They were all made for Sears, Roebuck & Company, the mail-order house. Before World War I, Columbia pressed a kind of Silvertone from its own masters. Single-sided, they usually had a lilac-mauve label printed in gold with ornate decorations. At least one of these is of interest as a very early example of genuine ragtime: Vess L. Ossman playing Tom Turpin's *Buffalo Rag*, on Silvertone 3360 (the original Columbia master number). No doubt similar examples will be found on this label.

Soon after the end of World War I, the name was reactivated and applied to a blue and silver Columbia product numbered in the late 5000's. These were short-lived. The best-known and generally most interesting are the tan-labelled Silvertones with gold lettering and design. They incorporate a lyre at the top of the label. The brand name in white script flows horizontally above the spindle hole. There were at least fifteen different blocks of numbers extant on this design, each with its own source of supply. Thus:

200	Harmony
1200	Pathe, and some Olympic
1600	Plaza (Banner, etc.)
2000	Federal (around 2400, some Emerson)
3000-3199	Vocalion, Brunswick, Gennett, Paramount
3200-3399	Harmony
3500	Paramount
3800	Gennett and Rainbow
4000	Gennett
5000	Federal (later Gennett)
6000	Autograph and Plaza
8000	Gennett
21500	Plaza
25000	Gennett

These issues appeared between 1920 and 1930, often concurrently. The issues using Federal, Harmony, Paramount and Plaza show the original matrix numbers on the wax and sometimes on the label. On the Pathe sides, they are dimly visible through the surface of the label. The later Gennetts and all the Brunswick and Vocalion masters show nothing anywhere of the original matrix numbers. Earlier Gennetts give the original Gennett matrix numbers as they appear on the Gennetts.

Some jazz and blues material of great importance can be found on Silvertone, originating as a rule from Gennett and Paramount. Where the Gennetts are issued under the correct name of the artist, however, the Paramount sides invariably use a pseudonym—not only for the artist but even for the title. As a result, there are some titles on Silvertone known to be of Paramount origin but unidentifiable beyond this. They are listed on some of the Silvertone sleeves along with readily identifiable issues, in the Paramount 3500 block; but no copies have so far been found.

Among the twenty or so issues between about 2397 and 2414, the original matrix numbers of the Plaza, Emerson, Olympic and Paramount were suppressed in favour of a kind of Silvertone control number in a range from 2600 to 2641, possibly higher. Why this was done, and why so many small blocks of numbers were used to accommodate material from the same source (e.g., Gennett), is not known. There are many unsolved mysteries among these smaller labels.

In 1940, and for about a year afterwards, the Silvertone label was revived yet again, this time by CBS. This edition drew on the Columbia-OKeh catalog of the period. The records are very rare, and nothing of any consequence seems to have been issued. As far as is known, all these Silvertones were already issued on Columbia or OKeh.

SIR HENRI

An exceptionally rare label that appeared briefly on the American market during the latter part of the first decade of this century. The few known specimens are double-sided, and obviously derived from Imperial. They have the Imperial 4500, 45000 or 74000 catalog number and the four-figure matrix number, suffixed D. Both are embossed or indented into the wax round the label, mirror-fashion. Nothing is at present known about the firm that marketed the label, or why it was given an exotic European-aristocrat identity.

SOLO ART

A very rare limited-edition label extant during 1939-1940, it was produced by a bartender named Dan Qualey. His taste for piano jazz induced him to record the work of musicians like Albert Ammons, Meade "Lux" Lewis and Jimmy Yancey. The records are twelve-inch, with plain black labels showing the make, title, artist and number in straightforward style. Apparently most of the sides were made in the same studios as the General label. The offices of Solo Art were at 1000 Broadway, New York. The numerical series was in a block beginning at 12001. There were only about twenty or thirty issues.

SPECIAL RECORD

This rather vague designation was applied by Columbia to items from its cheap Harmony label that were issued to theatres and movie houses to promote numbers from shows and films on view there. The songs were not recorded by cast members themselves, but the quality of the music was in no way substandard. Performers included star singers like Annette Hanshaw, Rudy Vallee and Kate Smith, and eminent dance bands like those of Ben Selvin, Sam Lanin, Bert Lown and the California Ramblers. There were two series of catalog numbers—though reference numbers might be a more suitable term: there were no catalogs as far as is known. The series were numbered 1000-P and 2000-P. The labels of both are black with gold lettering, and divide into three horizontal segments. The uppermost contains a montage of a sad and a happy mask, and patent references matching those found on Columbia and Harmony labels. The central one gives the name of the show or film from which the music comes, along with the brand name in heavy upper-case block letters. The lowest segment gives title, composer and artist credits, and the usual numbers. The quality of recording is superb. With the Harmony material all from its electric period from mid-1928 onwards, the high standard associated with Columbia products of that period prevails. The surfaces are likewise excellent.

STANDARD

The Standard Talking Machine Company of 198-202 Monroe Street, Chicago, Ill., was a pioneer in selling records by mail. Early in the century, its appearance led Columbia to sell its surplus stock to Standard. Thanks to this agreement, Standard could punch holes half an inch in diameter in the overstock. Then the records could fit the giant spindles on the disc machines Standard was selling in its catalogs. Standard would also paste its own label—black and silver, with an absolute minimum of decoration—over the original Columbia. Columbia made only one other stipulation: the identity of each artist must be cloaked in anonymity. Columbia not long before had abandoned anonymity on its own labels, so was careful to retain its new marketing advantage—especially since the price of a Standard issue was lower, at 60 cents.

The large spindle was a feature of Standard's Model A phonograph. Those who bought one from a catalog soon found that only Standard records would fit the spindles. Columbia, however, soon ceased to be a source of records exclusively for Standard. The Great Northern Manufacturing Company (see Harmony) and the Diamond Record Company (q.v.) also moved in and secured agreements with Columbia to siphon off surplus stock—and notch a half-inch central hole in it. With the entry of Montgomery Ward and Sears Roebuck into the record arena, it was only a matter of time before Standard and its competitors went bankrupt. It had pioneered something that was accepted in the 1950s as normal after RCA Victor launched its wide-holed 45 rpm seven-inch disc.

Records by Bert Williams and banjoist Vess Ossman have been found on Standard, and as there are several interesting rarities in the line of personalities and rag-time records on Columbia at that time, a thorough examination of any Standard record with an interesting-looking title may well bring its own reward.

STARCK

Little is known of this music store label beyond the fact that a few titles by Cliff Edwards ("Ukulele Ike"), recorded in 1925 for Pathe, appeared on it in 1926 and 1927. Numbering apparently started at 100 or 101. Just over a hundred issues were issued. All known examples were from the Pathe repertoire.

STARR

The earliest product of the Starr Piano Company of Richmond, Ind. was a vertical-cut record on the Edison Diamond Disc principle. It had a green label bearing the brand name in Gothic script outlined in gold and white surmounting two gold lyres. All other lettering was in gold. The name was changed to Gennett in America in 1917, but maintained as Starr in Canada for pressings issued there from the Gennett repertoire. The Canadian issues resemble the ornate hexagonal Gennett design, with all printing in gold. The catalog numbers are in a 9000 series. As far as is known, there are no issues of outstanding interest on the American Starr label. These records, while sturdy, were somewhat less bulky than the Edison on which they were technically based.

STERNO

The British Homophone Company launched its first Sterno records in 1926. They were ten-inch laterals recorded by the Gramophone Company in its studio in Hayes, Middlesex. Most of these S-100 series duplicated the same company's Homochord issues (q.v.). For quality of reproduction, smooth surfaces, and a high standard of dance music, they were as good as anything to be found on HMV and Zonophone. The attractive blue hexagonal design, with black and dark blue printing and a white credits panel printed in black, disappeared in 1928. It was superseded by a rich red label entirely printed in gold. The brand name, printed in the same Gothic lettering as before, was superimposed on a rising-sun motif. A lion reclined on a Union Jack listening to a portable phonograph, above the all-important legend, "Electrical Recording."

So it was; but it was metallic and thin compared to the superior HMV method. Over the next seven years the quality improved somewhat, but neither the quality nor the surfaces matched the Hayes product of former times. Pathe had pressed the first of the red labels. They began their catalog numbering at 100 and reached over 1,500 issues before the last in June 1935, when EMI and Decca bought the entire records side of British Homophone's business and shared the masters between them. From 1929, however, Homophone pressed its own products. By means of popular artists such as Charlie Kunz, piano soloist and bandleader, Mantovani, Flanagan and Allen, and some famous British bands, Sterno offered stiff competition to long-established EMI and newcomer Decca.

Sterno's place in this book is due to its having issued or reissued pressings from masters made by Gennett in 1920 or 1921 and Vocalion in 1923. These were inherited from the Homochord catalog. Both were Hawaiian guitar records. Their acoustic method of recording, combined with surfaces that seemed to be doing their best to obliterate the music, made them generally unacceptable to customers, even at 1s. 6d. Whether any other American recordings ever appeared on either type of Sterno remains to be discovered. Homochord issued pressings from Victor, so the chance is always there. The earlier Sterno label is among the rarer British makes.

STILLSON

Ray Stillson was a Midwest bandleader who recorded three sides with his band in the Richmond, Ind. studios of the Starr Piano Company on November 23, 1923. Two, *Trying* and *I Love You*, were allocated the number 20023 in Gennett's "Personal" series and issued with the bandleader's surname as the brand name. The rest of the label is exactly like a normal Gennett of the period, dark blue with gold hexagonal design. Curlicues, credits, and even the word "Stillson" are printed in the Gothic style used for Gennett. The number of copies pressed must have been infinitesimal. At least one is known to have survived.

STRONG

Only one Strong issue seems to have appeared, in May 1923. They were mostly popular music of the time. In a series beginning at 10001 they offered some interesting-looking titles by Abe Small and his Melody Boys. 10002 couples *Aunt Hagar's Blues* and *I Wish I Could Shimmy Like My Sister Kate*. The label is black with gold lettering. The design resembles prison bars—an allusion to the brand name? The design covers more than half the label, restricting the credits to a small segment in the lower part. Strong, not surprisingly, is an exceedingly rare make.

SUN

Another single-sided member of the Imperial group of 1905-1910, Sun bears the same 4500, 45000 or 74000 catalog numbers and four-figure matrix numbers suffixed D, all mirror-fashion, in the wax. The conditions of sale are printed in gold on a black sticker on the blank side. (See Imperial.) There was also a Sun Record Company operating from Toronto, Canada, in the very early 1920s. It produced a navy blue Sun record drawn from the OKeh catalog, maintaining the OKeh couplings and even its catalog numbers. In 1954, outside the scope of this book, there was a Sun Record Company in Memphis, Tenn. It earned a place in the Recording Hall of Fame for being the first to record the late Elvis Presley. These records, now of great rarity, command fantastic prices, well into the three figures.

SUNRISE

The earlier of two distinct labels bearing this name was a product of the Grey Gull Record Company of Boston, Mass. It seems to have been issued in at least three different series: 30000, 32000 and 33000. None of the known specimens gives any indication as to the scope of distribution or any particular customer, such as a chain store. It is unlikely that any material was issued on Sunrise that was not also released on Grey Gull, Radiex and Van Dyke, the three best-known of the group. The Grey Gull predilection for outlandish names for its house dance orchestra is very much in evidence. Carl Kendziora instances sides by the Bear Cat Jazzers and the Twilight Dance Orchestra. The Grey Gull label vanished in the summer of 1930. Known examples of Sunrise suggest that it made its debut about a year before that. For most of its life the economic condition of the record industry was precarious. It is hardly to be wondered at that the self-styled "Record of Today" soon became the unsalable record of yesterday.

The label is colourful indeed, not to say garish. The upper half shows an impressionistic rising-sun motif in deep orange against gold clouds. Below this is the brand name, all in futuristic lower-case lettering. The legend, "The Record of Today," is upper-case, in gold. There is a black background behind everything. The lower half has a pinkish-grey panel with all credits and numbers in black.

The later Sunrise was a lower-priced RCA product. It first appeared in the spring of 1933 at S-3100, and in just a year, issued its last, S-3467. The label was originally a conventional creamy-yellow sunrise effect against a pastel orange-red background. The same shade was used for the brand name in block letters encircling the like-coloured sun. Credits, including the equivalent Bluebird catalog number, were printed on a panel in the lower half of the label, the same creamy-yellow tint as the sunrise. Below the design, "RCA Victor Company Inc., Camden, N.J.," surmounted by the old RCA logo and the HMV trademark, appears in creamy-yellow on the orange rim. About half-way through Sunrise's brief career, the coulour scheme was changed, but not the design. The pastel orange-red became dark blue and the creamy-yellow a pale gold. The result was a slightly shoddy appearance. Nothing was issued on Sunrise that was not also on Bluebird. It may be that it was intended as part of a new distribution breakdown, but no details are known. The retail price was probably 35 cents, as for Bluebird.

SUNSET

Sunset records were recorded and pressed in California between 1924 and 1926. They were numbered in a block beginning at 1000 or 1001, and probably issued about 200 different items. A large, deep red label showed a gold sun setting on a rural landscape. There was a suggestion of waves in the foreground above the brand name, which was carried in large upper-case lettering. Nothing is known of the scope of distribution, but it is most unlikely that the label was sold in large numbers outside the Pacific Coast area—or indeed in large numbers anywhere. It is not at all common, despite such popular local bands as Carlyle Stevenson's El Patio Orchestra and (Anton) Lada's Louisiana Lads. A separate matrix number, mostly in three figures, was allocated to each take. The quality of pressing and recording, although the latter was acoustic, was remarkably good.

SUNSHINE

This was a label pasted on Nordskog records (q.v.) for six titles made in 1922 by Kid Ory's Jazz Band which on Nordskog was called "Spikes' Seven Pods of Pepper Orchestra," on Sunshine "Kid Ory's Sunshinne (sic) Orchestra." Four are vocals, two by Ruth Lee and two by Roberta Dudley, all accompanied by the Ory band. In any form they are rare indeed, but the recording quality matches the abysmally bad performances. The label is orange, black and white, and not unattractive.

SUPERIOR

The Superior label made its first appearance coincidentally with the disappearance of Gennett, from whose repertoire it drew. Both were pressed in Starr Piano Company's plant in Richmond, Ind. Starting in December 1930 at 2501, Superior records continued to appear until June 1932. The last issue was 2839. Mr. George W. Kay, in a series of articles in *Record Research* between August 1961 and January 1963, listed all 339 issues in minute detail from the Gennett ledgers, including the sales figures. During the last six months of life, only two Superior records, both country-and-western items, sold in the four figures. Most of the others reached a mere three figures with difficulty. In the last three months, only three sold over a hundred copies. The rest of the issues from 2813 onwards reached from 19 to 97 copies. It is interesting but sad to speculate on how many of these pitiful pressings still exist. Many are of great interest to the jazz, blues and country specialist. Indeed, relatively few Superior records are of commercial dance or vocal music, compared with the number of issues in the other three categories.

SUPERTONE

The story of the name Supertone is complicated. There are seven known varieties of records issued under this name. One was a Brunswick subsidiary of 1930 or perhaps a little earlier, issued in a series apparently beginning at S-2000 or S-2001. It utilized masters from Brunswick stock. Some interesting dance music by Benny Goodman and Red Nichols amongst others, and some Seger Ellis sides with good accompaniments, all of them under pseudonyms, appeared on this Supertone, which had vanished by the autumn of 1931.

Straus & Schram, a store in Chicago, sponsored four of the remaining six Supertones. It drew at different times on the repertoires of Pathe, Grey Gull, Columbia and Paramount. Each time the label was changed but slightly. Usually black with gold design and lettering, it is surmounted by a large Gothic S in an egg-shaped lozenge above two parallel bars across the upper half of the label horizontally. The lower bar is tangent to the spindle hole and contains the brand name in bold block letters. The credits, and the reference to Straus & Schram, are on the lower half of the label. An exception is the Columbia set, which depended more on Harmony for its material and is red instead of black. As far as is known, the catalog numbers followed those of the parent label, except for Harmony sides, which were in a 1000-S series.

The other two Supertone labels derived from Gennett (9000 series) and Olympic-Paramount (1000 series). Both types were sold by Sears, Roebuck by mail order. The earlier is the Olympic-Paramount derivative. The label is dull black with a broad gold rim, inside of which is a narrow white one; then a fairly broad black ring and finally a white one, broken at the top to accommodate a three-stringed lyre-like instrument flanked by the bells of two horns, all in gold. In an arc round the lower part of the label, on the innermost white ring, the name Sears, Roebuck & Co. is shown in gold. In an irregular figure below the three gold instruments, the brand name appears in fancy upper-case lettering across an empty stave, all in gold. From the popular titles on the specimens examined, we know that these were on sale in 1924.

The Gennett-derived Supertone was sold by Sears from the spring of 1928 until the end of 1930 and the demise of Gennett. It seems that Superior (q.v.)

took over when Supertone was discontinued. In those two-and-a-half years, nearly 800 records were issued. They had glossy black labels with a design in gold not unlike the one used in 1924, again with a symbol that might have been meant to represent a lyre, but with no horns above the brand-name shield. The words "Super Electrically Recorded" ran in block letters below the shield. About halfway through the series the reference to Sears, Roebuck & Co. was replaced by the words "Licensed RCA Photophone Recording." It was a curious change. Although by this time the Victor Talking Machine Company was about to be absorbed by the Radio Corporation of America, Victor had nothing whatever to do with these Gennett Supertones. It may be that they were recorded by a system akin to Brunswick's much-publicized "Light-Ray" process. In fact there is nothing particularly "super" about the recording technique of these records. They are much better than many early electric recordings, certainly. But Supertone was a challenging name, and obviously called for a slogan to match it.

SUPREME

Supreme, not the most appropriate name for a label that was not only cheap but looked and sounded it, was one of the Grey Gull complex during the middle and late 1920s, at least from 1926 to 1929. All known specimens have the same catalog numbers as the same couplings on Grey Gull, to which manufacture is credited. The pinkish-red label has black lettering, except for the upper part, with the brand name in crude pseudo-Gothic lettering, starting and finishing in the same size but increasing in the middle. This is in gold on a white band, surmounted by a lozenge enclosing a bird of indeterminate species, also in gold.

SYMPHANOLA

A nine- and ten-inch record produced by Emerson for the Larkin Company of Buffalo, N.Y. for a year or so immediately following World War I. Symphanola has a red label with all lettering and design in gold. The latter includes a lyre above the brand name across the top of the label. The typeface is obviously Emerson's. A few sides by the Louisiana Five were issued on this label, in a 4000 series that remained unaltered despite the change of size and which does not seem to have exceeded 4200. Apart from these, the catalog probably consisted of popular dance and vocal numbers, exactly as could be found on Emerson.

SYMPHONY

Another of the early Imperial-derived labels (q.v.). Single-sided and differing from its associates in that the condition-of-sale notice on the sticker on the blank side is printed in black on pink paper, Symphony apparently contains no music of importance.

TALK-O-PHOTO

All that I know of this label, as a collector of all kinds of recorded curiosa, is that it was announced in the *Talking Machine World* of July 15, 1920 as produced by the Talking Photo Recording Corporation of 334 Fifth Avenue, New York City, and that each record provided music on one side and a photograph of the artist on the other. The price was 35 cents, or three for $1. A list of artists was given. They included Mae Murray, Gloria Swanson, Lew Cody and H. B. Warner, stellar names in those days of silent movies. Did they in fact sing or speak on the recorded side of the records bearing their portraits? If so, these are among the most valuable entertainment documents of all. If not, what was the "music," and what connection did it have with silent movie stars of 1920?

TIMELY TUNES

At a time when even well established record companies were foundering, or at least finding it difficult to stay in business, Victor, mightiest of them all, introduced a cheap label devoted to the latest dance tunes and a sprinkling of hot jazz on this label. It began its career in April 1931 at number C-1550. It died quietly and unmourned three months and forty-one issues later. The quality of recording and pressing is up to the Victor standard, despite the 35-cent price tag. The label is pastel orange, printed in black, with a broad black band round the circumference. Most of the artists appear pseudonymously. Cab Calloway's sister Blanche even underwent a nominal sex-change and was renamed Fred Armstrong.

TREMONT

Tremont seems to have been the successor to Muse (q.v.) at the factory of the American Record Manufacturing Company of Framingham, Mass. It even continued the catalog numbers from the mid-400s to the mid-500s, between the early summer of 1924 and the summer of 1925. The later Tremont issues prefixed the number with O. The significance of this is not known, if it had any. Cameo masters were used throughout. Where Muse had plain black and gold labels, Tremont is black on the lower half and orange with black design on the upper. Credits are printed in gold. The brand name appears on a fancy shield in the form of a lozenge, with the letters increasing in size to the M in the centre and decreasing thereafter. Nothing was issued on Tremont that was not also on Cameo. Most if not all of the items in its brief catalog were labelled with pseudonyms. As with Muse, the Varsity Eight, for example, were described as "The Musical Comrades."

TRIANGLE

The first announcement by the Bridgeport Die and Machine Company of Bridgeport, Conn. that it was manufacturing Triangle records appeared in *Talking Machine World* on September 15, 1922. For slightly under three years, these turquoise blue-labelled discs were sold widely throughout the United States. The source of material was the Paramount repertoire, with some Emersons and such incunabula as Blu-Disc latterly. Triangle 11437 has on one side *Rainy Nights* by The Washingtonians, probably Duke Ellington's earliest band record (see Blu-Disc). The other side (*Then You Know You're in Love* by the Majestic Dance Orchestra) is simply another dance record of the late 1924 period, issued in December of that year. Other interesting jazz issues on Triangle that also appeared on the other B.D. & M. labels (Carnival, Ross, Cardinal, Mitchell and others) include two Jelly Roll Mortons (11397) and a generous helping of the Original Memphis Five playing rather more interesting titles than they did on other labels. There were some Fletcher Henderson sides, usually credited correctly, as indeed were the others mentioned above. These of course appeared on the labels of their origin as well as on B.D.& M. pressings. But there were also four sides by the Original Louisiana Five, recorded by Paramount but as far as is known never issued on that label.

The design on the Triangle label is simple and eye-catching. A double ring—the outer black, the inner gold—about quarter of an inch inside the rim of the label; a black-bordered white equilateral triangle inverted on the upper half and reaching below the spindle hole, and bearing the cryptic slogan "Equal all ways" (equal to what?); and the word TRIANGLE in gilt-edged black upper-case block letters—that was all. No maker's name, no source of supply, merely the price (75 cents—as much as the major labels were charging at the time) and the credits in gold, giving no more than the barest essentials. The catalog series appear to have been three: a 9000 block, for light popular instrumental and vocal records; a 15000 block for material of a slightly more serious type by ambitiously named symphony orchestras and concert instrumental soloists, usually violinists; and the usual B.D. & M. 11000 series that is common to most of the labels the firm pressed, embracing dance music and popular vocals. The first two series covered barely a hundred issues each. The 11000 block reached nearly five hundred issues.

UNITED

The United Talking Machine Company was a Chicago neighbour of the Harmony Talking Machine Company. They were only doors apart, United at 608 South Dearborn Street and Harmony at 618. Both were engaged, apparently not for long, in absorbing Columbia's unsold pressings, punching larger spindle holes in them and pasting on their own labels. Sometimes they were credited like the originals, and sometimes they were anonymous. Both firms sold the records by mail order. See also Diamond, Harmony and Standard.

UNITED HOT CLUBS OF AMERICA (UHCA)

In 1936 Milt Gabler of the Commodore Music Shop of East 42nd Street, New York City began issuing custom pressings of jazz classics on this label. There were double-sided records, at first issued only to subscribers. The handsome white labels included as much discographical information as could be traced at that time. Some were printed in green, some in blue, some in red. Many rare items from Paramount, Brunswick, Vocalion, and Gennett were reissued. Columbia (actually the American Record Corporation) was persuaded to provide masters from its vaults, including some OKeh material. Decca also provided pressings. The records were numbered according to side, so that 1 and 2 were coupled, likewise 3 and 4, 5 and 6, and so on up to 85 and 86 in October 1941. There do not seem to have been any subsequent issues on UHCA. In view of the early date at which the venture flourished, it is remarkable how fine the dubbings are. Several are indistinguishable from original master pressings, and these from records not noted for smooth surfaces. Such issues shame many subsequent LP transfers, with all the improved, sophisticated gadgetry with which they are made.

UP-TO-DATE

This is another label that must rank as one of the great rarities. It seems to have been a sister label to the exceedingly rare Blu-Disc (q.v.), and is just as interesting. Number 2019 offers *How Come You Do Me Like You Do?* sung by a girl described as Florence Bristol and accompanied by Duke Ellington at the piano and Otto Hardwick on alto saxophone. What other gems may have been issued on this label; how it was distributed; over what area; and at what price, are not known. The recording date of this super-rarity is about November 1924.

VAN DYKE

Of all the many labels produced by the Grey Gull Company of Boston, Mass., Van Dyke is perhaps the closest to its parent. It debuted in the late spring of 1929. For the first eighty issues it used the same couplings as Grey Gull (q.v.), with different artist credits. Sometimes it gave credits where Grey Gull was anonymous. This group was numbered with a 7 prefix to the Grey Gull number. Thus, the Dixie Devils on Van Dyke 71804 were the Memphis Jazzers on Grey Gull 1804. The Van Dyke series began at about 71732. Grey Gull 1811 is Van Dyke 71811, but Grey Gull 1814 is Van Dyke 81814. The prefix 8 to Grey Gull numbers was used until the company discontinued trading in the summer of 1930. The highest known Van Dyke in this series is 81894.

The same practice applies to other Grey Gull series. But there were other blocks of Van Dyke numbers for which there seems to be no Grey Gull equivalent: e.g., the 900s, which are probably identical to Radiex's 900s, and the 5000s and 7800s, which are unique to Van Dyke. The type of recording does not seem to vary from one series to another. A 35-cent product, it was aimed at an undemanding public that merely sought dance music, popular songs and light popular classics adequately recorded. These were provided, performed by the competent studio dance band directed by Paul Bolognese, under a bewildering variety of pseudonyms.

Despite the short life of Van Dyke records, they sold in prodigious numbers. Like Grey Gull, many were exported to Britain, there to sell cheaply in chain stores. As with Grey Gull, there are a number of interesting jazz items to be found on Van Dyke by such as Clarence Williams, Cliff Jackson and others; and the dance records frequently feature hot soloists. The recording is often overmodulated, so it can be tiring to listen to these records steadily. They are eye-catching and yet tasteful: black, white, red and gold labels with a cameo of a seventeenth-century man surmounting the brand name in white above the motto "Every Record A Masterpiece" in gold copperplate. The surfaces, however, are gritty.

VARIETY

Irving Mills, the music publisher, vocalist, dance-band impresario and agent, launched his Variety label at the same time as his Master records (q.v.), February 1937. It was an enlightened venture. He signed up outstanding talent like Cab Calloway and his Orchestra, various small groups from within Duke Ellington's Orchestra, Charlie Barnet and his Orchestra, Midge Williams and her Jazz Jesters, and many small bands whose members were recruited from established units and allowed to play jazz to their taste. The end of the year saw the end of both labels. Their catalogs were taken over by Vocalion, from the American Record Corporation stable.

The Variety label was purple and gold at the outset of its brief career. This soon changed to black and gold or black and silver. Unlike its label-mate, Variety was never pressed in laminated form. The catalog series began at 501. Nearly two hundred records were issued. Most are in Master's M series of matrix numbers, though some early ones made in Los Angeles are prefixed LO. The recording is quite good but the surfaces are inclined to be ashy. Several sides by the small Ellington units and others were issued after World War II on Parlophone in England, as the rights to the material became available there to EMI Ltd. The design includes a figure conducting an unseen orchestra while standing on the spindle hole. The figure is surmounted by the brand name, with extra-large first and last letters. Above this an array of stars and a semi-quaver provide the decoration.

There was another Variety record, drawn from Cameo's repertoire. It appeared on the market in 1927. It has a black label, with design and lettering in gold. There are three nymphs, one playing some kind of pipe and all dancing amid some foliage. They cavort above a banner bearing the brand name. The border for the whole label is cog-teethed like a gigantic clock wheel. The catalog series probably began at 5000 or 5001. It is not likely that more than a hundred issues ever appeared.

VARSITY

This was the principal label of the United States Record Corporation, founded in the autumn of 1939 by Eli Oberstein, late of RCA Victor. Varsity entered the American record scene with some panache. It offered a goodly selection of issues by top jazzmen fronting bands of the calibre of Harry James, Jack Teagarden and Frank Trumbauer. Johnny Messner, Van Alexander, Reggie Childs, Tommy Tucker, Will Osborne and Paul Whiteman's protegee of past years, Ramona, represented the sweet bands. There was crooner Buddy Clark, not then the star he became later. There were interesting, authentic folk artists, native and foreign. All appeared in various series on the new 35-cent label. The latter was blue, with the gold lettering. The design was simple and effective. A college pennant, with the brand name in block upper-case letters filling it, waved across the top part of the label, with the V as an implied support.

The matrix series began at 1 but was soon altered to US-1001. Some 900 numbers were used before the creditors closed in around mid-1940. The pressing plant in Scranton, Pa. refused further credit. By September, debts amounted to $250,000. Musicraft Records acquired the Oberstein masters and issued some of them in 1941 on their Masterpiece label, but this too was short-lived. Through the war years, Oberstein organized many small labels like Hit, Elite and Joe Davis. Though ephemeral, they sold widely, and during the Petrillo record ban of 1942-1944 Oberstein issued some new material on these labels and also resurrected many Varsity and Royale masters.

Varsity's principal popular and jazz series was in the 8000 block. The folk music block was 7000. "Race" issues, most of them reissues from Crown and Gennett of a decade earlier, were numbered 6000. The "hillbilly" series was in the 5000s. Serious works, some original but many from the German Telefunken catalog, also appeared on Varsity. One album featured the great contralto, Marian Anderson. Recording quality generally was spotty, the record surfaces much inferior to the products of competitors RCA Victor and Columbia; inferior even to those of Decca.

VELVET FACE

This was one of the subsidiary labels of the Edison Bell Company of London. It first appeared before World War I, in both ten- and twelve-inch form. The offerings were the customary middlebrow fare by middlebrow artists. The records hardly justified the claim implicit in the brand name. They were inclined to be gritty. All were recorded in London. The label was revived in March 1922 with much improved surfaces and a price tag of 3s. 6d. for the ten-inch and 5s. 6d for the twelve. The labels looked deluxe, with a linen surface printed in gold on violet in a sober, straightforward design that fitted all the necessary information into a small space. There was no adornment, yet the label never looked empty or bare. Latterly the label became bright green.

The catalog included the work of many front-rank concert artists then performing in England. When Edison Bell chief J. E. Hough concluded an agreement with the Starr Piano Company of Richmond, Ind., several titles from the Gennett label were made available under such pseudonyms as Joe Richardson's Orchestra, the Regent Orchestra, and the Pavilion Players. Jazz connoisseurs weep at the chances that were missed for introducing the pioneer recordings of King Oliver's Jazz Band, the Wolverines, the New Orleans Rhythm Kings, and Jelly Roll Morton to Britain on master pressings smoother than the original Gennetts. But J. E. Hough was a businessman, nor did he like jazz. Hough adhered stoutly to the mild fare of Bailey's Lucky Seven and ephemera of conventional dance bands.

Gennett masters used for pressing Velvet Face records bear the original matrix numbers. Here they are unsullied by tooling-out, as they were on most other British labels that used them. Edison Bell's own matrix number, which by then had reached the 7000s, was added in large, rather ornate embossed figures, followed by a stamper letter. The ten-inch series began at 1000, the twelve-inch at 500. Both produced slightly over two hundred issues each, priced at 2s. 6d. and 4s. In the summer of 1927 the label was withdrawn, though good sellers on Velvet Face remained in the Edison Bell catalog until that company died in 1933. By then prices had dropped to 2s. and 3s. 6d. The end of the Gennett agreement in 1925 meant no further American representation on Velvet Face, although it had never meant a great deal to the label. Most Gennett titles on Edison Bell had appeared on Winner (see Edison Bell Winner).

VELVET TONE

Velvet Tone was another sister label to Columbia's low-priced Harmony record (q.v.). It appeared first in September 1925. Numbering began 1001-V, in exact step with Harmony's but 1,000 numbers ahead of it. About 200 issues before the end of Velvet Tone in 1932, the label and its sister Diva (q.v.) began to get out of step with Harmony and with each other. Hitherto they had automatically issued everything identically, as a rule even using the same credits. Like Harmony, the Velvet Tone label is plain indeed, bright blue with gold lettering. The only decoration is an elaborate four-point star design above the brand name in bold upper case across the upper part of the label. When the label expired after seven years, it had issued some 1,500 records, including a brief 7000-V series in 1930 devoted to blues and other "race" items.

VICTOR

The fascinating saga of Victor records begins with Emile Berliner, inventor of the flat, lateral-recorded disc, and Eldridge R. Johnson, mechanic and cabinetmaker who designed the first spring-driven gramophone—the name the contraption was given to distinguish it from Edison's cylinder phonograph. (See Berliner.) Berliner's agent, Frank Seaman, had defected and was openly selling machines and discs based on the Berliner-Johnson concept (see Zonophone), while a court order temporarily restrained Berliner from marketing his own product. Johnson, facing bankruptcy with a stock of machines and no records, began producing records himself. Recording on wax blocks and thereby obtaining a much more natural, smooth sound than the jagged noise obtained from Berliner's acid-etched zinc masters, Johnson called his product the Improved Gram-O-Phone Record. He provided each copy with a paper label pressed into the shellac material. The labels were black with gold lettering. Though they are the product of an age noted for its love of superfluous ornamentation, they have very little decoration.

The legend on the Improved Gram-O-Phone Record label stated that it was manufactured by the Consolidated Talking Machine Company of Philadelphia,

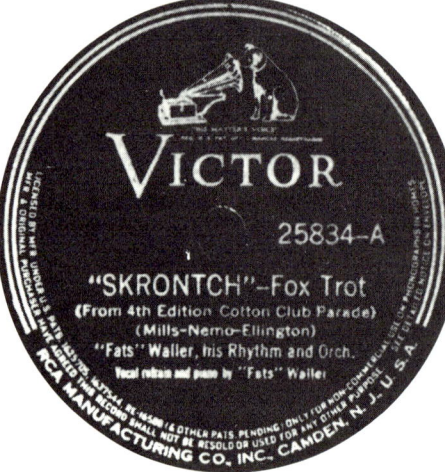

Pa. This was the name under which Eldridge Johnson began trading in the late summer of 1900. Soon he was turning his stock of machines and records into cash. He was helped by a sales promoter named Leon F. Douglass, who proceeded to make the nation Gram-O-Phone conscious by widely advertising in magazines with the largest circulation. He offered free records to all owners of a Gram-O-Phone, and spent $2,500—half of Johnson's capital—on the campaign. Then Frank Seaman struck again. Charging that the Improved Gram-O-Phone and its records were no more than Berliner and his prohibited enterprise under a new name, he asked for a similar injunction to restrain Johnson from making machines and records, and from even using the word "Gramophone." The court threw out part of the injunction, but Johnson could not use the magic word. Free again to earn a living by making machines and producing records, Johnson was not unhappy to accede to the court's direction over what they should be called. Johnson, advertising that he was continuing to make talking machines and records with the knowledge and blessing of Emile Berliner, incorporated the Victor

Talking Machine Company of Camden, N.J. on October 3, 1901. And why not—hadn't Johnson emerged as *victor* over Seaman?

Meanwhile, Berliner had regained the rights to his patents. Now he and Johnson pooled their resources, Johnson contributing his wax recording process and his new factory, which was working at full pressure to keep up with the demand for records and machines. Berliner contributed his patents.

About the same date, there was some opposition from Columbia (q.v.). Itself now embarking on the production of lateral discs in addition to their established cylinders, Columbia owned a vital patent for recording on wax discs. Johnson had never thought to patent the idea himself, believing it already covered by a much earlier patent. Common sense prevailed. Victor and Columbia pooled their patents and set out, if not always in friendly rivalry, at least in non-litigating coexistence to dominate the American record market for the next three-quarters of a century.

The first Victor records as such were seven-inch, as their Berliner and Johnson predecessors had been. Early in 1901, however, even before Johnson had won his right to make a fortune from machines and records, he had begun work on ten-inch discs. These were put on sale in the spring of that year as Monarch records. Both these and Victor records carried warnings on their plain black and gold labels as to penalties that could be incurred if the records were copied or used for any other purpose than the production of sound. Later, from 1902 onwards, when the famous "His Master's Voice" trademark appeared on the upper half of the label, the warning was printed on a sticker applied to the smooth reverse side of the record.

The first labels to use the painting by Francis Barraud (see His Master's Voice) were otherwise without decoration or typeface other than the brand name flanking the spindle hole, and of course the credits below. After winning first prize at the great national expositions in Buffalo, St. Louis and Portland between 1901 and 1905, the company proudly advertised the awards on its labels, around the upper rim, adding the words "Grand Prize" round the spindle hole. By now, twelve- and fourteen-inch records were in use. They were known as De Luxe records. Though the larger size never caught the favour of the public and was quickly abandoned, the twelve-inch disc remained to outlive even the ubiquitous ten-inch as the commonly accepted size. Ten-inch long-play records are rarely found now except occasionally as private recordings. The standard diameter of a long-playing microgroove disc is twelve inches.

The "Grand Prize" label remained in use until 1908, when the first double-sided records were issued in October of that year. The reference to the three first prizes remained in position, but around the lower rim of each Victor label (the three surviving sizes were all labelled as Victor from 1904, as was the short-lived eight-inch size) was added a three-tiered summary of all the patents owned by the company, with the dates of issue. This design was also applied to single-sided issues, and it was used until December 1913.

With the January 1914 issues, the Victor label again altered. This time it adopted an entirely different format that could not be confused with earlier styles. The rather old-fashioned typeface was replaced by a sans-serif style that is still in extensive use today, and still looks modern. The size of the trademark was drastically reduced and set in the curve of an arch above the brand name, in lower-case lettering. The patents were listed on the sleeves in which the records left the factory, and the legend around the lower rim of the label referred to this. The design of the label changed twice more, radically, in the twenty-eight years before the end of this survey, but not the typeface.

The design introduced in 1914 remained almost unchanged until the coming of electric recording—Victor's word for it was "Orthophonic"; or, more accurately, until Victor announced that its products were being made by the new process. That was in October 1926. From that date until October 1937 the design was again quite unlike any other used by Victor or its rivals. It consisted of an ornate device that broke with the established tradition of a circular rim to the label. It replaced this with what has long been described by collectors as a scroll. The trademark shrank yet again. The brand name was printed in upper case, in a fine, slender style that contrasted sharply with the heavy, thick type of 1914 onwards. Like its predecessor, it changed but minutely in the eleven years it was used. The November 1937 issues, and those that followed over the next five years to the end of this book's scope, reverted to a circular rim but used the same general design as the scroll label, with the trademark reduced even further, and a double ring to the rim. While later variants of the 1914-1926 type label listed a few patent numbers and dates, and the 1937-1942 style gave warning about the misuse of Victor records in similar language to that used on the first Victor labels around forty years earlier, the scroll design gave neither patent details nor fearful warnings. It concerned itself with assuring purchasers that it signified "Orthophonic Recording," advised the use of Victor needles, and latterly prohibited the unlicensed use of Victor records on the air.

One interesting feature adopted by Victor in April 1923, and gradually followed by most other makes (except Pathe, Decca, Gennett and Paramount, of the major-league labels) was the translation into Spanish of most of the popular titles. Titles couched in American slang presented some problems, of course. Even those employing normal idiomatic English must have sometimes given pause to the translators. *Here Comes the Show Boat*, transliterated from Victor's Spanish, became *Through Here Comes the Floating Theatre. Who's Sorry Now?* was presented as *And Now, Who Feels It?* Perhaps the most tortuous is *I Found You Out When I Found You in Somebody Else's Arms*. This was rendered as *I Knew Who You Were at the Sight of You in the Arms of Another*. The purpose of the translation was presumably for the benefit of customers in the Spanish-speaking areas of New Mexico, Southern California and Texas, not to mention those in Central and South American countries.

It was Victor's policy from the start to offer to the music lovers of the United States, and through its connections with the Gramophone Company in Europe to that continent and the rest of the world, the best performances that money could get on to wax. Once the great Milan recordings by Enrico Caruso had been issued on the new Red Seal series in 1902, others followed from the same and other European sources. In 1903, a Red Seal celebrity catalog was launched. It would set a standard that was never equalled. Calvin Child, the Red Seal artists' director, saw to it that all the Metropolitan Opera House stars were signed to exclusive Victor contracts. From 1904 onwards, there were no truly great singers of international reputation who did not appear in the monthly Victor supplements. The "middleman" who was invariably on hand to advise and soothe was a diminutive American of Spanish origin named Emilio de Gogorza. Possessed of a ringing but rich baritone voice himself, he added a formidable vocal technique, an ability to make crystal-clear recordings in many languages, and a natural charm that was more than a match for the temperamental *prime donne* and the posturing male artists who came to the studios in Carnegie Hall (until the spring of 1904), at 234 Fifth Avenue (until 1907), and at other New York locations. He was the husband of the American opera soprano Emma Eames. She contributed a number of records to the Red Seal catalog. Her methods of recording (under the admittedly trying conditions of projecting one's voice into an ugly, unsympathetic metal funnel, bound with tape to reduce certain resonances, while a small orchestra of predominantly wind instruments played accompaniment in close proximity) were however less successful than those of the Bohemian soprano Marcella Sembrich, who showed great interest in the whole procedure and cheerfully underwent the same difficulties with superb results. De Gogorza's affable personality also won over the superb French basso, Pol Plancon. Although he had recorded very successfully several times in London and Paris, the basso insisted on making a preliminary test at his first session in New York. He listened to the playback and exploded: "That is not me!" De Gogorza assured him it was. Eventually Plançon had to agree. "Yes, Gogorza, you are right. Who else could sing like that?"

According to an eyewitness in 1907, the studio was 16 feet wide, 22 feet long, and 11 feet, 6 inches high. The ceiling and one side were of steel. The other sides were brick. There were five windows, which in summer were all kept open, even during recording. Apparently this caused no recording problems in the days when auto traffic was minimal. But it is interesting to note that on October 16, 1908 the second take of a monologue called *Hoboken,* by Nat M. Wills, was ruined because, in the terse language of the recording ledger, "M. O. Noon whistle recorded." The usual instrumentation for the studio orchestra was two cornets, one trombone, two clarinets, one oboe, one flute, two Stroh violins with amplifying horns attached, one viola similarly amplified, one tuba, and one drummer who was in charge of all percussion. The instruments were placed at suitable distances from the two horns three feet long and used for recording. Each horn was ten inches wide across the mouth. The trombone sat in the rear, eight to ten feet from the horns. The cornets sat in front of him, six feet from the horns. The others were nearer in, the oboe to the left and the tuba at extreme left behind the second violin and viola. The clarinets were to the right of centre. To accompany a singer, three horns were used. The distances varied. The singer's (to one side) was two feet long and six inches wide. The middle horn was three feet four inches long and ten inches wide. On the other side, the horn was the regular three feet by ten inches. Military bands, which recorded extensively under the direction of Arthur Pryor, various other Sousa men, or resident staff conductor Walter B. Rogers, had a somewhat different placing, with the flute in front of the cornets and three clarinets all round him, and various horns to the right of the recording horn, the distances varying according to the pitch of the instruments.

By this time the old, gritty, scratchy surface common to most discs had given place to a much smoother, mirror-like surface. I have many Victor records made over seventy years ago that are as velvety and noiseless as anything in vinylite from the microgroove era. When sceptics with no knowledge of the subject deride me as a collector of "scratchy old 78s," I simply play one of them. The utter incredulity on their faces is an entertainment in itself.

The introduction in September 1906 of the internal-horn cabinet model known as the Victrola, which has become a loosely applied generic name for any machine playing 78s, continued the upward trend of the company's business. There was hardly a language not represented in the full catalog, from Korean to Albanian. Each was allocated its own numerical block. The Red Seal issues seemed to depend, for their first ten years or so, on singers and such instrumental celebrities as violinists Fritz Kreisler, Mischa Elman and Jan Kubelik, and pianists Ignace Jan Paderewski and Vladimir de Pachmann. But by the end of the second decade of the century Victor had added the imposing figures of composer-pianist Sergei Rachmaninoff and the Philadelphia Symphony Orchestra conducted by Leopold Stokowski. At the very end of 1920, the orchestra of La Scala, Milan, conducted by no less a virtuoso than Arturo Toscanini, paid its first visit to Camden. By that date, the catalog was filling up steadily with truly beautiful recordings by the Flonzaley and Elman String Quartets, two of the world's greatest interpreters of chamber music.

Victor recorded the voices of all the Presidents from Theodore Roosevelt to Warren G. Harding, taking the cumbersome equipment to the White House or even to their country homes in some cases. William Jennings Bryan was recorded in his home in Lincoln, Neb. Other unsuccessful Presidential contenders were also given a chance to perpetuate their views in their own voices. The latest Broadway musicals, the newest dance craze, outstanding opera singers newly arrived from Europe, all appeared on either the black, the purple, the blue or the Red Seal Victor label. Amelita Galli-Curci from Italy and John McCormack from Ireland sold in such numbers as to rival the popularity of Enrico Caruso himself. Neither was in the more expensive category he was, a category shared with Nellie Melba, Luisa Tetrazzini and Geraldine Farrar, among other exalted names. In the popular sector the monthly supplements, small magazine-like publications copiously illustrated and annotated with interesting material, forerunners of modern liner notes, were filled with records of the Victor Military Band, playing everything from light cafe music to *Alexander's Ragtime Band;* incredibly clear vocal records by Billy Murray, Arthur Collins and Byron G. Harlan, the Peerless and the American Quartets, and Ada Jones; and, on a more serious level, superb contralto singing by Elsie Baker and soprano work of effortless beauty by Olive Kline. There were enchanting records of little-recorded *morceaux* by the collective violin, cello, flute and harp of the Venetian and Neapolitan Trios, and the Florentine Quartet. When the Hawaiian craze hit the mainland in 1914, Victor rushed out some fine recordings of genuine Hawaiian music by genuine Hawaiian performers. One of them, a 45-year-old bass singer named George R. Nahadleus, fell dead while recording at 42 West 38th Street one day in the summer of 1920.

Into the midst of this talent burst the bombshell of jazz on February 26, 1917. The Original Dixieland Jass (sic) Band made its first Victor records. These were rushed out to the shops in a few days, and the sales rivalled those of the long-established serious and popular artists alike. The Jazz Age had begun. Yet in the early 1920s, with Paul Whiteman, Joseph C. Smith, the All Star Trio, and the Benson Orchestra of Chicago playing dance music that occasionally bordered on jazz, Victor tried to dissociate itself from the idiom that was being blamed for the moral laxity that seemed so prevalent in those days. Although Victor usually led, as it did with jazz at the outset, it was lagging behind Columbia, OKeh and Paramount in refusing to recognize a vast market for Negro artists. With the coming of "Orthophonic" recording, an attempt was made to mend fences. But a special "race" series was not started until January 1929. Although the quality of most issues was superb, the quantity was restricted. By the time economic conditions suggested that 75 cents was too high for records appealing to a poorer market, about 500 had been issued. Many were withdrawn after a matter of months, with sales in the low three figures. Most never made it to the general catalog at all. In the prosperous days of 1926-1929, however, Victor excelled in jazz and blues records by great names: Duke Ellington, Bennie Moten, Jelly Roll Morton, McKinney's Cotton Pickers, Charlie Johnson, the Missourians, and many more. All recorded for Victor's race issues in those years.

With the coming of the dancing years, Victor set about signing up the leading bands. John S. Macdonald, chief artists' manager during the pre-jazz era, had little time for this new music. His successor from June 1920, pianist and drummer Edward T. King, exercised authority over what was and what was not to be recorded and issued. Musical director Nathaniel ("Nat") Shilkret, a man of outstanding talent, taste and personal charm, was sympathetic to jazz as the present-day connoisseur understands the term. But it was not until King resigned in November 1926 and transferred his allegiance to Columbia (much to the relief of many dance-band musicians) that Shilkret was able to produce dance records featuring high-grade hot jazz solos, and to hire jazz musicians to accompany popular singers like Johnny Marvin, Gene Austin, Aileen Stanley, Chick Endor and Helen Kane.

Paul Whiteman's first record, *Whispering* and *The Japanese Sandman*, was issued in November 1920 and sold over a million and a quarter copies in the next five years. This eclipsed by some third of a million the vast sales of *Dardanella* by (Ben) Selvin's Novelty Orchestra, issued the previous February.

Few dance issues could match these figures, although the Benson Orchestra of Chicago's *Ain't We Got Fun?*, issued in July 1921, came close. There were countless records by other bands, well known and obscure, that reached five figures. One of these was the sophisticated Creole band from New Orleans under the direction of violinist Armand J. Piron. His *Mama's Gone, Goodbye* and *New Orleans Wiggle,* recorded in New York at the end of 1923, sold well over 80,000 copies.

The Wall Street disaster of October 1929 soon curtailed recording. By that date Victor was recording regularly in Chicago, Memphis, Atlanta and New Orleans, and sometimes in unusual locations like Houston, Oklahoma City, and Bristol, Tenn. There, at the end of a day's work in August 1927, a slim young man named Jimmie Rodgers quietly presented himself to the recording director of the field trip, Ralph Peer, and asked to record some yodelling blues. He did so, and for the next six years, until his death at 36 from tuberculosis on May 26, 1933, he recorded in almost every major city where Victor held sessions. His records were issued in all parts of the English-speaking world. People who never heard a genuine country singer from the Deep South were captivated by his wistful voice, his thrumming guitar accompaniment, and his plaintive yodelling, not to mention the wry humour of his lyrics. On the ninth of the series of his *Blue Yodels,* he did not use his guitar. Instead, the accompaniment was by a man-and-wife team, both Negroes, on cornet and piano. They were Louis and Lil Armstrong.

Victor, while belatedly sympathetic to jazz and blues, specialized in country-and-western recordings. Once the new type of recording by microphone had made field trips easy, Victor's talent scouts, headed by the expert Ralph Peer, combed the South, the Midwest and the Southwest for artists who could command sales comparable to Jimmie Rodgers'. Many thus recorded never made more than one or two sessions. But in the Carter Family, as nomadic as Rodgers himself (they recorded together in Louisville in 1931), Victor found a team of two girls and their father who sang old-time homey and religious songs in a way that caught the public fancy far beyond the confines of rural America and even the Western hemisphere. Like OKeh and Columbia, Victor is rich in genuine, superbly recorded Americana by artists whose authenticity is beyond question. On many of these field trips, Peer also recorded blues artists whose records are now top-priced among collectors. Furry Lewis, Ishman Bracey, Frank Stokes, Sleepy John Estes, the Memphis Jug Band, and Gus Cannon's Jug Stompers made Victor records that in their way match the supremacy of the Red Seal artists in theirs.

"Orthophonic" recording revealed to connoisseurs of concert music the true beauty of voices such as Tito Schipa's, Fedor Chaliapin's, Rosa Ponselle's and Lucrezia Bori's. All had made acoustic records for Victor, yet were still young enough to make the transition to the era of electrical recording. There were initial difficulties in recording symphony orchestras so that they sounded like symphony orchestras. These were overcome, and the art of recording in the Academy of Music in Philadelphia, Symphony Hall in Chicago, and the Lincoln Auditorium in Kansas City was perfected. Victor even secured the disused Trinity Church on Fifth Street, Camden, N.J. There was now no sound that could not be recorded quite naturally. A Victor record made in the ballroom of the Webster Hotel in Chicago in December 1926 by the Dixieland Jug Blowers—clarinet, saxophone, three banjos, violin and *two* jugs—was played in the 1960s to a sophisticated EMI recording engineer in London. Surrounded by thousands of dollars' worth of high-fidelity equipment, he was staggered by the clarity, natural resonance, balance, depth, and complete lack of distortion on the old disc. "Why can't we make records like that today?" was his response.

The piano had always been the most difficult instrument to record naturally. Solo piano records account for relatively few entries in acoustic-era catalogs, despite such masters as Ossip Gabrilowitsch, Shura Cherkassky (then a boy of eleven or twelve), and Alfred Cortot. It was Cortot who made the first electric Red Seal record in March 1925. Soon other stars of the concert hall were appearing on the deep crimson label: Pablo Casals, the greatest cellist of the century; the eleven-year-old boy violinist Yehudi Menuhin; faithfuls such as Kreisler, Elman, Zimbalist, Jascha Heifetz; pianist Vladimir Horowitz and harpsichordist Wanda Landowska. In the popular field, there were piano records by Frank Banta and Milton Rettenberg, and Victor Arden and Phil Ohman. In jazz and blues, Clarence Williams, Jelly Roll Morton and a superb but completely unknown artist from Savannah, Ga. named Sugar Underwood made classics in their genre.

What was true of the piano now also held for the organ. The great organ in the Paramount Theatre in New York could now be recorded successfully, so the Paramount's Jesse Crawford, greatest exponent of the mighty Wurlitzer, made dozens of records of popular songs. At the organ in the church in Camden on many occasions sat the huge figure of Thomas "Fats" Waller, composer and pianist. Fats loved the organ but made musical history at the piano by getting his message of good humour in jazz across to a public that still did not "latch on" (to quote him) to the more arcane jazz styles. Waller made hundreds of Victor records with his Rhythm from 1934 until his death at 39 in 1943. Today these classics sell in LP boxed sets, just like the voice of Caruso.

On December 7, 1926, Eldridge R. Johnson sold the Victor Talking Machine Company to a firm of bankers, Seligman & Speyer. Until his death nineteen years later he never ceased regretting the move, it seems. On January 4, 1929, after months of rumour, the bankers sold out to the Radio Corporation of America. When economic depression all but wrecked the American record industry, RCA slashed its catalog. There was no 1931 or 1933 edition. The 1932 version was a shadow of its predecessors, printed on inferior paper. To be sure, on September 17, 1931, RCA announced with much panache the first commercial lateral-cut long-playing ($33\frac{1}{3}$ rpm) discs. The timing was bad. A specially geared machine was obviously needed to play them. Pressed in gritty Victrolac, they bore little resemblance to the velvety quality of their 78 rpm colleagues. Although some music was recorded specially for the new discs, many were of existing performances dubbed from 78s—and they sounded like it. Many Victor customers could not, many would not afford them or the instrument for playing them. It was 1934 before the last issue appeared, but sales were always minute. (At that, they were better than the figure for a blues artist accompanied by Jelly Roll Morton. She was Billie Young. Her only record, Victor 23339, was issued in July 1932 and available only till September. It sold just 211 copies.)

In an economy measure, Victor pruned its Red Seal catalog to only the best-selling issues. Many were by Caruso, more than a decade after his death in 1921. For future releases, Victor would rely on its European branches, which were still flourishing. When better times came in the mid-1930s, many new artists and some old ones could be found on Red Seal records. Arturo Toscanini, Leopold Stokowski, Eugene Ormandy and Serge Koussevitzky commanded wide followings. But the majority of the best-selling artists were new, those who had made their names singing operatic and operetta roles in films. For this was the Golden Age of the Hollywood Musical. The Golden Age of Opera, of Vaudeville, of Jazz had strutted their little hour on the stage, or rather in the recording studios. Now it was Hollywood's turn. So to Victor's studios came Jeanette MacDonald, Nelson Eddy, Lily Pons, Grace Moore, Gladys Swarthout, Lawrence Tibbett.

Dance bands were popular across the country, even though most fans could not afford their records. Jazz was banished again, except for the occasional session reminiscent of a get-together of ex-members of a college fraternity. The only crooners who mattered were Bing Crosby, who after one solo date for Victor in March 1931 had transferred to Brunswick, then Decca; and Russ Columbo, who made a handful of Victor sides in 1931 and 1932, and died, accidentally shot, in 1934. Rudy Vallee still recorded with his Connecticut Yankees for Victor, after brief flirtations with Hit of the Week and Columbia. The main attraction among the dance bands were Paul Whiteman and Eddy Duchin, along with the imported work of British bandleader Ray Noble, who followed his records to America in 1934.

Then came another revolution in popular taste. In April 1935 Victor signed a young clarinetist from Chicago whose records on that label reached back to Ben Pollack and his various orchestras in the years from 1926 to 1929. Benny Goodman, soon to be the uncrowned King of Swing, began recording on the Victor black label with its gold scrolls and tortured Spanish. Along with his old rival, trombonist Tommy Dorsey and his Orchestra, Goodman made contributions to the archives of popular music that the passage of years has not dimmed in importance or value. Jazz standards, hot arrangements of popular songs (often interpreted by girls as easy on the eye as on the ear), new instrumental numbers—they all combined to make up an exciting decade in popular music, the Swing Era. New jazz that did not hanker after what had gone before nor gaze forward aggressively or falteringly into a misty future appeared on Victor from Lionel Hampton, Sidney Bechet, Bunny Berigan, and even the revived Original Dixieland Jazz Band. Duke Ellington, lost to Brunswick and its associates since 1934, resumed work with Victor in March 1940, and for the next two years produced some of his finest performances. Tommy Dorsey maintained a neat balance between commercial pop and earthy, basic jazz, the latter from his Clambake Seven as well as his band. The band changed in 1940. From then up to the ban in 1942, it featured vocal work by a hollow-cheeked, velvety-voiced young man named Frank Sinatra. Those who still liked their popular music for dancing flocked to Victor artists like Hal Kemp, and what the lordly connoisseurs termed the "Mickey Mouse music" of Sammy Kaye.

The ten-inch double-sided popular black-label series began its numbering at 16000 in October 1908. The last in the series, exactly thirty-four years later, was 27975. No series on any label can match the continuity of this. Prior to the spring of 1906, the matrix number was scratched into the smooth area round the label. The A- prefix denoted 7-inch, the B- 10-inch, the C- 12-inch, the D- 14-inch and the E- 8-inch sizes. This system was adopted on April 24, 1903. Up to that time, the catalog and matrix numbers were identical, and served the same purpose. From May 1906 until May 1928, Victor records do not divulge the matrix numbers on either the labels or the wax. Then, for about six months, they appear in both places, disappearing again in October or November. The matrix number is not shown again on the wax and labels of Victor records, apart from some Red Seals at sporadic intervals, until the 1950s.

The use of so many recording locations meant that maintaining the continuity of numbering became ever harder. Some studios used blocks of pre-allocated numbers more quickly than others, and the field trips complicated the system further. The matrix series that began in 1903 continued until August 1936, when it reverted from a six-digit number back to 1, prefixed 0. This was used until the recording ban of 1942. The last in the series is 075904. It had taken from 1903 until 1933 to reach 75904. The same span of numbers in the second series was reached in slightly over six years, a fifth of the time.

The following chart shows the approximate first number made *and issued in the principal domestic series* between 1903 and 1942. Red Seal records were all single-sided until 1923, fifteen years after the black- and blue-label categories had become double-sided.

	Matrix	D/S 10" Popular	D/S 12" Popular	D/S 10" Blue	D/S 12" Blue	10" Red	12" Red
1903 (April 24)	1					81001	85001
1904	880					81015	85007
1905	2107					81050	85040
1906	2972					64001	74001
						87001	88001
							89001
1907	4168					64052	74051
						87002	88038
							89006
1908	4989	16000	35000			64080	74093
						87014	88098
							89013
1909	6697	16113	35023			64096	74126
						87021	88141
							89022
1910	8528	16425	35091			64109	74147
						87035	88201
							89028
1911	9752	16681	35183			64153	74195
						87070	88275
							89049
1912	11427	17006	35210	45000	55000	64222	74251
						87086	88324
							89052
1913	12758	17200	35263	45050	55030	64253	74325
						87111	88390
							89058
1914	14262	17470	35334	45057	55031	64387	74368
						87173	88431
							89074
1915	15560	17656	35419	45059	55049	64470	74417
						87201	88492
							89072
1916	16951	17872	35500	45074	55060	64516	74455
						87208	88541

	Matrix	D/S 10" Popular	D/S 12" Popular	D/S 10" Blue	D/S 12" Blue	D/S 10" Red	D/S 12" Red	D/S 12" Red
1917		18894	18149	35590	45103	55080	64597 87261	74497 88559
1918		21323	18399	35663	45146	55093	64732 87282	74557 88589
1919		22494	18499	35682	45156		64791 87296	74575 88597
1920		23561	18620	35694	45173		64831 87306	74597 88614
1921		24768	18700	35703	45203	55135	64914 87322	74651 88626
1922		25931	18817	35713	45256	55153	66010 87329	74717 88647
1923		27275	18969	35718	45331	55179	66103 87350	74780 88663
1924	29169	19206	35730	45373	55202	969	6427	
1925	31565	19492	35748	45476	55255	1046 3034	6479 8067	
1926	34077	19844	35761	45526	55289	1132 3040	6555 8068	9000
1927	37331	20277	35797	4000 4002		1204 3042	6614 8069	9016
1928	41293	21015	35871	4027		1291 3045	6719 8084	9150
1929	48531	21796	35954	4066		1358 3051	6877 8106	9294
1930	57970	22220	35995	4147		1438 3053	7152 8163	9596
1931	64631	22574	36029	4194		1489 3056	7369 8194	9831
1932	71212	22830	36047	4198		1543	7439 8223	11169
1933	74769	24160	36081			1580	7580	11270
1934	81017	24420	36097	4244		1632	7821	11406
1935	87226	24767	36141	4279		1688	8389	11744
1936	98800	25167	36176	4303		1726	8859	11877
1937	03880	25448	36190	4323		1795	14162	11948
1938	018100	25702	36210	4375		1834	14614	12136
1939	030790	26080	36214	4409		1948	15225	12520
1940	044540	26399	36237	4446		2012	15737	12597
1941	053794	27200	36375	4536		2123	17529	13501
1942	068770	27622	36418	4565		2175	18275	13786

It should be emphasised that all the above numbers are approximate. In common with most labels, Victor did not necessarily issue its records in exact sequence. Some were occasionally held up, even though the catalog numbers already were allocated. The 4000 series was the successors to the blue 4500s. Most, if not all, were Red Seal records.

VICTORY

There have been several Victory records throughout the history of the industry. Only one, as far as is known, offered any American performances. This was the seven-inch product of the Crystalate Gramophone Record Manufacturing Company of City Road, London. It was introduced in the autumn of 1928 as exclusively Woolworth's merchandise, and thus cost sixpence. It enjoyed huge success for just over 300 issues, the last in March 1931. Most are from masters made specially for the Victory label. Those with a single- or double-figure matrix number, instead of a three- or four-figure one, are dubbings from ten-inch American pressings on Banner or one of its Plaza affiliates. Despite the claim on the label that Victory is a long-playing record, the duration of most titles is only about equal to that of a rather short ten-inch. The transfers from Banner are thus necessarily edited. (There are several examples of Imperial titles being treated in the same fashion and offered in truncated form to an uncaring public.) None of them is outstanding, although occasional hot solos can heard on records by Jay Whidden, the American bandleader, and his Band. Sometimes these are credited correctly, sometimes under nondescript pseudonyms such as the Victory Dance Orchestra, the Music Masters, Jayson's Dance Orchestra, and Jim Kelleher's Piccadilly Dance Band. Perhaps the most outstanding and unusual Victory record is a piano solo credited in the recording files to H. Peterson, the composer, whoever he may have been. The number is called *Classic Rag*. It was issued twice. Victory 234 gives it this title but credits the playing to "Miss Holsom." Victory 271 calls it *Le Chiffon Classique*, played by Herbert Richards. It is a frenzied, disjointed affair, hardly a rag and certainly not a classic example of its kind. Nevertheless, it is interesting in that by the time it was made in 1929, ragtime was long out of favour. Its double appearance is therefore a puzzle, especially since the artist made no other records at all, as far as is known.

Other Victory records of interest are the Aldwych Syncopators dance records, and those by the Hawaiian Serenaders which have vocal refrains (anonymous, of course) by Al Bowlly. The label is usually yellow, printed in dull purple. It includes a drawing of the British flagship in the Battle of Trafalgar in 1805, H.M.S. *Victory*, garlanded with red leaves of an unidentifiable growth. Some issues bear the same or a similar design, but on pale bluish-grey paper. Others dispense with the ship.

VIM

The Vim Company of Chicago appears to have operated on a very small scale indeed. It seems most unlikely that it would have recorded its own masters as far back as the first decade of the century. The only specimen known to me is a banjo solo by the great Vess L. Ossman. It is numbered 3003 and has no other discernible number. The record is single-sided, and has no outward characteristics that suggest Victor or Columbia origin. Nor does it seem to be from Odeon. The most likely source is Imperial (q.v.), in which case the numerical details of the original have been suppressed. The label is plain off-white or very pale grey, with the word VIM in red above the spindle hole and all other lettering in black, rather crudely printed.

VIOLA

The Southern California Phonograph Company of Los Angeles was apparently the maker of the Viola phonograph. In 1921 it seems to have begun producing records leased from Olympic (q.v.) and Black Swan (q.v.), and probably others, under the Viola name. The label is blue, with gold lettering. The design shows a phonograph encircled by a laurel wreath bearing the words "Viola Phonograph/The Soul Of Music/Plays All Records." As the emphasis is on the machine, it is probable that Viola records were given away—perhaps half a dozen or so with each machine. The catalog numbers, or perhaps they should be termed reference numbers, are those of Olympic on the only known copy. Since the couplings are not as they are on Olympic, being 17101 and 17109, Viola is another example of mismatching.

At the foot of the label is a bungalow or similar building between two trees.

These extend into the lower half of the label to such an extent that the artist's name is confined to two lines of type on the left-hand side. The maker's name and whereabouts are shown in block upper-case letters in blue on gold around the lower rim. The brand name is shown entirely in lower case *and in inverted commas* immediately above the spindle hole. It is impossible to guess at how many Viola records were announced or offered to the public. Their extreme rarity suggests that there cannot have been many.

VITAPHONE

An extremely rare and early example of piracy in the record industry, Vitaphone records are allegedly copies of existing Berliner products. I have never seen one, and know of no one who has. They are referred to in James R. Smart's *The Sousa Band: A Discography* (Library of Congress, Washington, 1970) on page 24, but without any information as to their appearance, numbering, or lifespan beyond the probability that it was from 1897 or 1898 until about 1900.

VOCALION

The story of the Vocalion record is long and complicated. It has died and been revived many times in England, and has undergone several ownership changes in the United States. Originally the Aeolian Vocalion label was the product of the Aeolian Company, piano manufacturers of Aeolian Hall, New York City. In 1916 Aeolian launched its machines and vertical-cut records in direct competition with the established firms. The design of the label is one which has won the approval of collectors of all kinds of records ever since. It may be the most tastefully ornate of them all. Whether British or American, the outline is the same: a square within an outer circle, each of the four segments being filled with curlicues, fronds and other decorations in gold on a coloured background. The background is tan at the outset. When the vertical-cut disc was discontinued and the first laterals announced in January 1920, the background became pale blue with dark blue decoration. Then followed a reversion to tan and gold, and finally a switch to black and gold. The upper half of the square, whether black or pale blue, always bore the brand name in truly olde-worlde script. It would be gold or cream on black, dark blue on pale blue. The lower half contained a panel of tan, or gold (on the first laterals), or cream, always with credits in black. Even after the summer of 1925, when Brunswick-Balke-Collen-

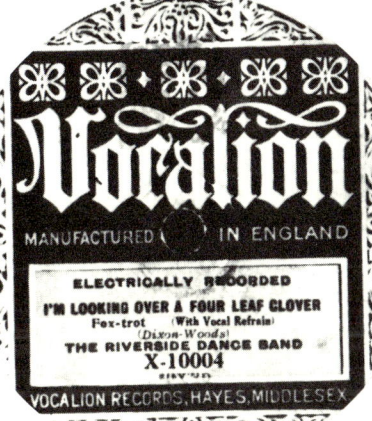

der took over Vocalion, the label remained almost unchanged, apart from the reference to the manufacturer.

Vocalion's absorption into the American Record Corporation's roster of labels at the end of 1931 resulted eventually in much the same design as before. But the colours were inverted. The credits and decor became black on gold, the brand name gold on black. Perhaps because this was too expensive, it was not in use for long. In 1935 a glossy black label, with a few much simplified curlicues and scrolls garlanded round a central scroll unfurled to display the brand name underlined by twelve single leaves and the usual credits, began a two-year life. From 1937 to 1940 the label was bright blue. Border lettering spelled out the conditions of sale. Within the three concentric rings that formed the border was virtually no decoration at all. The most gorgeous label of them all had become just another blue one with gold lettering. Columbia withdrew the label in 1940 and substituted the revived OKeh label (q.v.).

As long as Vocalion was an independent, its roster of artists compared quite favourably with those of Victor and Columbia. Operatic celebrities of the calibre of John Charles Thomas, Evelyn Scotney, Marguerite d'Alvarez, Armand Tokatyan, Vladimir Rosing, and Florence Easton made Vocalion records between 1917 and 1924. The merger with Brunswick meant the end of Vocalion as an all-purpose label. Thenceforth it was to feature mainly dance music, jazz, blues, spirituals and hillbilly music, with occasional ethnic records. For much of the time between the first laterals and the merger, Vocalions were pressed in a russet-hued material presented to the public as the Vocalion Red Record. Despite its striking appearance and the smooth surfaces surrounding a black, cream and gold label, the Red Record was no particular advance over its competition. Brunswick promptly withdrew it in favour of a conventional black one of fine quality. The Vocalions of the 1930s, however, betray a deterioration in the surface quality as the elegant 75-cent disc dropped to 35 cents or three for a dollar.

The recording on most Aeolian Vocalions was clear, rich and well balanced, once the "teething troubles" of the earliest laterals and their tendency to shrillness and a lack of bass had been overcome. With the Brunswick alliance came an almost immediate abandonment of acoustic recording, in favour of the "light-ray" system that in turn gave way to a more natural sound. The earlier ARC recordings of 1932-1936 or thereabouts are inclined to be thin and wiry. Those from the remaining years are generally much better.

The original vertical-cut Aeolian Vocalions were issued rather as Emersons were. There was a numerical prefix (e.g. 1200, which became 12000 after 1299). But the laterals were given entirely new serials and priced as follows:

14000* (Popular)	10"	.75-.85
20000	10"	1.00
24000*	10"	1.25
30000	10"	1.25
35000* (Popular)	12"	1.25
36000*	12"	1.35
45000	12"	1.50
48000*	12"	1.75
52000	12"	1.75
55000	12"	2.00
60000*	10"	1.50
70000	12"	2.00

*Double-sided

All except the 14000s, now entering on the 15000s, were dropped when Brunswick assumed control. In March 1926 a new 1000 series of "race" records was announced. Six years and just 746 records later, the series was temporarily suspended. As conditions in business generally and records in particular improved somewhat, it was resumed in September 1933, at 25001. This was changed after 25021 to 2522. This series, in which popular dance and vocal records mixed with race and hillbilly items (both these prefixed 0), continued right up to the substitution of the OKeh name in July 1940, and onwards far beyond the scope of this book. The original 14000 series reached 16026 in April 1942, when it was abandoned. It was still Vocalion, but from 15893 onwards, in 1933, all its issues were of Bohemian, Polish, Tyrolean and Scandinavian bands. Among them the names of Whoopee John Wilfahrt, Adolf and the Bohemians, the Bee Gee Tavern Band and the International Rhythm Boys occur with prodigious regularity.

Vocalion had a branch in England, the Aeolian Company, Ltd. of Aeolian Hall, New Bond Street, London, W.1. This was a concert hall, and the building also housed a complex of offices. One was used from 1920 to 1926 as a recording studio. The first Vocalion records in England appeared in December 1920. They were of remarkably good quality in all respects. They retained the American label design, with a bewildering array of tints for the credit panel below the spindle hole. Pale pink served for the most expensive category. Through the years the less elevated divisions of the repertoire rejoiced in dark green, with black lettering that was extremely difficult to read; and also bright scarlet, pale blue, and yellow. For the popular series, black graced the more expensive ones at the outset. For the short-lived dance and light vocal M series, the entire label was maroon with gold printing.

The prices asked for these beautiful-looking records were formidable for 1921, a year of recession. Almost all the Vocalion categories cost more than their equivalents on HMV and Columbia. Further, the latter two had most of the best artists under exclusive contracts. Vocalion did prune some of its categories after a while, and reduced the prices of the remainder. But even after introducing a form of electric recording known as "the Marconi Co.'s process" in the summer of 1926, it found that there were too many top popular artists on other labels for Vocalion to compete. In September 1927 the last ten- and twelve-inch Vocalions appeared—now being made by British Brunswick. These are the prices of the numberous label prefixes in 1921, the first complete year of business. All are double-sided except the A-, B-, C- and L- series:

A-0100	12	8s.
B-3000	10	6s.
C-01000	12	7s. 6d.
D-02000	12	7s. 6d.
J-04000	12	7s.
K-05000	12	6s. 6d.
L-5000	10	5s. 6d.
M-1000	10	3s. (introduced in February 1922)
R-6000	10	5s. 6d.
X-9000	10	4s. 6d.
Y-8000	12	5s.

The dollar was worth about 5s. at that time, so the high prices of Vocalion in England become obvious.

A black and yellow Vocalion B-200 series was issued briefly during the last days of the Brunswick regime in England. It offered most interesting jazz and dance records. Some came from American Brunswick, including two sides by Johnny Dodds's Black Bottom Stompers and two by Duke Ellington's Washingtonians. Some were from Gennett, usually under the pseudonym "The Harlequinaders." These were invariably sold with a black sticker bearing the word "Kildare" in ornate white lettering over the Vocalion name.

In March 1932 Crystalate bought Vocalion and all its labels, by then embracing various kinds of Broadcast (q.v.). In May 1936 the Vocalion name was reactivated. The new series started at 1 (soon to be prefixed S-) and cost 2.s 6d. It was devoted to the new jazz fashion, Swing Music. This too was discontinued in February 1940 after Decca took over Crystalate and its family of labels. In the four years, 247 issues had appeared. Many are of considerable jazz value, but pretentious commercial rubbish almost outweighs the good music. The bright red, black and gold label, based closely on the original design, is nevertheless attractive to jazz collectors, and not only for its artistic appearance. The last fifty or so issues are entirely black with the same design in gold. In November 1936 a group known as the Vocalion Celebrity Series also began, at 500. It disappeared within two years and eighty issues, most of them American dance bands identical to those on Brunswick, Decca, Panachord and Rex at the same price (or 1s.!).

It was October 1951 before Decca again resurrected the Vocalion label. Again it was on glossy black with gold design and lettering, again an approximation to the original style of the early 1920s, again devoted to jazz: "Origins of Jazz," according to the label. The series started at V-1001. Although a wealth of fine jazz was issued, most of it was from dubbed masters, some of dubious quality. After forty-one issues in three years, the project folded. One of its issues was a double-sided "actuality" recording of the wedding of Sister Rosetta Tharpe, the gospel singer. How this was deemed an example of the origins of jazz is obscure, to say the least.

Vocalion as a label has always been held high in the esteem of jazz collectors. From the beginning it employed front-rank musicians. Recording sessions in New York originally took place in Aeolian Hall. To this awesome edifice came the Original Dixieland Jass Band (so labelled) for six sessions between July 29 and November 24, 1917. In May 1918 new studios were ready at 35 West 43rd Street. There does not seem to have been any field recording by Vocalion until the Brunswick merger of 1925. After that the matrix numbers were the same for both labels, although Vocalion had its own E- series added to some Brunswicks. (See Brunswick for date charts on both labels.) After the merger, recordings made in Chicago, Atlanta, Dallas, San Antonio, Fort Worth, Los Angeles, New Orleans, Knoxville, Hot Springs, Birmingham and Memphis proliferated on the Vocalion "race" series.

It was the Vocalion label in England that sparked (Sir) Compton Mackenzie's interest in the gramophone. On a wet afternoon in March 1922 he was looking at the player-pianos in the Aeolian Hall showrooms. The great novelist was interested in an instrument that would reproduce his favourite music. He had experienced the older forms of gramophones and had not been at all favourably impressed. Yet the catalog of available piano rolls did not offer him anything he wanted. The salesman suggested he buy a gramophone and some records instead. A demonstration of the Schumann Quintet for Piano and Strings, Op. 44, by Ethel Hobday and the London String Quartet on Vocalion convinced him of the strides made in recording and reproduction. His enthusiasm led him to found *The Gramophone*, a monthly magazine that first appeared in April 1923 and flourishes to this day. Some of the early covers incorporate the outline of the Vocalion label in the design. The original Vocalion disc that started the magazine on its way now hangs in a glass case in the home of the present editor.

The following chart shows the approximate number of the first title cut each year on American and English Vocalion as independent companies:

	American	British
1917	100? (vertical)	
1918	500?	
1919	1260	
1919 (September)	5000 (lateral)	
1920	5420	01000
1921	6900	02200
1922	8430	02600
1923	10760	03100
1924	12500	03450
1925	190 (new series)	03750
1926		04270
1926 (August)		M-01 (electric)
1927		M-0180

It should be noted that the American studios allocated a different number to each *take*, so there are no take letters or digits. The matrix number is not on the label. It can usually be seen showing through one of the ornamental segments in small, neat handwriting. Early laterals have this number in much larger, thinner figures that are rather difficult to make out.

WESTPORT

Westport was the sister label of Portland. It was produced by Edison Bell for Curry's, the British electrical and cycling equipment store, from 1922 to 1924. Its repertoire was drawn from Edison Bell Winner's. Consequently, several examples of Gennett products can be found on Westport. The artist credits were the same as on Edison Bell Winner, most of them pseudonyms like the Diplomat Orchestra, the Regent Orchestra and the Pavilion Players. The crimson label is printed entirely in black. It shows only the title, artist, catalog number (in one of three series: a three-figure block around 400-500, a 2000, and a 3000. Each of the last two produced nearly 200 items each). There was a minimum of decoration. Unlike Portland (q.v.), Westport has only one sales slogan advertising itself. The words "Curry's Value" extends across the centre, one word on each side of the spindle hole. Again unlike Portland, the address of Curry's is shown on two arc scrolls surmounted by a geographical globe, 24-26 Goswell Road, London, E.C.1. A segment on either side of the globe informs us proudly that Curry's Ltd. was established in 1884, and had over 100 depots.

While it is most unlikely that Westport issued anything more interesting than straightforward dance music and popular songs of the time, it is fascinating to speculate on exactly what else remains to be discovered on this plain but striking label. We know that Edison Bell Winner produced little in the way of collectors' items at this time. But there exists the remote possibility that material from Gennett, considered unsuitable for Winner, *may* have found an outlet in Westport's four or five hundred-strong catalog.

WILHELM

From seeing the brand name of this label, we might guess that it had some connection with the last reigning representative of the German royal house of Hohenzollern, perhaps in a propaganda capacity. But in fact it is nothing more than yet another personal record produced at the artist's expense by the Starr Piano Company of Richmond, Ind. The artist was a lady named Ruth Wilhelm, who composed *Spring Frolic* and *April Morn*. Along with an unidentified *Grande Valse,* she accompanied herself at the piano while whistling her two compositions in Richmond on January 18, 1923. The first and third of these have been found by American collector Les Zeiger. The label is green, with gold design and lettering like the usual Gennett of the time. The surname of the performer serves as the brand name. There is no catalog number, not surprisingly. The matrix numbers 11288-A and 11290 are shown in the wax.

WINNER

WISE

This is a type of Bell record produced by Emerson during the mid-1920s. I have never seen one, and know no more than this concerning it. It was made for William H. Wise and Company of 50 West 47th Street, New York City (see Roycroft), a book publisher that sold mainly by mail.

WONDER

Of all the obscure labels referred to in this book, Wonder must rank as the hardest to find. The Wonder Talking Machine Company of New York was a subsidiary of the Conn Instrument Company of Elkhart, Ind., which became involved in the talking machine industry in the late 1890s. Its machine was built on the example of the early Eldridge R. Johnson-Emile Berliner model, but with a special attachment holding two brass horns, presumably to increase the volume and at the same time divert the sound to another part of the room. The machine is rare enough. But in eighty years, no Wonder records have been discovered, although a catalog of them, thirty pages in length, was published at the time. The contents tally exactly with those of the Berliner catalog of the same presumed date (1898), except that the figure 1 precedes the Berliner number in every case but one (Wonder 243, listed as Sousa's Band playing *The Brusto Eleck March,* which does not appear as a Berliner issue, and which must surely be some rather myopic typesetter's attempt at interpreting *The Bride Elect March,* a Sousa composition). James R. Smart, in his magnificently documented book *The Sousa Band: A Discography,* published by the Library of Congress, Washington, D.C. in 1970, suggests that the Wonder records were supplied to purchasers of a Wonder machine, by arrangement with Berliner; or that Berliner made custom pressings for the Wonder Talking Machine Company to publish on its own label. If so, these must rank as the first disc records to bear a label. But until one of the dozens in the catalog is found, this must remain a matter of conjecture.

WORLD

World record today signifies the enormously popular reissue label produced as a subsidiary of EMI Ltd., on which some of the finest performances of the past in serious music, theatre and film personalities, dance bands and jazz have appeared. But in the days before LP there was a World record that was unique in that it too was a long-player of sorts. The earlier World record, a twelve-inch product of the Vocalion factory in Hayes, Middlesex, was the strange invention of an eccentric Englishman named Noel Pemberton-Billing. He had seen active service in the Boer War in South Africa in 1900 and in the Royal Naval Air Service—he was a keen aviator—between 1914 and 1916. He entered Parliament on retiring from the service and remained there until 1921. Pemberton-Billing wrote articles for various journals, including one involving him in an action for criminal libel, with unprecedented courtroom scenes as he conducted his own defence. He also wrote some plays, and patented the World record.

By means of a gearing device designed to keep the velocity of the record surface under the needle constant throughout the record (since the velocity of the outer grooves was faster than that of the inner), World records could be made to play on any machine to which the patented gear was fitted. As the track was cut very finely, almost in microgroove dimensions, it was possible to obtain seven and a half to eight and a half minutes of playing time on each side, an unheard-of length at that time. (Playing a World record without the Pemberton-Billing attachment produces a weird effect: unintelligible gabble gradually making more and more sense, until the last third of the side sounds normal, if the nominal speed is 78 rpm. If 33⅓, then the side begins sanely enough, but gradually reduces pitch to the point where the turgid mass of sound becomes insufferable.)

Much of the World repertoire is from the Vocalion and Aco roster, serious and dance music alike. Pemberton-Billing went to New York in 1923 and also made an arrangement with Emerson records (q.v.). Thus, on some very rare World records, can be found such interesting items as Fletcher Henderson and his Orchestra, expertly transferred two to a side on World. By the end of 1924, however, it had become clear that the British public had no time for gadgetry on gramophones. They spent their mechanical or scientific leanings on crystal sets and the like, leaving their gramophones to play at 78 rpm. When they bought records, they bought HMV, Columbia, Edison Bell, Imperial and their affiliated labels, at less cost on the whole. Pemberton-Billing emigrated to Australia. By June 1925 he had set up a factory in Bay Street, Brighton, Victoria, in an attempt to interest Australian gramophiles in his invention. For a year he persisted, but with the same results. He returned to England and died in November 1948.

The later World label is white, with a black and gold rim. The design on the lower half includes the customary theatrical masks representing Tragedy and Comedy, numerical and copyright details, and two World records. All performance credits are on the upper half, together with the playing time, an innovation for that period. The earliest World records are Pathe-supplied vertical-cut pressings produced by the World Phonograph Company of Chicago in late 1919 and 1920. They bear the same material under the same catalog numbers as Operaphone (q.v.). A black label carries all the printing in gold. The brand name is in bold serif upper-case letters around the entire upper rim. A keyhole design above the spindle hole shows a phonograph of the cabinet type in front of a geographical globe of the world.

YERKES DANCE RECORDS

The *Talking Machine World* of March 15, 1924 reported that Yerkes Dance Records were to be made in a studio at 102 West 38th Street, New York City. Yet the label gives the home base of the Yerkes Recording Laboratories as in the Metropolitan Opera House, New York, while a couple dance happily down the left side of the label. Harry A. Yerkes, long associated with Columbia also appeared on Victor, Vocalion, Olympic, Lyric, Paramount and Federal as director of all kinds of bands from saxophone sextets and the Southern (or Novelty) Five to the S.S. Flotilla Orchestra, the Happy Six and the Jazarimba Orchestra. He was a percussionist and xylophone soloist who recorded in his own right for Columbia as long ago as 1906. He formed a dance band in 1917. His venture as a promoter of records does not seem to have prospered. The October 15, 1924 issue of the same trade paper reported that the Harry Yerkes Orchestra, henceforth to be known as "the Wattle Path Palais Orchestra," was about to embark on an eighteen-month tour of Australia and New Zealand, for a handsome $200,000. No further records by a Yerkes band on any label are known, either in the United States or the Antipodes. The few known to have been issued under Yerkes's brand name are of little interest, although many of his earlier recordings used pioneer jazz musicians from New Orleans like trombonist Tom Brown and clarinetist Alcide Nunez, and have a quality and originality that sets them apart from conventional dance records of the time.

ZARVAH ART

The brand names of records are sometimes inexplicable. There can surely be fewer more bizarre identities than Zarvah Art. It was apparently a semi-private label that existed during the autumn of 1922, and possibly for a short time before or after. The name is derived from the first names of two individuals, presumably men, who launched the venture, Zarh Myron Bickford and Vahdah Olcott-Bickford. Or were they husband and wife? One record they produced was a single-sided pressing on a red label with gold lettering and simple design, the brand name appearing in offset red on gold in an arc across the upper half of the label. The price is shown as $1.25, the same price Victor was charging at that time for Red Seal artists of the calibre of Enrico Caruso, Ernestine Schumann-Heink, John McCormack and Fritz Kreisler. The specimen reported by Carl Kendziora is as strange musically as its trading identity. It offers a performance of *Romance* from Halévy's little-known opera *L'Eclair*—as a guitar and mandolin duet by the founders of the company! Another example of Zarvah Art is a black- and gold-labelled double-sided issue, without catalog number or stated price, of two dance tunes of late 1922 played by the Red and Blue Orchestra. A sticker on one side refers to at least that particular copy having originated "from Lewis P. Smith, Jr., The Taft School, Watertown, Conn." Can it be inferred that the record was made by the Taft School orchestra and distributed privately to relatives and friends? The matrix numbers, 1094 and 1095, are shown. They do not fit any known sequence. The address of the Zarvah Art Record Company is given as 616 West 116th Street, New York. The business was probably not there for long, and nothing more is known of the Bickford production team.

ZONOPHONE

When Emile Berliner's double-dealing agent, Frank Seaman, seceded from the business in 1899, he set about building a business of his own. Using his knowledge of Berliner's products, he openly touted a machine and discs that were almost exact replicas of Berliner's. As we have seen in the section on Berliner, the latter's engineer, Eldridge R. Johnson, continued producing records when Seaman secured his famous (and infamous) injunction barring Berliner from making his own product (June 25, 1900) on the grounds that Seaman's National Gramophone Corporation and its subsidiary, the Universal Talking Machine Company, now allied to the American Graphophone Company and the Columbia Phonograph Company, held patent rights in the manufacture of machines and records. Johnson (see Victor) appealed successfully against injunctions to stop *him* from making machines and records. By 1903, Seaman and his National Gramophone Corporation, together with the Zon-O-Phone name he had used for them, were absorbed by the Victor Talking Machine Company in the

United States, and overseas by Victor's European associates, the Gramophone and Typewriter and sister companies.

Victor continued the Zon-O-Phone record as a sort of poor relation until 1910. In England its fortunes continued successfully until the EMI merger that brought His Master's Voice (and thus Zonophone, as it has always been spelt in Europe, with no hyphens) and Columbia (and thus Regal) into the same family. From January 1933, the alliance was marked by the appearance of Regal Zonophone (see Regal). The original American Zon-O-Phone records were seven-inchers, of course, single-sided and without labels, in the Berliner style. The brand name and title and artist credits were engraved in ornate lettering, filled in with some kind of white paint to make them easier to read (as long as the paint was not removed by wear). Eventually they became ten-inch, with black and gold labels. An Italian product under the Zonophone name had turquoise blue labels with gold lettering, and offered top-rank operatic singers including Enrico Caruso—his rarest records. The French branch recorded Pol Plançon on a now very rare orange Zonophone.

The American Zon-O-Phone was based in Camden, N.J. It has a dark bottle-green label, with three lines of minute upper-case lettering around the outer edge that gives details of the patents under which it was made by the Universal Talking Machine Manufacturing Company and the date, which varies. All this is outside an inner gold ring containing ZON-O-PHONE RECORD around the upper rim, and a line-drawing of a child listening with pleasure to a disc machine with a flower horn above the caption "On Speaking Terms." A more flagrant parody of the famous "His Master's Voice" painting would be hard to imagine.

The price of a double-sided Zon-O-Phone Record was 65 cents. The numbering began apparently at 5000 or 5001, and is shown in the wax in the Victor manner, with the same typeface. A matrix number, nothing whatever to do with Victor's, is given in fine, often barely visible digits in the wax across the label from the catalog number. The original single-sided catalog number is also shown as a rule. This can be three- or four-figured, like the matrix number itself.

In England, Zonophone continued in single-sided green-label form, first as a seven-inch disc, then as a ten- and eventually a twelve-inch as well. In October 1908 a double-sided disc known as "The Twin" appeared. It had a buff or ochre label and brown or dark green lettering and design. This too used Zonophone masters. In June 1911 this format disappeared in favour of the Zonophone Twin record on another dark green label with gold. It too used the Twin design, two cherubs wreathed in scrolls. In 1920 the cherubs were replaced by the "His Master's Voice" trademark on a dark green label that in almost every detail was a replica of the HMV design of the period. This continued for three years. Then, in 1924, the dog and gramophone were replaced by a circle containing the brand name twice at right angles to each other, the letter P being common to both. The whole was set in a pair of ornate segments with the monograms Z and R to the left and right. In 1926 the brand name was changed from Zonophone Record to simply Zonophone. The dull, almost funereal green became a verdant, pleasing colour like fresh grass, and with minor alterations in size and occasionally the wording in small print. This remained constant until the end. The Twin numbers at the outset varied from side to side. When numbers were allocated as catalog references, common to both sides in the normal manner, they sensibly started at 1 and continued through to 6274, except for a block from 3000 to 4999 which was used for pressings made in Hayes for export to Australia and New Zealand.

Much Victor material of interest to jazz and dance-music collectors appeared in this series. Very few Victor dance bands were represented in the English Zonophone catalog, but a fair number of Victor vocalists and instrumentalists turned up on Zonophone, from Sir Harry Lauder—on the bright scarlet GO (Grand Opera!) series—to Kirilloff's Balalaika Orchestra, various Hawaiian groups, and all four Victor titles by the Five Harmaniacs, a pioneer "spasm" band using unorthodox instruments.

The English Zonophone catalog introduced Jimmie Rodgers to Britain. His records enjoyed a long and steady sale, even years after his untimely death. Other country-and-western artists such as the Carter Family were also issued by Zonophone. There were any number of novelty items, from the American Black Jacks (a copy of Columbia's Two Black Crows) to the sexton of a Sussex church singing genuine Sussex folk songs. *The Old Sow*, beloved of Rudy Vallee, was first recorded unaccompanied by this worthy, Albert Richardson, with all the customary snorts, whistles and razzberries associated with the number.

Zonophone is now a much sought label by dance-band and jazz collectors because of the superb sides recorded in England by Anglo-American bands like Bert Firman's (also known as the Arcadians Dance Orchestra, the Cabaret Novelty Orchestra, the Carlton Hotel Dance Band, the Devonshire Restaurant Dance Band, the Orpheus Dance Band, and above all, usually many degrees hotter than any, the Rhythmic Eight). In 1923 and 1924 the Original Capitol Orchestra from the Mississippi riverboat of that name played in London and recorded for Zonophone. Though many sides are straight arrangements of popular dance numbers, several, including a spirited *Tiger Rag*, are as hot as anything recorded on location by OKeh or other American labels.

Zonophone masters recorded in England use the same series as HMV, but from 1921 with prefixes Yy- (ten-inch) and Zz- (twelve-inch) replacing the HMV Bb-/Cc- prefix. The later OB- and 2B- on HMV became OY- and 2Y- on Zonophone. Best-selling Zonophones remaining in the Regal Zonophone catalog after 1932 retained their original numbers, prefixed T-. They offered quality at a popular price: 2s. 6d. for ten-inch, 4s. for twelve. Today they can still be found in considerable numbers—except, of course, the jazz gems. The American Zon-O-Phone repertoire was no more exciting than that of many other cheaper labels of later date. An occasional ragtime title can found, recorded by the Zon-O-Phone Orchestra or Vess L. Ossman, the ubiquitous banjoist. Reproduction is adequate, surfaces reasonably clean.

GLOSSARY

The terms most frequently met with in this book may not be clear to anyone but experienced record collectors.

Acoustic Recording: One made with the artist performing before a large-mouthed horn, usually of metal and of varying lengths and widths according to what was being recorded. The horn was often strapped with tape to reduce overtones and resonance that would mar the reproduction. The tapering end of the horn was attached to the cutting head and the diaphragm. The recording stylus attached to the latter traced the vibrations of the sound in a thick wax block, without the aid of any electrical device. By 1927 almost all companies had abandoned this method, which is also known as pre-electric recording.

Catalog Number: The number common to both sides of most records. It is used to refer to the contents in the company's catalog, and is frequently suffixed -A and -B. The -A side was the company's guess as to which would prove the more popular.

Control Number: A number stamped in the surface of the record, usually outside the label. Often used when a company leased a master from another company. Used in addition to, or instead of, the one allocated by the parent company.

Cylinder: A tubular body, usually five or six inches in length, made of wax or shellac or sometimes a type of vinyl, with vertically cut grooves holding the recorded sound. The earliest type of device for sound recording, invented by Thomas A. Edison in 1877 but obsolete as a commercial product by 1930.

Dub or Dubbing: The result or process of transferring the sound from one medium to another to obtain a copy.

Laminated: The method used principally by Columbia, its subsidiaries and its associates (and occasionally by other makes) whereby the recorded surfaces have a core of tough composition sandwiched between two very thin paper layers. The thin outermost plastic layer carrying the soundtrack is pressed on the paper enclosing the core. The result is a long-living record, less easily destroyed.

Lateral Cut: A record on which the soundtrack is cut with the sound on the *walls* of the groove, so that the pickup or soundbox vibrates from side to side, thus picking up the signals of the soundtrack.

Location Recording: A recording made in a building not necessarily constructed as a studio: usually a hotel ballroom, a church, a theatre or an auditorium in a city visited by mobile recording units looking for local talent (usually jazz, blues, and country music).

Master: The original wax block on which the sound was recorded.

Matrix Number: The number allocated to each *master* for identification purposes. Usually this is shown on the smooth part of the record surrounding the label, often on the label also, but sometimes on neither. It can be used as a rough guide to the date of a recording, since matrix numbers were issued as nearly as possible in chronological order.

Pantograph: An early method of recording whereby cylinder and disc versions were cut simultaneously. Alternatively, a master cylinder would play on to a battery of other cylinders to make one or more exact copies, depending on how many machines were involved.

Run-Off: The spiral groove extending from the recorded track to a locking device, eccentric or concentric, around the label of the record. Used for activating the automatic stop on machines equipped with these, or at least for stopping the stylus from dragging the pickup across the record surface.

Shellac: The basic ingredient of manufacture of the majority of 78 rpm records. Produced from the resin of certain Indian and Burmese trees.

Spindle Hole: The central hole of all disc records.

Take (Number): The number, or letter, allocated to each recording of the same performance. It is usually shown on the area around the label, is sometimes visible under it, or, rarely, is not shown at all. Comparison between records bearing the same matrix number but different take numbers can be interesting and instructive, especially when the performance is improvised.

Vertical Cut: A record on which the soundtrack is indented into the surface so that the sound is recorded on the bottom of the groove. This necessitates a soundbox or pickup designed for such recording. Suitably adapted modern stereo equipment can be made to reproduce vertical cut records quite well.

Wax: The term loosely given to the shellac-based material of which 78 rpm records were manufactured. More correctly, the term given to the original circular block (see Master), some one or two inches thick, on which the sound was recorded until the adoption of lacquered discs in the 1940s.